D1539346

BRILLAT-SAVARIN

BRILLAT-SAVARIN

The Judge and His Stomach

GILES MacDONOGH

IVAN R. DEE
Chicago

For Natasha

"il est un faux artiste celui qui n'est pas gourmet et un faux gourmet celui
qui n'entend rien à la beauté d'une couleur, ou à l'émotion d'un son."

Marcel Rouff, *"Dodin-Bouffant"*

BRILLAT-SAVARIN. Copyright © 1992 by Giles MacDonogh. First American
edition, published by arrangement with John Murray (Publishers) Ltd. All
rights reserved, including the right to reproduce this book or portions thereof in
any form. For information, address: Ivan R. Dee, Inc., 1332 North Halsted
Street, Chicago 60622. Manufactured in the United States of America and
printed on acid-free paper.

Library of Congress Cataloging-in-Publication Data:
MacDonogh, Giles, 1955–
Brillat-Savarin : the judge and his stomach / Giles MacDonogh
p.   cm.
Includes bibliographical references and index.
ISBN 1-56663-028-2
1. Brillat-Savarin, 1755–1826.   2. Food writers—France—Biography.
3. Judges—France—Biography.   I. Title.
TX649.B75M33 1993
641'.01'3092—dc20
[B]   93-13879

Contents

Preface

IT WAS THE late Caro Hobhouse who first suggested I write this
book. Having read my earlier work on Grimod de La Reynière, she
believed that a fuller treatment could be given to that other founding
father of French gastronomy, Brillat-Savarin. The difference between
the two books, however, was to be clear from the outset: with Grimod
I had been content to examine the subject's gastronomic writings
alone, leaving aside the bulk of his theatrical criticism. The Brillat
book, on the other hand, was to be devoted to the whole man.

My first thanks must go to Caro for the constant encouragement she
gave me right up to her tragically early death in 1991. Others naturally
also played a role in seeing the manuscript reach completion. I thank
Hugo Dunn-Meynell of the International Food and Wine Society for
letting me have a copy of a lecture on the subject by the Australian
Brillat scholar, Graham Pont; Paul Dymond, former editor of *Taste*,
commissioned an early article on Brillat which helped me to crystallize
my thoughts on the book; Catherine Manac'h of *Food and Wine from
France* facilitated a research trip to Bourg-en-Bresse among other
things; and my sister, Katharine Sheppard, not only cleared up one or
two points about the Empire, but also located and copied a missing
article from the *Revue des deux mondes*. My thanks also to Professor
Nicolas Kurti for providing me with the whereabouts of Brillat's tomb
in Père Lachaise cemetery.

In the little town of Belley I never wanted for help and encouragement. Special thanks to M. David Genin for acting as an intermediary

with the town hall and driving me about during my stay; to M. Gerald Crétin of the Hôtel Ibis who organized my life while I was under his roof; to M. José Carron of *Le Progrès de l'Ain*; to M. Olivier Nicolle for showing me Brillat's town house and M. Michel Perrin for taking me over Brillat's *gentilhommière* at Vieu. M. Paul Troncy at the town hall sent me photographs and the Député-Maire's *chef du cabinet* arranged a meeting for me with the leading French Brillat scholar, Professor Louis Trénard. Professor Trénard was kind enough to give me a copy of his latest article on *La Physiologie du goût*.

Another helpful person I met in Belley was Louis Augustin Barrière. Barrière gave me copies of the two articles he has written on Brillat and sent me a precious fragment from Brillat's pornographic *contes*.

I thank my friends Tim and Stephanie Johnston in Paris for making their camp bed available once again. Also in Paris Gerald Long, the unrelenting critic of my articles in the *Financial Times*, was kind enough to set down his own views on Brillat; my former teacher Professor Romuald Szramkiewicz of the University of Paris I provided me with biographical details relating to Brillat's financial friends. Professor Jean-Louis Halperin of the University of Lyon helped with the revolutionary *Tribunal de cassation* and Dr Pierre Amalric was also helpful with details concerning other members of Brillat's circle.

I am grateful to the staffs of the British Library in London, the Archives nationales and Bibliothèque nationale in Paris, the Archives départementales in Bourg-en-Bresse, and the Bibliothèque municipale in Belley.

Lastly, once again I must offer special thanks to my friend Roderick Blyth for taking so much trouble reading the manuscript. He covered it not only with his helpful emendations but also put down any number of amusing insights into the characters of both subject and author.

Giles MacDonogh

Introduction

IN THE COURSE of a Biblical human span, Jean-Anthelme Brillat-Savarin contrived to exercise a very large number of professions. Despite a popularly held view, one *métier* which he never embraced was that of cook. Nor did he ever write, or even attempt to write, a cookery book. The nearest he came was the book for which he has gained everlasting fame: *La Physiologie du goût.** Nor is *La Physiologie du goût* really a food book; rather, it is a discussion of the nature of eating in its widest sense, what our ancestors in the nineteenth century would have called the 'phenomenology' of taste.

La Physiologie du goût was published in the last three months of Brillat's life. There is no substantial evidence that during the seventy years which preceded the publication of his book, the author was abnormally interested in his stomach, or indeed in any major branch of the culinary arts. Brillat's preoccupations were those of a minor public figure in one of the most fast-moving periods of European history. During the 25 years between the outbreak of the Revolution and the downfall of Napoleon, Brillat rose occasionally to pre-eminence, sometimes fell from view; in all he did he proved the perfect measure of his troubled times; in his own provincial way, he was no less accomplished a survivor than Talleyrand or Sièyes.

The first 34 years of Brillat's life show him an unabashed provincial.

---

*English edition, *The Philosopher in the Kitchen*, trans. Anne Drayton (Penguin Books, 1970; paperback edition, 1981).

Before 1789 he had visited the court at Versailles only once, and Paris possibly not at all. In his home town, the sleepy cathedral city of Belley, he occupied an important position in the landed bourgeoisie which was beginning to challenge the supremacy of the local nobility. Like his father and grandfather before him, Brillat was a popular lawyer with a busy practice. Like so many other provincial lawyers throughout the length and breadth of France and Navarre (one has only to think of Robespierre in Arras), he had an insatiable appetite for the new thinking extolled by the *philosophes*. He was passionate about Voltaire and almost as keen on Rousseau. On the other hand, the earthy, sensual side to his character prevented him from embracing the whole package of moralistic, puritanical thinking which attracted so many of the younger generation. The obsessive imitation of Roman virtue which was held to excuse so many atrocious acts during the years of the Terror did not appeal to Brillat.

Until the spring of 1789, Brillat's political preoccupation was maintaining the importance of his own region, the rugged semi-Alpine province of the Bugey, and of its capital, Belley. The Bugey had only become a part of France 150 years before Brillat's birth, having previously been a part of the Italian Duchy of Savoy. Its annexation by France after the 1601 Treaty of Lyon brought with it untold complications. In theory, at least, the region should have retained its customary rights and laws, but as the years went on a greater and greater centralizing tendency began to erode local rights, to the extent that the people started to complain that they were worse off under the French Crown. As a politically ambitious young lawyer, Brillat listened to their grievances and tried his best to find answers.

The immediate pre-revolutionary years saw the collapse of royal authority in the provinces, notably when a local revolt went unchecked in neighbouring Dauphiné in 1788. Brillat saw a chance to use the Estates General as a means of redeeming some of the region's autonomy and countering the ineluctable extension of central power.

Elected to represent the Bugey at Versailles, and later in Paris, Brillat spent the next two years on the periphery of the events of the Revolution. He was a failure as a politician; he could not convince the other members of the assembly of the need to check central power by means of local power bases like the Bugey, and his province was abolished as an entity and absorbed in the newly created *département* of the Ain with the old rival city, Bourg-en-Bresse, as its capital.

If his achievements were few, they were not non-existent: at the very least he was able to retain the Ain's cathedral and seminary in Belley and prevent them from migrating to Bourg. In other matters he spoke as a lawyer, voicing his opposition to juries and his support for the death penalty. In the former he failed to carry the day, in the latter (ironically as it turned out) his views swayed deputies on both sides of the chamber. His efforts were appreciated by his fellow citizens; when he returned to Belley they made him President of the Civil Court; the understudy to the department's envoy to the new national appeal court, the *Cour de cassation*; and, in the last month of 1792, Mayor of Belley.

If Brillat thought he would live out the rest of his days as the biggest fish in his small pond, he was much mistaken. A former member of the Jacobin Club, he now switched his allegiance to the Girondins; and when war broke out with the nations on France's borders (a war advocated by the Girondins against Jacobin opposition), provincial Girondin opposition to the revolutionary measures being enacted in Paris was interpreted as treachery which would lead to a civil war, to the benefit of France's enemies. The Jacobin-dominated assembly dispatched representatives to the provinces to arrest local Girondin leaders. Brillat had been party to one or two imprudent discussions in the past; knowing that to face any trial in Bourg, Lyon or Paris would be tantamount to putting his head under the guillotine, he vanished over the border into Switzerland.

Disguised as one Benoît Sattner, Brillat managed eventually to reach safety in the United States. Forced to earn a living by teaching French, he awarded himself the title of *Professeur*, by which he jocularly referred to himself to the end of his days. He also played first fiddle in America's only professional orchestra; at the John Street Theater, New York. Despite later protestations to the contrary, it is clear that Brillat's gaze remained firmly fixed on his native land and the chance of an early end to his exile. Changes in the political structure of France marked by the downfall of the Convention in 1795 made him optimistic about an early return, but time dragged on without any clear indication of an amnesty. Eventually, encouraged by his influential cousin Jacques-Rose Récamier and his beautiful wife Juliette, he decided to run the risk. In the autumn of 1796 he landed in Le Havre.

Brillat's rehabilitation was frustratingly brief. A new *coup* from the left in the autumn of the following year forced him to quit Paris once again; he became secretary to the General Staff attached to the French army in the Black Forest. His experience of army life was dismal, enlivened only by occasional bouts of whoring in the company of a sympathetic general. He left the army at the first opportunity, and re-entered the judiciary as President of the Criminal Court in Bourg at the beginning of 1798.

Brillat's brief sojourn in Bourg-en-Bresse opened up a new chapter in his life; for the next 29 years he remained a judge, first in Bourg, next as State Prosecutor in Versailles, and finally as a member of the bench of the *Tribunal* (later *Cour*) *de cassation*. It was in this last post that he died, in February 1826. However, it would be a mistake to assume that from 1797 onwards he had put the years of anxiety behind him: France itself was far from stable. But Brillat was at least on the winning side. The *coup d'état* of 18 Brumaire which brought Napoleon to power as First Consul led to Brillat's reinstatement as a member of the appeal court. Ensconced in the capital once more, he had the time and income to enjoy its delights: restaurants, the secret pleasures of the Palais-Royal, the company of Madame Récamier. In his idle moments he wrote, planning a major study of the judiciary and producing a long essay on political economy.

While Bonaparte's star was in the ascendant, so too was Brillat's. As one of the judges of the *Cour de cassation* his appointment was guaranteed for life by the Emperor, and he was decorated as a Chevalier of the Légion d'honneur. Brillat's heart filled with pride as his emperor's armies subdued the European continent from Cadiz to Moscow. When Napoleon's fortunes turned at Leipzig in 1813, however, Brillat must have thought his luck had also come to an end. He took refuge in the Bugey and, with little to occupy his mind but the business of mending fences at the new royal court, wrote a few pornographic stories. However, King Louis XVIII seemed prepared to accept the assurances of Brillat and his colleagues that they had always been His Majesty's most stalwart defenders. Brillat was reappointed to the bench.

Nor was Napoleon different from the plump Bourbon Louis: returning to Paris for the Hundred Days, he too accepted the judiciary's claims of loyalty. After Waterloo this collection of Bray vicars in judges' robes achieved a hat-trick: their petition was accepted once again. Who, after all, had not apostatized during the previous quarter-century?

Brillat was now 60, and there was as yet no sign of the book which brought him fame. An essay on duelling was well received, and one more short story was produced.

The judge's years had followed a set pattern since his promotion to the bench. Every September he returned to the province he loved so much in order to shoot, read and idle away the evenings in gossip with the local rakes. Sometimes he would try the virtues of the local matrons, but always with a light-heartedness born of considerable experience. His generosity of spirit was at its most noticeable during the two months he spent annually at his manor house in Vieu, where he organized the feasts and dances which were the high points of the local shooting season. At the beginning of November he made his way back to the capital and the court, to Paris's restaurants, and Madame Récamier.

The mid-1820s were a time of intense interest in food and restaurants, and the word 'gastronomy' was on everyone's lips. A number of writers, including the young Balzac, took advantage of the public enthusiasm. Brillat's mind also turned increasingly to his stomach. Encouraged by his friends, he too set about writing a study of taste, drawing on all aspects of the subject and paying special attention to the medical side, as elucidated by the many leading physicians he called his friends.

By the summer of 1825 the manuscript was ready, and it was privately printed when he returned from his annual leave at the end of the year. It was an immediate sensation. Paris was mystified by this extraordinary study and by the puckish wit of the tall, portly judge who had put it together. For the next two months, many people angled to meet the now-famous author; but the judge's triumph was to be literally short-lived. Two months later, at the age of 70 years and 10 months, Brillat was dead.

As a young man Brillat epitomized a generation of thrusting lawyers who formed the cadre of the Revolution; yet Brillat was much more than just a metaphor for his time: few people assembled such varied talents, and even if many travelled widely in exile Brillat was almost unique in wanting to adopt the manners and customs of his host country. In his surviving letters and papers we see samples of the quality of his wit and judgement and finally, in his swansong, a work which in 165 years has never gone out of fashion.

CHAPTER ONE

Belley and the Bugey

I

S OME FIFTY MILES to the east of Lyon and about the same distance to the south of the departmental capital, Bourg-en-Bresse,
lies the small city of Belley. One might hesitate to use such a grandiose
term as city were it not for the presence of the cathedral church of
Saint John the Baptist. With its 8,000 inhabitants, Belley falls in size
somewhere between a small town and an overgrown village.

In a country so rich in beautiful small towns, few tourists come as
far as Belley. There is surprisingly little to see, anyhow: just the
remains of the college where both Brillat-Savarin and the poet,
traveller and diplomat Alphonse de Lamartine first construed the
Latin poets, the Episcopal Palace, and the aristocratic houses of the
Grand'Rue, their bleak façades hiding, as many do, beautiful Renaissance courtyards. The gastronomically minded judge, Jean-Anthelme
Brillat-Savarin, was born at No. 62.

For the late twentieth-century traveller what is best about Belley is
the surrounding countryside. Where the Bresse is sleek and flat, perfect land for nurturing its famous poultry, the Bugey is rugged and
wild. In the far north of the region the remote, sleepy town of Nantua
is perched on the end of its lake, its densely wooded banks rising
steeply towards the Alps. To the south two ranges of mountains
enclose the pretty Valromey, or 'valley of the Romans', protected
from the worst of the Alpine climate by two peaks, the Crêt du Nu
and the mighty Grand Colombier. On the Grand Colombier's south-
eastern slopes are a few clumps of vineyard, with those of Vongnes the

only relics of a previously prosperous wine industry in the region. The Rhône forms the borders of the Bugey to the south, and also on its way to Lyon in the west.

The Bugey had already enjoyed a long history before it came under French domination. Until the sixteenth century the Rhône Marches, as they were called, paid homage to the Holy Roman Emperor. The Dukes of Savoy held sway over the Valromey from their capital of Rossillon, protecting the powerful abbeys of Saint-Sulpice, Saint-Rambert and Ambronay.

In 1535 François I annexed the Bresse and the Bugey, but was careful to guarantee the rights of his new subjects. The people of the Bugey, the Bresse and the Valromey might now be part of Greater Burgundy, but retained a body of local laws and rights derived from the Savoyard dukes.

These Dukes of Savoy had by no means abandoned their claims to the area. Emmanuel Philibert's attempts to win back the Bresse by laying siege to Bourg ended in humiliating defeat, but with the signature of the Treaty of Câteau Cambrésis in 1559 Marguerite of France was promised to him as his bride: part of her dowry was the Bresse, the Bugey and the Valromey, and 24 years of French rule came to an end.

When Emmanuel Philibert died in 1580 he was succeeded by Charles Emmanuel who, eight years later, chose his moment to strike. Believing France to be crippled by her religious wars, and confident in his alliance with the King of Spain, the Duke of Savoy invaded the Marquisate of Saluces.

In 1594, Henri IV put an end to the French wars of religion by converting to Catholicism. Attempts to arbitrate between France and Savoy were hampered by Charles Emmanuel's failure to keep his word. Henri IV remained attached to Saluces: 'I ask only for my property, whatever the arrangement I want my marquisate.'[1] He was easily able to subdue the armies of the Duke of Savoy and take the region by force. In the event, by the Treaty of Lyon signed on 17 February 1601, Charles Emmanuel retained the Marquisate of Saluces, but at the cost of the provinces of the Bresse, the Bugey, the Valromey and the Pays de Gex. These regions now became irrevocably part of France, their inhabitants French.

II

Very soon the French Crown began to infringe on the privileges formerly enjoyed by the *bugistes*. In July 1601 Henri created the *Présidial* in Belley's rival, Bourg-en-Bresse. Belley and Gex, previously on an equal footing with Bourg, were awarded the subsidiary judicial jurisdiction of *bailliages*. Subservience to Bourg was bad enough, given that very little contact existed between the two cities (for instance, they were not served by the same bishop); worse was the appellate jurisdiction, the *Parlement* of Dijon. For the most part Burgundian law, like that of the rest of northern France, was based on common law. Like much of the *Midi* or the south of France, Belley and the Bugey adhered to written, Roman law. In 1789 the inhabitants of Culoz expressed their displeasure at a situation which had rankled for nearly two centuries after the Bugey became a province of France: 'The Province of the Bugey was included in the jurisdiction of the *Parlement* of Dijon after the exchange of 1601. It is unfortunate for the inhabitants of this province to have to travel fifty leagues to have their cases heard by a common law court, while they should be able to render such judgments themselves according to Roman law.'[2] They would have preferred to belong to the Dauphiné, whose *parlement* at Grenoble was closer and, moreover, adhered to Roman law.

A similar problem beset the local assembly which the Bugey preserved after the exchange of 1601, the *Tribunaux d'élection*. Theoretically, at least, the Bugey, like the Dombes, the Bresse and the Pays de Gex, had the right to an assembly every three years where the three orders of France, the Church, the nobility and the third estate, met to decide how their people were to be taxed. As the eighteenth century wore on, the right to free election in the case of the third estate was replaced by royal nomination, often overriding strong local feeling.

Part of the resentment felt by the *bugistes* was engendered by their remoteness from the throne of France and the comparative proximity of the court of Savoy. In 1820 Brillat-Savarin noted:

a province built on such terrain had by necessity little communication with its neighbours. In the middle of the eighteenth century before the opening of the *routes royales*, you wrote your will before undertaking a journey to Dijon (50 leagues). Any man who had spent any time in Lyon was deemed *Lyonnais* (20 leagues) and one of our compatriots alone was thought to deserve the glorious epithet of 'Parisian'.[3]

Even today, roads leading out of the province and into the Bresse are poor, slow and hazardous.

In 1760, the same year that reforms went through for rebuilding the tortuous mountain roads of the Bugey, the Treaty of Turin concluded between France and Savoy (now united with the kingdom of Sardinia) finally resolved border disputes between the two countries, removing from Savoyard control a strip of land on the borders of the Gex which had formerly been used to afford Spanish troops access to the province of Franche-Comté. To the immense chagrin of its inhabitants the Valserine came under the feudal jurisdiction of the Cistercians, provoking Voltaire to an exchange of correspondence with the minister in Paris. To the south, the border with Savoy was advanced to the middle of the Rhône.

To end this catalogue of despotism (as felt by the inhabitants of the former Savoyard provinces), the little principality of the Dombes bordering the Bugey to the west was suppressed by 'a simple notarial act' in 1762. The last sovereign, the comte Louis-Charles d'Eu of the House of Bourbon-Montpensier, ceded his lands on the Saône in exchange for estates in Normandy. Local laws were swept aside as the estates were rolled into those of the Bresse. In 1771 the minute but proud *Parlement* of Trévoux was abolished and replaced by a modest seneschalsy; from now on its *intendant* resided in Dijon. In 1789 the nobility of the Dombes still preserved the bitter memory of this 'illegal act'. The *cahiers* (books of grievances which were presented to the King on the eve of the Revolution) talk of 'the most despotic abuse of power' and of 'slavery'. 'This', they add, of the abolition, 'is our foremost grievance.'[4]

III

The remoteness of pre-revolutionary Belley was the source of much of its charm: local traditions were strong in an area so infrequently penetrated by agents of the outside world. Life centred on the village, where Belley's 4,000 or so inhabitants made it a formidable metropolis. Young people rarely left the village to marry, and the men positively prevented the beautiful girls of the community from being snapped up by a neighbouring commune – interested parties met strong-armed opposition.[5]

Brillat-Savarin, explaining his native land to Parisian savants in

1820, happily detected a survival of Roman manners in the *vallis romana* (Valromey). One of these was 'a sort of saturnalia'. In the distant past in the valley this had taken the form of inviting servants to eat at the tables of their masters at Christmas. 'This practice has been replaced by the following,' wrote Brillat-Savarin in 1820: 'in the houses of the comfortably-off or those of rich landowners, the servants go out to find the biggest log they can, which they call the *grobaz dè noíez*. This they roll on to the kitchen hearth and during the time it burns they eat white bread and have the best of times.'[6]

'*Grobaz dè noíez*' is an example of the local *patois* which successive rulers of Savoy and France were at pains to stamp out. Brillat-Savarin took a particular interest in his local dialect, indeed he was fascinated by language in all its forms. The 'th' of the *bugiste*, wrote Brillat in *La Physiologie du goût*, is found elsewhere only in English and Ancient Greek. Similarly, the *aou* sound as found in *baou* (cow-shed), *laou* (wolf), *taou* (tufa) and *saou* (elder tree) was unique in its monosyllabic pronunciation. Clearly Brillat had trouble undertaking his research into the language: 'This *patois* disappears from day to day, and when on my travels I use it to talk to the elders of the countryside, they reply almost without exception in French.'[7] Brillat would be even sadder to find how little the language survives in our time. The only *bugistes* who keep it alive now are a few old village-dwellers and a handful of well-meaning local scholars.[8]

The regional dress of the Bugey was also distinctive. On Sundays the well-off farmer wore a pointed hat in the shape of a medieval helmet, exposing his face but protecting his neck. His hair was worn long, falling over his shoulders. He wore a black tie, and a blue or grey tunic which reminded Brillat of a Roman *sagum*, covered by four or five jackets or waistcoats 'according to the importance of the person'.[9] On his legs he wore short breeches, with woollen stockings rolled at the top. He carried a stick. His wife wore a sort of cornet, a *fichu* crossing her breasts, a spencer or woollen under-bodice tight at the waist, 'the elbow decorated with an appendage shaped like a dog's ear'.[10] Her skirt was short, her heels high.

The women, without being remarkably beautiful, have freshness and possess good health. Their blood has been kept pure. The men in general are of the same stock as the Gaulois, tall with blond or light brown hair, their faces rectangular. Very few have Roman or Greek noses but there are few if any snub-nosed types either.[11]

IV

More distinctive still was the food and cooking of the region. The character of *bugiste* cuisine has now largely disappeared, so that one is hard-pressed to find a restaurant in the region which is a conscientious exponent of the once famous local style. This was not so before the war; when the great geographers of French cuisine Curnonsky and Marcel Rouff visited the region, they were able to declare:

> If the Bresse and the Bugey are the incontestable masters [of French cuisine] . . . it is because the goddess Nature, by her special grace, is pleased to endow this blessed corner of the globe with all those elements indispensable to the culinary art.[12]

Lucien Tendret, the model for Marcel Rouff's delightful novella *La Vie et la passion de 'Dodin-Bouffant'*, has left the best picture of the *bugiste* cuisine in his book, *La Table au pays de Brillat-Savarin*, although he is careful to add that at the time he wrote it (1892) much had already disappeared. The Bugey's secret was not just the wealth of raw materials, but also the remoteness of the province: 'means of communication were either insufficient or non-existent, everyone remained at home and the pleasures of the table were virtually the only ones available.' Tendret quotes a passage from Balzac:

> In the provinces the tedium and monotony of existence attracts mental activity into the kitchen. One does not dine as luxuriously in the provinces as one does in Paris, but one eats better as the dishes are better thought out. In every provincial hamlet there is a Carême wearing an apron, an unsung genius who can make a dish of beans worthy of that nod with which Rossini* greets some perfectly executed recipe.[13]

In such a varied terrain the woods and forests were a great source of game, kindling and, in season, wild mushrooms. In the springtime, woodland gleaners on the slopes of the Grand Colombier found morels, both black and white, 'the black not altogether black and the white not wholly white'.[14] In the woods around Belley a profusion of ceps, Caesar's mushrooms and chanterelles grew throughout the summer and autumn months. Between Belley and the vineyards of Culoz there were field mushrooms, which Tendret thought the best of all and which, by the end of the nineteenth century,

---

*To his Parisian contemporaries, Rossini was as well-known for his *gourmandise* as he was for his musical compositions.

had virtually disappeared 'like our freshwater crayfish and our good wines'.[15]

The greatest of all fungi is the truffle, of which the best in France come from Périgord and northern Provence. 'They are also found in the Bugey,' writes Brillat-Savarin in *La Physiologie du goût*, truffles 'of the highest quality, but the breed has the drawback of not being preservable.' Tendret found them from September to February 'in fallow or rocky stretches of countryside or on the edges of woods . . . the first truffles are white inside and have virtually no bouquet but they are excellent cooked with fresh butter, white onions and cream.' The blacks, unearthed after Christmas, Tendret calls 'a *sine qua non* for transcendental cuisine'.[16]

Game also was to be gleaned from the land, if you were lucky enough to possess a *seigneurie* in pre-revolutionary France. The fiefless commoner could not hunt, although he probably poached. Brillat-Savarin correctly set great store by the nature of the soil on which an animal was nurtured. A leveret from the sunbaked slopes of the Valromey or Upper Dauphiné was for him incontestably superior to one shot on the outskirts of Paris, and possibly 'the most aromatic of four-footed beasts'.* Lucien Tendret once again goes further, stipulating that the best hares were those caught on the Combe à la Done or the Rock of Talbaçon – those from the latter 'a more refined delicacy than a haunch of venison'.[17]

Another *bugiste* speciality was the fig-eater, a small bird of the garden warbler, blackcap, waxwing or pipit variety, which nourished itself on grapes and figs around harvest time. In *La Physiologie du goût* Brillat tells the story of the Jesuit Honoré Fabi. This man, who disputed Harvey's claim to be the first to chart the circulation of the blood, was a *bugiste* with a passion for fig-eaters second only to his love of science. As soon as the birds appeared in the vines and fruit trees, the locals would cry ' "Look, fig-eaters, Father Fabi is on his way . . ." This was indeed the case, he always arrived on 1 September accompanied by a friend and the two feasted themselves during their whole visit; everyone was more than happy to invite them to dinner, and they departed around the 25th.'[18]

Lucien Tendret considered the mutton of the Grand Colombier superior to that from the famous *pré-salé* of Normandy, where the sea-breezes impart a special flavour to the animals' flesh. The small

---

*Martial: *Inter aves turdus, si quis me judice certet, Inter quadrupes prima gloria lepus.*

bâtarde sheep ate wild herbs on the mountainside, rather like the lamb from Sisteron in Provence: 'Today, the memory of these juicy *gigots* puts into even starker perspective the strong taste and stench emanating from the thighs of those infamous billy-goats which are impertinently dished up under the name of *pré-salé* legs of lamb.'[19]

Lamb from the Grand Colombier was one delicacy which has already disappeared before the end of the nineteenth century; another was the local small black pig, now confined to parts of Italy, Corsica and Spain. In the course of the nineteenth century it was phased out in favour of fast-growing, heavyweight white pigs from Britain and Scandinavia.[20] The introduction of the Large White with its 'insipid flesh' presaged the disappearance of the *saucisson de Belley*, which had formerly rivalled its counterparts in Lyon and even Bologna. Proper feeding even of the black pigs of the Bugey was vitally important if the flesh were to have taste: 'If they are fed on cooked plants, vegetable leaves, kitchen scraps, dirty water and bran, the flesh will be flabby, tasteless and grey. It will be firm, juicy and red if they are fattened on cooked potatoes, coarsely ground barley, a purée of little beans, maize, buckwheat, acorns, chestnuts, oats and rye flour.'[21]

The Bugey could not vie with neighbouring Bresse for the quality of its poultry. Even in Brillat-Savarin's time the capons and *poulardes* of the Bresse had a reputation which reached Paris and beyond. The turkeys, however, had a fine, delicate flavour and could rival those of the Berry for size. The superiority of the region was noticeable again when it came to the rare sorts of fish which teemed in the rivers and lakes. First among these were the fresh-water crayfish or *écrevisses*, which made the gastronomic reputation of the town of Nantua in the Haut-Bugey. Even today dishes containing crayfish tails (and even many which don't) are styled *à la Nantua*.

The famous crayfish were not restricted to the lake at Nantua. In those days before the general scarcity of crayfish was felt all over France they were to be had in the rivers Gland, Rousses and Furens. On the Furens was the original site of the Convent of Bons, later transferred to Belley, and then made over during the Revolution for the use of the seminary which Brillat-Savarin was instrumental in founding there. The reason for the nuns' removal from the country is revealed by Tendret: under Louis XIII they had been leading a scandalous life 'and were busier with their *courts-bouillons* than with the reciting of the psalms.' Attempts by the Bishop to call them to order were met with abuse and indecent gestures. Intervention by Richelieu himself

was necessary before they would consent to leave the fish-rich Furens and move in under the eye of the Bishop in Belley. The nuns took with them, however, a recipe for the crayfish of the Furens which they continued to perfect right down to the abolition of the convent at the time of the Revolution.[22]

Besides *écrevisses*, the Bugey supplied excellent pike and trout. From Lake Bourget on the far side of the Rhône came perch, pollan, and char – 'the best freshwater fish, its milky-white flesh lighter and more refined than that of a trout'.[23] Despite its lightness, Tendret suggests for char a sauce composed of black truffles, coxcombs, carp roes and pollan *quenelles*, adding with characteristic vehemence, 'Aren't you disgusted by the eternal turbot with *hollandaise* sauce?'

The dairy herds which fed on the abundant pastures of the mountain valleys produced excellent butter, as Brillat-Savarin discovered on his visit to the Cistercians of Saint-Sulpice in 1782. As for cheese, Tendret claimed that *bugistes* had no reason to be jealous of other regions of France, but sadly gave no details. Patrick Rance, visiting the region in the 1980s, found two goats' cheeses, *chevret* and *tomme*, native to Belley, both soft with patchy red crusts. In the Bugey he found another cheese called *Bugey*, or *petit Bugey*, similar to a *crottin* from the Berry but made from cows' milk rather than goats'. In addition to these there were *ramequins*, small goats'-milk cheeses allowed to grow strong with age and used for flavouring *fondues*. The best cheese of the region was and is the *bleu de Gex*, one of the world's great blue cheeses, made from the milk of Montbéliard cows which graze 1,000 metres above sea level. The cheese, now all dairy-made, has existed since the fourteenth century, and it is inconceivable that it did not find a place on the tables of the rich bourgeois of Belley in the eighteenth century.[24]

Visiting the Cistercians at Saint-Sulpice, Brillat-Savarin marvelled at the quality of the vegetables grown at that altitude, 1,066 metres. Tendret heaps praise on the turnips of Parves in the Lower Bugey, where Brillat's father was responsible for administering feudal justice for the monks of the Charterhouse of Pierre Châtel. Tendret describes the turnips as having 'a black skin, their white flesh having a particularly sweet flavour stemming from the mountain soils in which they are grown'.[25] The best potatoes were the Marjolin and the long Quenelle which, dug up in spring and rubbed with a cloth to remove the skins before being tossed in a pan of clarified butter, became 'véritables soufflés à la crème'.[26] The best fruits came from the sunny

plains below Culoz. Of particular note was the *angurie*, a species of water-melon with red pips which was cooked to make jam.

The *salé* was another Belley speciality, bread rubbed with walnut oil and baked with onions and chopped walnuts, eaten at children's *goûters* or teas. Tendret and Curnonsky and Rouff list hosts of culinary preparations for which Belley and the Bugey were famed, such as the *gâteau de foies blonds*, the *noix de veau farcie entourée de morilles noires de Valromey* and *oreilles de veau farcies*. One recipe given in *La Physiologie du goût* is for the *fondue de Belley*: 'Fondue comes from Switzerland. It is nothing more than scrambled eggs and cheese mixed in proportions decreed by time and experience.'[27] Swiss or not, the *fondue de Belley* had for a long time been one of the classics of local tables. Brillat tells the story of a M. de Madot who arrived to take up his office as Bishop of Belley in the seventeenth century and who, thinking the *fondue* a cream, ate it with a spoon rather than a fork. Even his great-uncles, says Brillat, used to laugh over the Bishop's gaffe. Predictably, Tendret improves on the basic recipe by showering the *fondue* with black truffles.

V

Writing in 1820 Brillat-Savarin told the history of the vine in the Bugey in his *Mémoire sur l'archéologie de la partie orientale du département de l'Ain*. As in so many other parts of France, the vines of the Bugey were first introduced by the Romans, who 'gave the name of Falernum to the hillside which nourished the first plantations'. The hillside still preserved the slightly deformed name of 'Falère' in Brillat's time, leading patriotically minded *bugistes* to confuse references to the famous Falernian of Roman times with the products of their local slopes.

Brillat's own vineyard was the Côte-Grêle in Machuraz, producing a wine which, we are told, could be fermented to an impressive strength: the bawdy song which Pierrette Brillat-Savarin sang on her wedding day has been put down to the fact that she 'had dipped her wings in the *crus* of Machuraz'.[28]

The bad jokes made about *vins du cru* [*cru* has a second sense of 'invention'] have not prevented me from offering it to a *selected few**

---

*In English in the original.

who have looked at its colour, nosed it and rolled it round their palates with signs of satisfaction which I have every reason to believe genuine.[29]

Sadly, like most of the wines of the Bugey, the Côte-Grêle has disappeared. Wine-making had ceased there even before the scourge of phylloxera eliminated most of the vineyards in the region. But Curnonsky and Rouff were still able to sing the praises of the wines of Virieu and Seyssel, 'the liquids which crayfish and fish dream of',[30] and of those of Manicle, de Pontet and Culoz 'which leave the mouth fresh and the mind clear'.[31] Curnonsky and Rouff leave an impressive list of vineyards, which sadly have since proved uneconomic and have been turned over to dairy farming; the grapes were, broadly speaking, those grown in Burgundy, with the addition of one or two Savoyard types, Chardonnay, Pinot Noir, Gamay, Mondeuse and Roussette. Few survive today apart from those on the villages of Flaxieu, Vongnes and Culoz.

The vines are emblematic of the general decline of this picturesque region of jagged rocks and tiny valleys, of torrents and mountain lakes. The decline had set in long before Brillat's death in 1826 and was a result, at least in part, of the character-obliterating, centralizing tendency which began under the *ancien régime* and achieved total victory during the Revolution. As a member of the Constituent Assembly Brillat-Savarin fought hard to preserve his native province. He, more than anyone, knew the world he had lost:

Civilization and fashion everywhere extend the veil of uniformity; the ancient ways are gone, tradition is forgotten; our people no longer wear the patriarchal tie or use our *patois*; painted cloth has replaced wool; young women in the villages twist their hair on to elegant combs; *fichus* open as shawls, those creations of the devil, multiply. We have lost our former ways, above all, the empire of marriage has been destroyed and now when I go to breathe the air of my native land I am astonished to find, despite the one hundred and fifty leagues that I have travelled, all around me the same behaviour that I thought I had left behind me on the sunny banks of the Seine.[32]

The Proud Provincial

I

IT WAS INTO this remote world of plunging ravines and fertile valleys that Jean-Anthelme Brillat-Savarin was born on 2 April 1755.[1] His father, Marc-Anthelme, was one of the three dozen or so local lawyers who, together with the canons and officers of the cathedral, formed the élite of the provincial city.[2] Claudine-Aurore, his mother, also hailed from a family of *robins* or lawyers. Her father, Claude Récamier, held the office of Notary Royal in the city, and also a lucrative post as manager to the *seigneurie* of Rochefort.[3] At the beginning of the previous century, the Récamiers had been among the founders of the Collège de Belley. Jacques-Rose Récamier, whose wife Juliette became Châteaubriand's mistress, was Claudine-Aurore's third cousin.[4]

Claudine-Aurore had made a good marriage: the Brillats were distinguished by a more ancient lineage than the Récamiers, and clerical Savarins were even present at the assemblies of the 130-strong nobility of the Bugey.[5]

The Brillats came from Lochieu, near the Charterhouse of Arvières in the mountainous Haut-Valromey.[6] Until the Bugey passed from the House of Savoy to the Bourbons, the family had hovered on the fringes of nobility. Several Brillats had used the title of *miles* or knight, while during the sixteenth century they profited from a sale of offices to raise money for the Savoyard princes, thereby becoming *nobles à cent écus*, or 'hundred-crown nobles'.

After the Bugey was ceded to France in 1601, Clair Brillat moved to

Belley where he practised as a lawyer at the *bailliage* or local court. In 1673 Clair's son, Jean Brillat, another lawyer, married Claudine Savarin.

The Savarins or Savarinis had their origins in Venice. As Savarinis the family had produced a brace of cardinals for the Roman Church. Under the Bourbons, the Savarins rapidly established themselves as one of the leading legal families in Belley. In 1619 Paul Savarin became *procureur royal*, or King's Prosecutor, at the head of the Belley bar.

The first Brillat to become *procureur royal* for Belley was Melchior, in 1687. On 7 October 1723 Étienne Brillat took over the office. On 12 September 1748 he was replaced as *procureur royal* for the Valromey, Gex and the Bugey by his son Marc-Anthelme, the father of the author of *La Physiologie du goût*.[7]

Twenty-two years before his birth, Jean-Anthelme's fortunes had been considerably advanced by the death of a great-aunt, Marie-Gasparde Savarin. Marie-Gasparde left her house in the Grand'Rue of Belley together with a *gentilhommière* (a small country house) to Marc-Anthelme on condition that he make 'an honourable marriage before the age of twenty-five, and bear the arms of the Savarin family in perpetuity'.[8]

At the time of Jean-Anthelme's birth, then, Monsieur and Madame Brillat-Savarin were the possessors of a fine town house in the most prestigious street in the provincial capital and of a manor house in Vieu in the shadow of the Grand Colombier, about thirty kilometres to the north. Jean-Anthelme was born in the house in the Grand'Rue: a solid, stone-built construction, dating back to the beginning of the seventeenth century when the *robins* of Belley had first begun to make their homes in that street. The house still stands, a chemist's shop filling two of the ground-floor arcades on to the street. From the inner courtyard a Renaissance staircase gives access to vaulted galleries with a view over a secluded garden. The only major alteration dates from the Directory, when part of the courtyard range was rebuilt in a pretty, contemporary idiom.

Marc-Anthelme and Claudine-Aurore had been married in 1753, and Jean-Anthelme was their first child. At his christening the future politician, judge and gastronome was given the name of the city of Belley's favourite son, the twelfth-century Saint Anthelm. This Carthusian was a 'fearless and uncompromising bishop' of Belley who in 1175 excommunicated the local magnate, Count Humbert de

Maurienne, and refused to back down even when the Pope had lifted the excommunication. Earlier, Pope Alexander III had chosen Anthelm to mediate between King Henry II of England and Thomas à Becket. Sadly for Becket, Anthelm's mission never took place.[9]

Marc-Anthelme and Claudine-Aurore had eight children in all. Their second, Pierrette, married a notary from Lhuis to the west of Belley. Pierrette died in Lhuis at the age of 99 years and 10 months, having lived long enough to tell stories of her famous elder brother to the young Lucien Tendret. Tendret tells us that she died, 'sitting up in bed. Finishing her dinner she roared "Bring me my dessert".' The maid ran to her side, but she was too late; 'her mistress had missed out on dessert, she was already on her way to take her coffee in the next world.'[10]

Only two of the other children married: François-Xavier, or plain Xavier, whose descendants carried on the Brillat-Savarin name into our century, married a Marie Chevrier and followed his elder brother into the law. Anthelmette or Thelmette married the clerk to the magistrates in Lhuis, Marc Carrel. The youngest brother, Frédéric, became a professional soldier, ending his days as Colonel of the 134th Regiment of Foot. The three remaining sisters, Gasparde (Padon), Marie (Marion) and Joséphine (Joson), died spinsters, 'they only lived for Anthelme'.[11]

The reluctance of the Brillat-Savarins to marry seems odd: three marriages for eight children is not an impressive total in the circumstances of their wealth and station. The reason lies, perhaps, in the overbearing character of their mother, 'la Belle Aurore'. According to the *livre de raison* or family bible of the Récamier family, Claudine-Aurore 'had a pretty figure and a pretty face as well as a deal of natural intelligence. Her upbringing had been neglected, and she had been spoiled and flattered by her aunts, which hindered the development of her talents. Her heart was frank, generous and grateful. The only thing one might reproach her for would be a little severity towards her children.'

The same source informs us that la Belle Aurore was 'very strict about the way her children were dressed. She insisted that they only appear before their parents decently clad, that they be well-scrubbed and that they refer to them only using the polite form *vous*. If, by chance, the children entered a room where their parents were to be found and for some reason forgot to greet them, they were sent out again with the reproach, "You have forgotten something".'[12]

In 1855, just before her death, Pierrette Guigard told Lucien Tendret the story of a severe admonition meted out by Aurore at the time of her wedding. After a blessing from the Bishop of Belley, Mgr Cortois de Quincey, the family and guests sat down to dinner. 'Bidden to sing, the newlywed broke into an extremely bawdy air. The bride's mother, la Belle Aurore, listened to the song in silence; but once it was finished, she rose to her feet and, ignoring the presence of that Prince of the Church, administered two resounding slaps to Pierrette's cheeks.' The same medicine was administered to her eldest son one day when he 'had had the effrontery to contradict this oracle [Aurore Brillat]! She rewarded him with a magisterial whack, adding: "Let it be known, *Monsieur*, that anyone who talks back to their mother deserves a hiding".'[13]

II

While the young Jean-Anthelme was taking his first steps under the strict supervision of his mother, Marc-Anthelme was consolidating his position in Belley. We learn that his practice was flourishing to the extent that clients came to consult him 'from a distance of fifty leagues around the city'. Brillat-Savarin *père* added to his income by becoming *juge civil et criminel des seigneuries de Nattages et Parves pour les vénérables chartreux de Pierre Chastel*,[14] meting out justice for the local Carthusians in their domains to the south of Belley.

By all accounts Marc-Anthelme was a civilized man. His library showed no evidence that he took his church work too seriously; indeed, for one so close to the Bishop of Belley, some of his books were decidedly controversial. He had read deeply in Voltaire, Rousseau and Condillac and owned the seven volumes of the *Encyclopédie*, as well as volumes on the Vatican's index of banned books.

At least one of Brillat-Savarin *père*'s friends had a close relationship with Voltaire, who lived nearby at Ferney in the Pays de Gex. Doctor Jean-François Coste, fresh from his studies, had been called upon to deal with an epidemic raging in the Pays de Gex. Within three months the epidemic had been stamped out - largely, we gather, as a result of Coste's vigilance and ability.[15]

From that moment onwards, Voltaire lent his full support to the young doctor. In 1769, finding it difficult to survive on his earnings as a country physician, Coste asked Voltaire for help. The venerable sage wrote to Louis XV's chief minister, the duc de Choiseul:

> To Monsieur le duc de Choiseul, a request from the Hermit of Ferney, presented by Mr Coste, physician.
>
> Nothing is more fitting than the supplication of an infirm valetudinarian in favour of a young physician, nothing is more equitable than an increase in revenues when the burden of labour increases.
>
> Monsieur is aware that formerly we had only scrofula in this desert of Gex, and that now that we have troops stationed here, we have something more virulent to deal with. The old hermit, who, to tell the truth, has received neither of these two benefits of providence, but who maintains a sincere interest in those people who are so honoured, takes the liberty to present in misery and respect, M. Coste. M. Coste is a most endearing physician who believes he may be able to prevent our death, but who has nothing to live on, which is quite the contrary to all those great physicians in Paris. He begs *Monseigneur* to kindly take pity on a little territory for which he is the sole hope.[16]

Choiseul took Voltaire's somewhat mocking letter in good part. Coste was given a pension of 1,200 *livres* and made physician in charge of the hospital at Versoix. More prestigious appointments followed, at Nancy and Calais.[17]

Marc-Anthelme must have been eager to hear stories of the Hermit of Ferney from one who spoke from personal knowledge. His son Jean-Anthelme also became a convinced Voltairean, and anyone who had known his hero was bound to achieve an important place in his affections.[18]

Jean-Anthelme received his early education from his severe mother and from a Sieur Chavance, who had been contracted to teach the boy his letters.[19] Instruction took place during the legal terms at the family house in the Grand'Rue, and during the holidays at the *gentil-hommière* at Vieu in the Valromey. The house in Vieu still exists, a Savoyard *maison forte* of which the earliest parts date from the mid-sixteenth century, when the ravages of the Wars of Religion made small fortresses necessary for protection against itinerant bands of Protestant or Catholic thugs. The main body of the building was constructed almost a century later under Louis XIII, after the Valromey became part of France. The Edict of Nantes which proclaimed religious liberty within the state had removed the necessity for fortifications. The impressive towers and machicolations which decorate the present building were added in the nineteenth century.[20]

21

The young Brillat-Savarin entered the prestigious Collège de Belley in 1764 or 1765.[21] Coste had been an earlier luminary, while Brillat's friend and future member of the Convention Anthelme Ferrand,[22] was a near contemporary.

The colleges of Bourg, Thoissey, Nantua and Belley were the best schools in the area, and noble families of the district sent their children there to board, 'where they rubbed shoulders with the sons of rich commoners who made up the lion's share of the pupils'.[23] The young nobles were not the most academically dedicated elements in the school; in 1803 Brillat-Savarin described them as having gloried in their ignorance. The Revolution, he added, made all classes 'realize the advantages of study, and the children of historic families began to bow down before the equality of public education.'[24]

The Collège de Belley was not cheap: the fees for boarders amounted to between 400 and 450 *livres*, which can be compared to the annual salary of a country clergyman – only 700 *livres*. The school was therefore accessible only to the wealthy: wholesale merchants, office-holding bourgeois, financiers, lawyers like Marc-Anthelme, *rentiers* and a smattering of nobles. The school was clearly good, and its fame such that it attracted pupils from as far away as Voiron and Grenoble in the Dauphiné and from Chambéry across the border in Savoy.

In 1770, while Jean-Anthelme was a pupil, the Antonines who ran the Collège gave place to the Missionaries of the Congregation of Saint Joseph, whose mother-house was in Lyon. New buildings for the school, begun a year or two before Brillat started his studies, were finished in 1770. The handsome chapel is still one of Belley's best buildings, although it is no longer used for its original purpose.

The rebuilding had been made possible by the will of Monseigneur du Dousset, who had intended to re-endow the college as a *collège-séminaire*. His will was not respected, and although most of the teaching staff were in holy orders there was no theology class. The presence of so many priests among the staff did not inhibit the interest in science which was sweeping through France; indeed, Belley decided to open a *'Cabinet de phisique [sic], méchanique et histoire naturelle'*. The inquisitive Jean-Anthelme must have been pleased to find the library contained books on agriculture and chemistry as well as the usual collections of Latin authors.[25] It was during his years at the Collège de Belley that he read the works of Lavater, Pascal, Vauvenarges, La Rochefoucauld, Montesquieu and Rabelais, not to mention those who remained his life-long favourites: Voltaire, Rousseau, Fénelon and Buffon.[26]

The growing influence of Voltaire notwithstanding, Jean-Anthelme grew to appreciate in some degree the wisdom of his priestly tutors. In a small cathedral city like Belley it must have been difficult to avoid becoming involved in the affairs of the religious community, especially one led by such a bishop as Gabriel Cortois de Quincey.

Lucien Tendret has left us this stylish picture of him.

> It is said that Mgr Gabriel Cortois de Quinsey [*sic*] was named Bishop of Belley as a favour to Madame de Pompadour, that he possessed a very handsome face, and an imposing figure, that he spent his time at court and that Louis XV used to say mischievously: 'Watch out Mesdames, Monsieur de Belley is coming.'
>
> It is not true for one moment that Mgr Cortois de Quinsey owed his crook and mitre to the kindly protection of Madame de Pompadour; he never went to court, being continually resident in his episcopal palace; however, it is true to say that he was extremely gracious, grand in his manner, and that his features were remarkably fine.

Tendret maintains that de Quincey owed his bishopric rather to his education and sharp wit, used in defence of religion in a dispute with an abusive, free-thinking young officer whom he encountered while journeying to Paris in quest of preferment. It chanced that a witness of his verbal triumph was a young monk who, it transpired, was the brother of Mgr. de Mirepoix, who held the portfolio of Church appointments.

Mgr. de Mirepoix proposed making him Bishop of Belley to replace Mgr. de Tinseau, who had recently been promoted to the see of Nevers. He added that the Bishopric of Belley was worth a mere 4,500 *livres*, but that he would think of some means of increasing the emoluments.

M. Cortois de Quincey became Bishop of Belley and shortly afterwards he was named Abbot of the Abbeys of Conches in Normandy and Ambronay in the Bugey. These two benefices brought in a further 40,000 *livres*, which he put to use in constructing a new bishop's palace.[27]

In fact Cortois' income from the see of Belley was considerably greater than Tendret suggests, though if his figures for the pluralistic Bishop's emoluments are wrong, he is correct as to the use Cortois made of his funds. Cortois wished to construct the most magnificent building in Belley. The famous Jean-Jacques Soufflot made a plan for the project, and soon there rose the palace of the bishops of Belley. '*Monseigneur* loved the arts,' wrote Tendret. 'He commissioned the magnificent statute of the Virgin, which one can still see in the Cathedral, from the sculptor Chinard. It cost him 12,000 *livres*.'[28]

The Bishop was also a gourmand of note. Brillat-Savarin has left us a story about a spear of asparagus found growing in his kitchen garden:

> As quickly as they could get to their feet, the entire company descended on the vegetable patch to see if it [really existed]; as even in bishops' palaces one is enchanted to find something to fill the hours.

Great was the excitement; and the local cutler was commissioned to make a special knife for the Bishop's use when the asparagus should be ready for cutting. Its progress was closely watched, and a fine dinner ordered when it was judged that the day was at hand. The Bishop bent to his task:

> But, imagine the surprise! The disappointment! The chagrin! The prelate rose to his feet with empty hands . . . the asparagus was made of wood.
>
> This possibly slightly wicked prank was the work of Canon Rosset who, being from Saint-Claude, was an excellent carpenter and painted extremely well.[29]

This episode gives something of the flavour of Cortois' reign, as well as an idea of the futility of life in Belley at the end of the *ancien régime*.

Brillat-Savarin was not immune to the charms of clerical existence. In old age he reminisced contentedly of his childhood in the cathedral city and of the many gourmandizing figures connected with the church and college. One of these was the meticulous Canon Chevrier, who taught the young Brillat a recipe for spinach which involved starting the cooking on Sunday for a dish to be consumed on the following Friday: it was 'put back on the hob each day with a fresh addition of butter'.[30]

When Brillat was about 15, Canon Charcot taught him how to eat small birds and get the full benefit of their delicate flavour. 'Few people know how to eat small birds,' he wrote in 1825; 'here is the method . . . take a properly fat bird by the beak, season it with a pinch of salt, remove the crop and stick it neatly into your mouth. Holding your fingers close to your mouth, bite hard and chew vigorously: the result is an abundance of juice which is sufficient to envelope the entire palate. By this method you will experience a pleasure quite unknown to the plebeians.'

One presumes that the bird was cooked first. Ortolans are eaten in the same way in the Landes of south-west France:

> Take a properly fattened ortolan and plunge it into a glass of armagnac (this instantaneous death gives it a unique flavour). Pluck it and roast it carefully, serving it on a little pastry base: a few minutes only is sufficient. Now you come to the moment you have been waiting for. Place the bird in your mouth cutting off the head with your teeth. Fill your mouth with a slug of Burgundy, cover your head with a napkin to avoid distraction, and suck. It takes between fifteen and twenty minutes for the ortolan to "melt". It is fit for the table of the Gods.[31]

The monasteries before the Revolution were grand repositories of culinary and gastronomic wisdom. The secrets of many of France's best cheeses were known only to monks before 1789, and the various orders possessed their own recipes for cakes and sweetmeats which they guarded jealously from the outside world. But sometimes an interested boy could penetrate the mysteries. It was Madame d'Arestel, Mother-Superior of the aristocratic Convent of the Visitandines in Belley, who taught Brillat the secret of chocolate-making, before his fifteenth birthday: '*Monsieur*, when you would like some good chocolate, make it the night before in a pottery jug and let it repose. A night's rest concentrates the flavour and gives it a velvety texture which makes it altogether better. The Good Lord cannot complain of this little refinement, for He is excellence itself.'[32]

The humbler Ursulines were famous for their method of preserving walnuts (possibly by bottling them in vinegar), and part of their production found its way into the pockets of the cathedral preacher, Canon Delestra who, we are told, was in the habit of popping one into his mouth during those awkward moments in the homily when the audience tended to break out into spontaneous fits of coughing.[33]

There were bibulous canons, too, in Belley, such as the Canon Rollet who breathed his last at about the time Madame d'Arestel was imparting her secrets to the adolescent Brillat. Rollet was forbidden wine by his doctor. Visiting his patient, the physician discovered the Canon's bedside table arranged with a touching *nature morte*: 'a crystal goblet, a fine-looking bottle and a cloth for wiping his lips, all laid out on a snow-white napkin.' The doctor was incensed to see his instructions flouted, but the Canon was able to explain: ' "Ah! Doctor, you will recall that you forbade me the use of wine, but your instructions did not forbid me the sight of the bottle." '[34]

Not all Brillat's memories of the clergymen of his youth centred on their eating and drinking. At least one contributed to his later interest in the nature of sleep. Through his father's administration of seigneurial justice for the Charterhouse of Pierre Châtel, Brillat was familiar with the Carthusian monastery and its *cadre*. Among them was the former Prior, Dom Duhaget, a military man and Chevalier de Saint-Louis turned monk. It was from Duhaget that Brillat heard the story of the somnambulant brother.

In the monastery which he had administered before arriving at Pierre Châtel, Duhaget had under his charge a monk of 'a melancholy disposition, a gloomy character who was well known to be a sleepwalker'. Before the incident in question took place various cures had been attempted, and with the incidence of the monk's nocturnal wanderings somewhat lessened it was thought that he was better, and the community ceased to worry about him.

One night the Prior was working late at his desk, somewhat later than his usual bedtime, when he saw the door open and the lugubrious monk enter. His eyes were open, but his stare was fixed. He was dressed in a nightshirt and carried a long knife. The monk went directly to the Prior's bed and, testing the covers with his free hand as if to determine where the Prior was sleeping, struck three times with the blade, hitting the covers with such force that he not only penetrated the blankets but also cut deep gashes in the mattress, 'or rather the matting which served as such'.

When he had entered the room, the monk's face had been disfigured, his brows knit in hatred. Once the deed was done, his features relaxed and he wore a satisfied air. Taking his knife, he made his way back to his cell. Not surprisingly, the Prior did not feel like sleeping that night. Instead, he thanked Providence for sparing his life. The next morning he called the sleepwalking monk to him and asked him about the dreams he had had during the night. The monk seemed embarrassed; he told the Prior that he had had an awful dream which he did not wish to recount. 'I command you to tell me,' said the Prior. 'A dream is always involuntary; it is only an illusion. Speak truthfully.'

The monk told him of his dream. The bloody corpse of his mother had appeared to him to tell him that she had been murdered by the

Prior. Her image told the monk to seek him out, and avenge her death. Thus incited, he had gone to murder the Prior. Waking the next morning, the monk 'praised God that such a terrible crime had not been committed'.

'It was more *committed* than you think,' replied the Prior, who then showed the monk the cuts in the sheets.

The judge Jean-Anthelme became wrote this action off as *meurtre involontaire*, or manslaughter.[35]

III

Like many other adolescents growing up in the second half of the eighteenth century, Jean-Anthelme was impressed by the tales of virtue he discovered in the Latin poets. Archaeology, too, was all the rage, inspired by the excavations of Pompeii and Herculaneum and the recent pictures of the antiquities of Athens which had been brought back by Julien-David LeRoy.[36] Hoping to find no lesser splendours in the Roman settlement of Villaca (i.e., Vieu), Brillat-Savarin *fils* set to work on the family garden with a pick-axe. He struck lucky: 'we found a tomb which must have belonged to a musician: he had been buried with the instrument of his profession.'

> It was a flute, or a fife rather, made up of three parts. The damp had eradicated the gelatinous part but one could still make out how thick it had been.
>
> It had been severely damaged by a blow from the pick-axe, but I was still thinking of mending it when the Revolution obliged me to go on a journey. During my absence the instrument disappeared.

Brillat was luckier with another object revealed by those early garden digs, 'a quite remarkable vessel: it is a sort of vat which can contain about twelve hectolitres, cut into a stone which still shows the marks of the primitive carvers. This basin was probably used for ablutions, which were much in vogue in the religions of the ancient world. The conservation of its primitive form seems to indicate Celtic origin, where some gatherings of crude stones constituted national monuments.'[37]

Jean-Anthelme's discovery of the Roman fife was apt: they were a musical family. Marc-Anthelme was an amateur violinist, and from his earliest days his eldest boy had been encouraged to take up the instrument as well, possibly serenading his father's guests at family meals.[38]

Voltaire's influence, either through his father or his father's friends, or as a direct result of his own reading in the family library, made Brillat increasingly an enemy of superstition. At the same time as he was excavating the kitchen garden at Vieu, he observed a man driven to madness by the influence of the local *curé*. The man was 'almost in the same condition as the Greeks depict Orestes.'

> A foolish confessor had persuaded him that he was damned, and this idea had become an obsession; from time to time he imagined he saw several devils' heads emerging from the ground, looking at him with burning eyes. Some of them reached out their claws to seize him.
>
> He fled into the fields, reaching out to Heaven with his arms and making the most frightful noise; he screamed and ran in this manner until all his strength left him; at that moment he fell to the ground, slept for a few hours and woke calm.
>
> He died in the course of a similar fit, his last gasp a ghastly scream.

'What is remarkable', added Brillat later, 'is that I recognized, first with Larive and later with Talma,* some of the same muscular contortions which furrowed the brow of this unfortunate fellow.'[39]

In January 1771, when Jean-Anthelme was 15, he witnessed the death of his great-aunt, Christine Brillat, at the age of 93. She had been bedridden for some time, but despite her extreme old age 'she had kept all her faculties and one would not have been aware of her impending death had it not been for her declining appetite and the weakening of her voice.'

Relations between the boy and his great-aunt had always been close and he was happy to act as nurse. However, this did not 'prevent my watching with a philosophic eye – which,' he added, 'I have always employed for everything that has come under my gaze.'

> 'Are you there, my nephew?' Christine Brillat asked in the faintest of voices.
>
> 'Yes, aunt, I'm at your service, and I think it might do you good to take a sip of old wine.'
>
> 'Pass it to me, my friend. I can still manage liquids.'
>
> I acted speedily; gently lifting her from the pillow, I made her swallow a half glass of my best wine. The sip gave her instant strength and, turning those eyes on me which had once been so beautiful, she said:

---

*Notable actors of the Revolution and Empire.

'Thank you from the bottom of my heart for this last service. If ever you should live to my age, you will know that death becomes a need, just like sleep.'[40]

In later life Brillat-Savarin totally abandoned the Catholic Church, and his observation of its festivals became merely an expression of his notable prudence. Watching Christine Brillat's calm and resigned attitude to death, lacking all fear of divine retribution, had a profound effect on him and one which shook his faith in the afterlife. Elsewhere he quotes the *philosophe* Bernard Bouvier de Fontenelle who, like Pierrette Guigard, died in his hundredth year. When Fontanelle was asked on his deathbed what he felt, he replied: 'Nothing more than a difficulty in living.'[41]

Fontanelle was also well known for the fact that his interest in the opposite sex continued into those twilight years. Walking, at the age of 89, into the bedroom of Madame Helvétius, he found her in the process of putting on her clothes. Stopping for a moment to take in the scene, he announced, 'Ah! Madame, If I were only eighty!'[42]

While Fontanelle was bowing out gracefully, the adolescent Jean-Anthelme was just beginning to show an interest in women. A tantalizing fragment of one of the destroyed *contes* tells of his first *liaison amoureuse*. The story was called 'Ma première chute'.

My father and his family lived on two floors of a large house. At the bottom of a vast courtyard there was a second building which had been converted into a coachhouse, maids' quarters and haylofts; behind all this was a garden affording sufficient space for a rendezvous which could not be seen from the house . . .[43]

Beyond the garden of the elegant house in the Grand'Rue was an alley-way, which has since disappeared, where adventures beckoned for the 17- or 18-year-old Jean-Anthelme. Brillat's biographer, M. Callet, who had access to the *contes*, tells us that the lane was a 'disgusting . . . haunt of vagabonds' which had already been earmarked for demolition in 1778, when Brillat's adventure took place. Ideal, he adds, for 'flirtatious escapades in the quest for forbidden fruit'.[44] Unless some descendant of Brillat-Savarin decides to produce the missing story, however, we will remain ignorant of the circumstances of Jean-Anthelme's 'first descent'.

IV

In the spring of 1774 Jean-Anthelme Brillat-Savarin left home for the first time. Like so many of his ancestors before him he had elected to become a lawyer, and had to qualify at a university before he could practise at the Belley bar.[45] His choice of Dijon University was predictable. Dijon was after all the seat of the *parlement* which heard appeals from the court in Belley, and its university was therefore more popular with Belleysans than Grenoble (for all its Roman law). The University of Lyon did not, as yet, possess a legal faculty.

Brillat-Savarin took lodgings in the rue des Forges, in a house belonging to a relative of Bishop Cortois de Quincey. Almost at once, we are told, he adapted his name to include the noble particle *'de'*, styling himself Brillat de Savarin, or plain Monsieur de Savarin, to give himself a more aristocratic air.[46]

It was by no means rare for bourgeois like Brillat, finding themselves nudging against the blurred margins of nobility in late eighteenth-century France, to take that little leap into the noble camp through the addition of the tell-tale *'de'*. One has only to think of Messrs *de* Robespierre, *de* Saint-Just and *d'*Anton. Significantly, perhaps, Brillat does not appear to have used the particle at home in Belley.*

Possibly Brillat's desire to advance his social station was partly explained by a wish to be seen as a *bon parti* by the daughters of the Dijon parliamentarians.

In 1775, only a year after Brillat's arrival in Dijon, the death of Louis XV brought to an end a reign fraught with cripplingly expensive wars which left a country on the verge of bankruptcy to be inherited by his grandson, Louis XVI. That same year, Dijon was shaken by serious rioting. The so-called *guerre des farines* was yet another bread riot underlining the terrible vulnerability of the common people whose sustenance revolved almost entirely around the four-pound loaf. Brillat was made forcibly aware of the problems confronting France.

The following year, the Hermit of Ferney took up his pen to inform the Court on an issue concerning the people of Gex. On 23 February 1776 Voltaire wrote to Dupont de Nemours, assistant to the reformer,

---

*His father had acquired the *seigneurie* of Pugieu the year before Jean-Anthelme went up to university, from Joseph-Marie de Barral, comte de Rossillon and marquis de Montferrand. It may have been felt, in the family, that by its very possession the fief conferred nobility.

Turgot, whose administration had made a brief attempt to demolish France's still feudal structure. Voltaire tried to draw Dupont's attention to the plight of his neighbours, the inhabitants of Chezery.

I am aware, *Monsieur*, that I have chosen my moment badly, and that our worthy minister has other things to do than answer the screams of a few bipeds buried under 500 feet of snow who are being ravaged by monks and taxmen . . .

In the middle of the rocks and abysses which form the frontiers of the Pays de Gex, on the far side of Mount Jura on the banks of a torrent called la Valserine, there is a settlement containing some 1,200 spectres who formerly belonged to Savoy and who are rumoured to be French since the exchange made with the King of Sardinia in 1760.

The lords of the manor are the Cistercians . . . all the inhabitants are slaves to the Abbey, slaves in both their bodies and their belongings. Were I to buy a *toise* of land in the *censive* of *Monseigneur l'abbé* I would become *l'abbé Monseigneur*'s serf and all my property would thereby belong to him without distinction even were it to be situated in Pondicherry. At my death, the monastery would begin by placing the seals on my effects, would appropriate my best cows and drive my relatives from the house.

The most favoured inhabitants of this area feed themselves with a little barley which they sow themselves and on which they pay a tithe of one in every six sheaves to *Monseigneur l'abbé*, who excommunicates anyone who has the insolence to make out that they don't owe him the tenth sheaf as well.

On 20 January 1762 the late King of Sardinia abolished this Christian slavery in all his lands . . . So it transpires, *Monsieur*, that the farmers of whom I have spoken would have been free had they remained Savoyards until 1762, and that they are slaves to the monks today only because they are French.

Chézery is the name of this little place. If God gives me the strength, *Monsieur le Contrôleur-général* may expect me to come and throw myself at his feet along with all the inhabitants of Chézery and say '*Domine, perimus, salva-nos*'. But what is both more admirable and more Christian is that France has the good fortune to possess more than 50,000 men who are in the same position as the people of Chézery, and as a result, just below the level of the oxen which plough the monastic fields . . .

Voltaire received no reply from Dupont de Nemours. On 3 April he wrote again: '*Monsieur*, I believe that the fruit of the tree of liberty is not ripe enough to be eaten by the people of Chézery, and that they will have the consolation of going to Heaven after dying of hunger as slaves to the Cistercian monks.'[47]

Such local grievances as these can have done little to inspire the young Brillat-Savarin with any great love of religion or the religious.*

That same year, Jean-Anthelme had the sole romantic adventure he felt important enough to record for posterity. The girl's name was Louise. Possibly she was the daughter of a counsellor at the *Parlement* of Dijon, enthralled by the young 'Monsieur de Savarin'.

Louise, as he recorded in 1825, was one 'of the prettiest people I can remember'. The young couple exchanged whispers and confidences, but so innocent, by virtue of their ages, that 'the mother was not in the slightest alarmed'. One of Louise's most attractive features was her *embonpoint classique*, which was enchanting to see, and 'the glory of the imitative arts'.

Although Brillat claimed to be only a friend, he was 'far from being blind to the charms that she exposed or allowed one to imagine'. One day, having examined his friend with more than usual interest, he said: 'My dear, you are unwell, it occurs to me that you have lost weight.'

> 'Oh no!' she replied with a slightly melancholy smile, 'I am well, and if I have lost a little weight, I can in my condition lose a little without worrying about it too much.'
>
> 'Lose weight!' I replied passionately. 'You have need neither to lose weight nor to put it on: stay as you are, delicious' – not to mention other phrases of the same sort which the 20-year-old always has at his command.

But Louise got thinner and thinner, 'her cheeks sank, her complexion paled and her charms faded with it'. Encountering her at a ball, Brillat persuaded her to rest between two *contredanses* and, using the moment profitably, got her to confess that, 'tired of jokes from a number of her friends that in a couple of years she would be as heavy as Saint Christopher, and with the advice of some other friends, she had decided to slim. To that end she had drunk a glass of vinegar every morning for a month . . .'.

> I was shaken by this confession; immediately seeing how great the danger was, I informed Louise's mother the following day. The latter was no less alarmed than I, as she adored her daughter. Not a moment

---

*It is interesting to note that when the locals sacked the Cistercian monastery in 1793, there were only three monks and the Prior, Martin, still resident in the building. Seeing the angry crowd approach, they took to their heels. Denis Varaschin, *L'Ain de Voltaire à Joubert* (Bourg, 1988).

was lost; deliberations, consultations, medications, but it was all for nought. The sources of life had been bitten to the quick . . . At the very moment that we were first aware of the danger, there was no longer a shadow of hope.

Louise died in Brillat's arms at the age of 18, 'casting a baleful glance at a future which could no longer exist for her.'[48]

Brillat had added some extra-curricular medical studies to his law course, and so was particularly interested in what sounds like an early example of anorexia nervosa. Nor was medicine the only science which intrigued him during his student years in Dijon. In 1777 Louis Bernard Guyton de Morveau, *avocat-général* in the *parlement*, had begun a series of public lectures on chemistry. At the time Guyton enjoyed a reputation as a chemist second only in France to the *fermier-général*, Lavoisier. Brillat was an enthusiastic pupil of Guyton and the two men became friends. Later Guyton gave him useful advice when, as Mayor of Belley, Brillat looked set to fall foul of Robespierre and the Committee of Public Safety, of which Guyton was a member.[49]

Brillat-Savarin received his law degree in the summer of 1778. To obtain his licence to practise at the Belley bar he was obliged to travel by boat to Lyon. In one more surviving fragment from the missing *contes*, the future appeal-court judge left a description of himself at this time, at the age of 23.

He was tall, with a good figure but rather more ugly than handsome. His physiognomy had something of a dizzy air, frank and carefree, not altogether unprepossessing, or at least so others have said.

His blond hair curled naturally; it was in a mess as a result of having been pinned up for the night [*relevé au fer*], but one could see that the day before it had been carefully combed. He wore a big hat, a green coat, a white waistcoat and red breeches.

This young man, *mesdames*, was me, and casting a glance . . . at the clothes I was obliged to wear, it seems to me that they had a good deal more grace than the formless trousers under which, whoever we are, young or old, wise or foolish, we conceal our nullity, deformity and infirmity.[50]

So speaks the gouty Brillat-Savarin of 1820, musing on his triumphal entry into Lyon 42 years before. Apart from the business of securing his right to plead before the bar of his home town, Brillat-Savarin had relations in the city, and doubtless he was able to spend some time in their company. One was his cousin Philippe Delphin; another was Jacques-Rose Récamier, his mother's third cousin, a successful banker who, it was said, was carrying on with the wife of the banker Bernard. Later Jacques-Rose married Bernard's daughter, Juliette, in what was rumoured to be purely a *mariage de convenance.*[51]

CHAPTER THREE

Belley's Advocate

I

JEAN-ANTHELME BRILLAT-SAVARIN returned to Belley in the summer of 1778 and sank into the monotonous if amiable round of provincial society. Had the French Revolution not broken out in 1789, it is doubtful whether we should ever have heard his name. As Charles Monselet wrote in 1879, Brillat can be pictured 'at one time ensconced in some rustic inn while chickens roasted by the dozen on a spit, at others immersed in conversation with some jovial clergyman, or being one of the lads in a throng of noisy huntsmen . . .'[1]

Henri Roux, a friend to the last, was another scion of Belley's medico-legal bourgeoisie. After Brillat's death he gave a description of the man at the outset of his career as a lawyer in Belley.

> He was tall, with a finely chiselled head and regular features. His eye was lively and alert. If a fine face betokens a beautiful soul, this would have well applied to him. His physique and his bearing, at once impressive and graceful, served to conceal qualities more tangible and more admirable.
>
> His début at the bar in Belley at once highlighted his knowledge of law, his erudition, his talent for logical disputation and the lucidity of his judgement. As an advocate he had numerous clients [and they were his life until] the need to reform the abuses in the administration brought about the convocation of the Estates General.[2]

Brillat had scarcely moved into the quarters made over to him in the family town house when he made his first appearance before the bar on 2 September 1778. It is probably fair to say that the small-town judiciary was relatively unsophisticated. Fernand Payen, a former *bâtonnier* of the Paris bar, gives an example of a case of the sort heard by magistrates.[3] The action concerned the payment for an annual mass for the soul of a distant ancestor. The petitioner asked to be relieved of this duty, his counsel adding, 'Masses have been said for the deceased for such a long time that the soul in question must have passed on to purgatory or Heaven. In either case, they are useless.'

Despite the cogency of his argument, the lawyer lost his case. After the settlement, he complained to the judge:

'How on earth were you able to award against me in that last case?'

'Your argument was misconceived.'

'Misconceived! What the hell do you know about it?'

Payen goes further and insists that proceedings in the Belley court came to an abrupt end whenever a wild boar was sighted in the district. That assertion, however, ignores the fact that only the few magistrates in possession of noble fiefdoms would have had the right to pursue the boar, and even then only on their own land.[4]

The courts may have been unpolished, but Belley's lawyers were acutely conscious of their status and privileges. The local bar had a lengthy tradition, but there was an increasing anxiety here and throughout France lest these small institutions which depended on autonomous *parlements* and which were barriers to 'ministerial despotism' should be swept away prior to the imposition of some monstrous tyranny.

These anxieties were prompted by such events as the suppression in 1771 of the little *Parlement* of Trévoux, despite cries of 'despotism' from the inhabitants of the Dombes.[5] Perhaps in order to form what might be described as a better lobbying unit, the Belley bar was reorganized in 1772 to create a new hierarchy of offices; the *bâtonnier* was the honorary head of the bar, with a *syndic* to assist him and a *secrétaire* to take the minutes at the lawyers' meetings.

Whatever the rusticities and anxieties of the Belley bar, Brillat-Savarin had joined a privileged coterie.[6] The law was respectable. There was no question of derogation in even the great and ancient families of the *noblesse d'épée*, who had won their titles through feats of arms, practising at the bar. Indeed, the *conseillers* and presidents who constituted the judges of the Dijon Sovereign Court or *Parlement* had to be noble to acquire their *charges* or offices. This was a recent change; only a few years before, nobility could have been

36

acquired with the purchase of the office. With enough money, Brillat-Savarin could have become a legitimate 'Monsieur de Savarin'.[7]

If there were few nobles at the Belley bar (only, it seems, the Rubats), the lawyers' code of practice stressed their chivalry: they were not allowed, for example, to demand fees, which had to be paid 'voluntarily' in the form of *honoraires*. Advocates were still required to work gratis for the poor when required, though one wonders how often the common people were made aware of their rights to the lawyers' time in the late eighteenth century.[8]

None of the three dozen or so lawyers practising at the court was exactly poor. The Brillats had their estates in Vieu and Pugieu, the Peyssons owned four domains besides their house in Belley, the Rubats possessed four fiefs, the Chevriers were substantial vineyard owners; other large tracts of land were in the hands of the lawyers La Bâtie (cousins of Brillat), Nivière, Parra, and Parra Brillat. As Brillat's own family demonstrates, the local bar was an hereditary clique. After Jean-Anthelme was sworn in in 1778, only one other lawyer was included on the roll before the Revolution, and that was yet another of his cousins, François Brillat. In the words of one of the present members of the Belley bar, they were 'a great deal richer than the man in the street, a sort of caste which was at once rich and respected'.[9]

It was not long before Brillat was lifted out of the ruck of the court and into a position of authority. In 1781 he became *lieutenant civil du bailliage* for Belley, a magistrate empowered to deal with civil cases within the jurisdiction. One of the perks which went with the job was exemption from the *taille* (a tax levied on all non-noble Frenchmen), one of the most hated of the taxes which infested *ancien régime* France.[10]

Life for the lawyers of Belley cannot have been enormously busy even with the hunts, the shoots, the clients to see and the usual round of large meals taken in an essentially expanded family circle (they were mostly related). One means at Brillat's disposal for dealing with his long hours of leisure was his violin. In the 1770s he had formed an informal band of musicians to play concerts on demand. Now the group was brought back to life, and Brillat increased his knowledge of the region as he travelled around with his strolling players.

In the summer of 1782, Brillat and his friends were invited to play at the Abbey of Saint-Sulpice on the occasion of the feast of Saint Bernard, founder of the Cistercian Order. The Cistercians, originally famed for the austerity of their routine, had developed a reputation as the most gourmand of the monastic orders. Brillat maintains that the Cistercians advanced the science of the kitchen in a number of ways, and Grimod de La Reynière made them the butt of several anecdotes in the pages of the *Almanach des gourmands*.[11]

Brillat's description of his day with the Cistercians provides a delightful glimpse of the gentle *far niente* which characterized his pre-revolutionary existence. Perhaps he was there seeing to some legal work; at all events, one day after dinner, the Abbot Dom Charles Claude took Brillat aside and said: '*Monsieur*, it would be most kind of you if you and your friends could come and perform a little music on the feast day of Saint Bernard. The Saint would be all the better glorified for your presence, and our neighbours would be esctatic. You will also have the honour of being the first sons of Orpheus to penetrate these lofty regions.'[12]

As the Abbey was high up on the ridge of the Grand Colombier, Brillat and his friends had to set off at one o'clock in the morning that 20 August in order to arrive in time for morning mass. Before the players left Belley they played 'a vigorous serenade to the beauties of the town who enjoyed the privilege of exciting our interest.'

The monastery was to be found in a small valley enclosed to the west by the summit of the mountain and to the east by a lesser peak. On the western side there was a forest of pine trees, while the valley floor was made up of a vast meadow 'where clusters of beech trees created a number of irregular compartments, huge models for those little English gardens of which we are so fond.'

Arriving at daybreak, the musicians were received by the cellarer, 'The Venerable Dom Crochon, a passionate huntsman who lived and died for his food',[13] who was responsible for an expression much in use in the Bugey in the last century: 'visiting people always gives them pleasure; if your arrival doesn't make them happy, your departure will'.[14] Brillat described Dom Crochon as having 'a square face with a nose like an obelisk'.

'*Messieurs*,' said the jovial Crochon, 'you are most welcome. The Reverend Abbot will be delighted when he hears that you have arrived. He is still in his bed, as he was rather tired yesterday. Please follow me, you'll see that we have been expecting you.'

The party followed Dom Crochon in the direction of the refectory:

There, all our senses were regaled by the sight of a most seductive breakfast, indeed, it was more like a truly classic lunch . . . In the middle of a large table stood a pâté as big as a church. To the north it was flanked by a quarter of cold veal, to the south by a huge ham, to the west by a monumental slab of butter and to the east by a big bunch of raw artichokes . . . In addition we saw different sorts of fruits, plates, knives, napkins, silver heaped in baskets and, right at the end of the table, lay brothers and servants ready to act at our bidding, even though they were a little bleary from having been obliged to rise at such an hour of the morning.

In a corner of the refectory we saw a stack of over a hundred bottles being continually sprinkled by a natural fountain which spurted to the tune of *Evohë Bacche* [Hail Bacchus] and if the aromas of mocha did not tickle our nostrils it was only because, in that heroic age, we had not yet begun to take coffee in the mornings.

Dom Crochon enjoyed their astonishment but could not stay to eat with them, as his presence was required in the Abbey church. The musicians laid into this huge breakfast *con brio*, but were unable to make much of a dent in the feast. The brothers led them to their beds, replete.

Brillat was woken from his slumbers by 'a robust friar who almost pulled my arm off'. He ran to the church where he found his fellows assembled at their music-stands. They performed a symphony during the Offertory, a motet at the elevation of the Host, and finished with a wind quartet.

Despite all the bad jokes about amateur musicians, all the respect I owe to accuracy requires me to affirm that we performed extremely well.*

We accepted benignly the praise which they were happy to bestow and after receiving thanks from the Abbot we were ushered in to dinner.

The dinner was served in the style of the fifteenth century: few entremets, few superfluities but an excellent choice of meats, simple but substantial ragoûts, the kitchen was good and the cooking perfect, above all when it came to the vegetables, which had a flavour unknown to us, coming from the marshes, and which we had never missed because we had never known how good it could be. . . .

There was no absence of liqueurs, but the coffee deserves a special mention . . . It was clear, aromatic and wonderfully hot, above all, it was not dished up in those base receptacles which we have the

---

*'Three things to avoid: "a little wine which I bought directly from the grower", a dinner which is described as "just among friends", and amateur musicians.' Grimod de La Reynière. Giles MacDonogh, *A Palate in Revolution: Grimod de La Reynière and the Almanach des Gourmands* (London, 1987).

effrontery to call *cups* on the banks of the Seine, but in lovely deep bowls into which the thick lips of the reverend fathers could slobber to their hearts' content, sucking up the life-giving liquid, making a noise which would have done justice to a school of sperm whales before a storm.

After this memorable bowl of coffee the musicians played again at Vespers, performing antiphons composed especially for the occasion. As Vespers marked the official end to the day, Brillat was able to take a refreshing stroll on the monastic lawns before saying good-night to the Abbot.

His retirement was the signal for the monks to put aside the more sombre mien they had worn throughout the day, and the company became noisier as jokes were told of the sort 'reserved for cloisters, jokes which meant very little and at which one laughed without knowing why'. At nine a supper was served, 'carefully presented, delicate in a way which was far removed from dinner.' After supper came more laughter, jokes and songs, and one of the monks read some verses of his own composition 'which weren't at all bad considering they had been written by this tonsured fellow.' At the end of the evening one of the monks cried out to Dom Crochon, 'Father Cellarer, where is your special dish, then?'

'You're quite right,' replied the reverend father. 'I'm not in charge of the cellar for nothing.'

He left the hall for a moment and returned accompanied by three servants, of whom the first carried a tray covered with slices of bread and butter while the others bore a table on which stood a basin filled with *eau-de-vie*, sweetened and boiling hot, almost a punch, which wasn't known at that time.

These newcomers were received with cheers. We ate the bread and butter and drank the mulled *eau-de-vie*. When the abbey clock struck midnight everyone retired to his chamber to enjoy the pleasures of a sleep to which the labours of the day had not only entitled us; it was our just desserts.[15]

II

La Physiologie du goût tells us much about Brillat-Savarin's provincial existence before the summoning of the Estates General in 1788 changed his life for good. The book's autobiographical pages provide a rare picture of the characters of Belley, and above all, of their eating habits. One clergyman whom Brillat in his old age seems particularly to have admired was the *curé* of Bregnier, whose appetite was famed throughout the province. Visiting him on business some time in the mid-1780s, Brillat witnessed a prodigious feat of gluttony:

> Although it had only just gone midday, I found him already seated at table. The servant had already removed the soup and boiled meat and in the place of these two essential dishes was a leg of mutton cooked *à la royale,* * a decent-looking capon and a copious salad.
>
> As soon as I walked in he asked for a plate to be brought to me. I refused this, and I did well to do so as, alone, unassisted, and effort-lessly, he demolished the lot; to wit: the leg of mutton down to the bone, the capon as far as the carcass and the salad to the bottom of the bowl. Not satiated by this, he had brought a pretty big cottage cheese of which he ate precisely half, moistening the whole with a bottle of wine and a carafe of water. After this he took himself off to bed.

Brillat tells us that the whole performance took no longer than three-quarters of an hour, and did not prevent the *curé* from talking or laughing. The meal was demolished with no more effort than if he had lunched off 'three larks'.[16]

The priest's feat is all the more remarkable when one considers that it was unlikely to have been the only large meal he consumed that day. Elsewhere Brillat gives a description of the eating routine of an aver-age day before the Revolution, and of its modifications during the Lenten fast. Breakfast (as we have seen, without coffee) was taken before nine in the morning, a substantial meal involving bread, cheese and fruit as well as pâté and cold cuts. Between noon and one came lunch or *le dîner*, with soup and stewed meat as well as other dishes 'according to wealth and occasion'. At four was the *goûter*, princi-pally for children. Sometimes there were *goûters soupatoires*, which started at five and went on till bedtime. Brillat says that these were particularly favoured by women, and that the result was 'a lot of nasty stories and gossip'. If no *goûter soupatoire* was an offer, dinner or *souper* was served at eight with a panoply of entrées, roasts, entremets, salad and dessert.

During Lent the meaty breakfast was suppressed. 'When the time

---

*Possibly 'a thick velouté to which cream and chopped truffles have been added'. R.J. Courtine (ed.), *Larousse gastronomique* (English translation, London, 1988).

came one lunched as well as one could, but fish and vegetables don't fill one up for long and one was dying of hunger by the time five o'clock came round. Everyone looked at their watches, they waited, they put everyone in an ill temper while they looked to their salvation.' At eight, instead of dinner, there was a collation where neither butter, eggs nor anything else which had 'seen life' could be eaten. 'We had to make do with salad, jam, fruit: dishes which, it is sad to say, have little in the way of consistency if you think of the appetites we had in those days; but we were patient for the love of God . . .'

There was one consolation in the form of the *collation rigoureusement apostolique*, a clever subterfuge which allowed for the eating of fish *au bleu*, cooked alive or just dead in a *court bouillon* containing vinegar, *coulis* made from root vegetables, and pastry using oil rather than butter. If one did not resort to such tricks, there was the *décarêmement*, the first meat meal at lunch on Easter Sunday, to look forward to. 'I saw two of my great-uncles, wise and serious men, go into raptures on Easter Sunday at the moment when they first saw a slice cut from a ham or a scoop taken from a pâté. Now, degenerates that we are, such powerful sensations are simply not enough.'[17]

III

If Brillat and the *curé* of Bregnier were sufficiently well-off to enjoy the pre-revolutionary *douceur de vivre*, the lowlier mortals of the Bugey were not. An economic crisis wracked the region from 1770 virtually without a break until 1787. In 1783 Belley's town clerk, Gaudet, drew up a lengthy report for the *intendant* or provincial governor, pointing out the principal problems besetting the region. For the most part the land was given over to the growing of corn, although a few dairy herds supplied milk for butter and cheese. Some business was done in bringing down timber from the southern Jura, floating the trunks down the Ain and Rhône rivers. The wines of the region enjoyed a certain reputation, and sold to customers as far away as Geneva and Lyon.

Much of the Bugey, however, was mountainous, rising to 5,000 feet and more. A gradual increase in the price of wheat during the 1770s was particularly hard on peasants living in these areas. 'During the reign of Louis XVI the years 1779, 1782 and 1783 have been the dearest,' wrote a Nantua official in 1783. 'In 1783, the price of a *bichette* of wheat rose to 86 *sols* (a little more than four *livres*).' In mountainous areas staples like grapes were hard to ripen, and the women of the Bugey eked out a living by taking in children from Lyon to breast-feed. Others spun hemp, selling the coarse cloth to the Lyonnais hospitals, while their menfolk spent three months of the year picking the raw material in the provinces of Alsace and Lorraine. The migrating workers were a mixed blessing, 'returning at Christmas with a few crowns, some hemp, new habits and the occasional fever contracted in those low countries.'[18] Many emigrated to Lyon, where some became carpenters (like Canon Rosset; carpentry seems to have been a local talent) or went to work in the silk factories.

The economic crisis of 1779–83 was compounded by the tax position of the province, which was particularly difficult when it came to shipping wine. Technically, the Bugey formed part of the *cinq grosses fermes*, the territorial units of central and northern France which were allowed to trade freely with one another. This was not helpful, as the Bugey's best customers were in Savoy and Switzerland, and duty had to be paid on passing the frontier; and in Lyon, the Franche-Comté and the Dauphiné, which lay outside the *cinq grosses fermes*. The 1789 *cahiers de doléances*, or books of grievances commissioned for the region, were united in their demands for the suppression of these trading restrictions.[19]

Possibly the Brillat-Savarins were also affected: their wealth was to some extent tied up in land. On 28 March 1783 Jean-Anthelme leased part of his property to a Matthieu Laboureau. In January 1785 he leased off another part to a clergyman, Canon Guillot. We don't know whether he did this because he needed money, or simply lacked interest in farming.[20]

The winter that year was particularly harsh, lasting from 1 November 1784 to the end of April 1785. Up in the mountains, a certain C.A. Bellod committed his impressions to his family bible: between 27 March and 4 April, 'the weather was so abominable that no one could come to Mass from the mountains. During those days another four feet of snow fell to the three we had already. The storm blew it into drifts in such a way that we could not leave our houses. Everyone cried for mercy and forage, and we no longer had any idea how to feed our animals.' The priest at Champfronnier, Genolin, wrote: 'In the memory of man there has not been a winter as long, as hard or as beset by snow as the winter of 1785.' In Lhuis, where Pierrette Guigard had gone to live with her husband, the population was forced to decimate its reserves for the future by selling off its livestock rather than see it die of hunger. By 1787 good milch cows had become a rarity in the Valromey, and the price of butter and cheese was exorbitant.[21]

Possibly Brillat-Savarin had a chance to speak to Amelot de Chaillou, the *intendant*, about this; Amelot's progresses were occasioned by the need to fix the *taille* in each area under his supervision. His sub-delegate for Belley was Jenin de Montègre.[22] Brillat had become one of the *notables* (or leading officials of the town) of Belley, so was required to wait on the *intendant* during his visits.

As the representative of Louis XVI's government in Burgundy, Amelot must have felt increasingly harassed during those waning years of the *ancien régime*. The untenable financial situation in which the Crown found itself had led to increasing belligerence on the part of the *parlements*, or local sovereign courts. The King responded with increased use of his *lit de justice*, a royal veto allowing him to override the *parlements'* objections to his measures. Recalcitrant members of a *parlement* could be exiled to their estates by means of *lettres de cachet*.

It is possible that the worsening economic situation and the gradual erosion of local liberties were the reason for Brillat-Savarin's visit to Versailles in the course of 1787. All we know about this first excursion beyond the confines of his region is that he stayed in the house of a fifer in the King's Swiss Guard, a M. Schneider. There he witnessed the death of another member of the guard who, having drunk himself to a stupor the day before, had taken a foolish bet not to drink any liquid for a period of 24 hours.

Brillat would have gleaned enough in Versailles to know that the Crown was short of funds; the riots which broke out in Grenoble, the capital of the Dauphiné, on 7 June 1788 – 'the first blood shed for the Revolution' – must have convinced him in the general opinion that the King would soon be forced to consult his people by summoning a meeting of the Estates General, the closest equivalent in France to the English Parliament. The Estates had last met in 1614, thirteen years after the Bugey became part of France.[23]

The riots in Grenoble occurred in response to edicts of 8 May 1788, which linked a much-needed reform of the law and judicature with the abolition of what amounted to a veto in the hands of the *parlements*. Previously the regional *parlements*, in addition to their judicial functions, registered royal edicts; in regions such as the Dauphiné which had been ceded to the Crown by treaties replete with solemn pacts

44

guaranteeing them in the enjoyment of their local laws and institutions, this amounted to a right to criticize or even to refuse to register edicts which impinged on these jealously guarded local rights. In addition to instituting legal reforms, the edicts of May 1788 proposed to relieve the provincial *parlements* of their duty of registration, which would henceforth be carried out by a new *cour plénière*, whose members would be nominated by the King,[24] and leave the *parlements* with a purely judicial function.

The *parlements* naturally resented this, and trouble flared throughout France. It was only in the Dauphiné, however, that the *parlementaires* succeeded in reaping political advantage from their protest. Crowds intervened to prevent the counsellors from being forced into exile on their estates. Troops were brought in, but only one of the two regiments involved fired on the mob; the officer commanding the other regiment declined to follow suit. When the *parlementaires* finally did leave the city, the local estates were convened, for the first time since the seventeenth century. The Crown tried to suppress the meeting, at Vizille, but the local military commander refused to execute the order. Much of the credit for this act of local rebellion went to Jean-Joseph Mounier, a lawyer in the Grenoble *parlement* who later became one of the leading lights of the Constituent Assembly.

The attempts of Loménie de Brienne and his Minister of Justice, Chrétien-François de Lamoignon, to break the resistance of the *parlements* failed in Grenoble. Revolts by other *parlements* were no less heartfelt and no less popular, even if they were less violent and less successful. In Dijon the news that the political power of the local *parlement* had been scrapped in favour of a new sovereign court in the form of a *grand bailliage* (which would not have recruited its members from the old cadre) provoked the *parlementaires* to a written protest that they would have no dealings with the new courts. On 11 and 12 June the resisters were exiled to their *châteaux* by *lettres de cachet*, without such scenes as had led to the successful rebellion in Grenoble on 7 June.

The changes in the structure of the courts improved the status of Belley; from a mere *bailliage* the court became a *présidial*. This might have been a considerable cause for local pride, had it not been that Bourg-en-Bresse was elevated to one of the three *grands bailliages* of Greater Burgundy. Now cases involving sums over 4,000 *livres*, as well as important criminal actions, were to be heard in the rival city of

Bourg. Moreover, judges in the *grands bailliages* obtained 'personal', in some cases even hereditary nobility. Belley had been snubbed.

Lamoignon thought that he could rely on the support of the bourgeois courts in his attempt to dispossess the aristocratic *parlements*. He was wrong in the case of Belley. Influenced on the one hand by their neighbours in the Dauphiné, and by their jealousy of Bourg on the other, the officers of the Belley court lent their support to the exiled *Parlement* of Dijon refusing to carry out the royal command until it had been ratified by that *parlement*.

As Brienne's government appeared powerless to deal with the meeting of the Estates of the Dauphiné in Vizille or later in Romans, it was hardly in a position to deal with a rebellious *bailliage* or *présidial* in Belley, or elsewhere. Royal authority collapsed with the toleration of such open protests. Less than two months later, on 2 August, Louis XVI announced the summoning of the Estates General for 1 May the following year. Even sleepy Belley had made its opinion felt, and Jean-Anthelme Brillat-Savarin was about to become a politician.

IV

The Estates General will be composed of deputies elected by the clergy, the nobility and the third estate. The representatives of the third will be equal in number to those of the two privileged orders put together.

The elections will be held in each *bailliage* or *sénéchaussée*.

The elections will be direct for deputies of the nobility and clergy but in two stages for the third estate. At the first stage the communities meeting in a general assembly will write their grievances [the *cahiers de doléances*] and name their deputies. At the second stage the deputies from the communities will assemble in the main town of the *bailliage* or *sénéchaussée* to write the collective grievances of the third estate and to elect their deputies to the Estates General.

The Council meeting at Versailles on 7 February has decided that the number of deputies to be elected in the *bailliage* of Belley will be in the order of one for the clergy, one for the nobility and two deputies for the third estate.[25]

By asking the people to tell him their grievances, the King fostered the fatal illusion that he was willing or able to solve them. (The result for the next year or more was that virtually all civil disobedience was committed in the name of the King!) As a picture of France on the eve of the Revolution, however, the *cahiers de doléances* are historic documents without equal.

In the vineyards of Culoz, built into the side of the Grand Colombier and overlooking the Rhône, the inhabitants complained bitterly, for example, of the dues paid to their lord:

> The inhabitants of Culoz still make considerable payments to their *seigneur*, as each household must make an annual contribution of a *bichet* and a half of wheat, three periods of labour service and a hen for the rights to gather wood in the forests, to graze their flocks (*abérgeage*), and for the use of ferries in the said parish. Not enough wheat is grown in these parts to provide for the tribute and the inhabitants are for the greater part obliged to buy in. If there has been a poor grape harvest and the *seigneur* demands payment to the letter it is just one more handicap to the happiness and subsistence of the people of the parish.[26]

As it was, the growers of Culoz, Vongnes and Machuraz, the top *crus* of the Bugey, had been hard hit in the 1780s, not by poor harvests but by their abundance and quality. All the vintages from 1780 to 1787 had been excellent (the best were 1781 and 1785) and had caused a slump in prices. In 1785 one *vigneron* threw up his hands: 'We have wine at eight *livres* a tun and we don't know where to put it.'[27]

The third estate of Virieu-le-Grand in the Valromey, where Brillat-Savarin's lands of Vieu were to be found, painted a harrowing picture in their *cahier*:

> Ten thousand peasants of the Valromey are presently shivering under the burden of misery as wealth and credit have simply taken their mountains from them, which were their sole resource. Now there is hardly enough kindling to heat the bread kilns, even though they still pay the same dues. They take advantage of the permission which the good king has granted to them to throw themselves at the feet of the throne and to crave justice and commiseration from His Majesty . . .

One detects the hand of a lawyer in the phraseology of many of the *cahiers*; perhaps the lawyer who was to represent the Valromey at the Estates General – Brillat-Savarin – had to do with that for Virieu-le-Grand.

The despair was all the worse for another frightful winter. One report even compared it to the terrible winter of 1709, when the sea had frozen for some miles off the coast of France and much of French agriculture was destroyed. In November and December several people died in the first onslaught of cold. At −21° centigrade, 16 to 18 inches of ice settled on the ponds and rivers, bringing the mills to a standstill and killing the fish. The town clerk of Belley made a report on the situation in the town:

> Excessive cold on 31 December and the two days preceding. The thermometer has gone down to a degree below the lowest temperature recorded in 1709. From the last days of December to 12 January 1789 you could cross the Rhône on the ice in several places. Even in the warmest lodgings practically everything has frozen. Wine has turned to ice in its barrels, fruit and vegetable plantations have been ruined, corks have popped out of their bottles, partridges can be caught by hand, etc. . . . Most of the game has been destroyed, breath freezes on the sheets on our beds at night. A light rain which came down in the form of a fog a few days before Christmas froze as it fell, forming drops of ice on the vines and branches of trees; with the ensuing frost this has burnt the buds off the vines and walnut trees. Many walnuts and vines have perished. There will be little wine and few walnuts. Fortunately the ground is covered with three or four inches of snow, else all the corn would have died from the cold, which has killed off a number of old people and exhausted the young.[28]

All this was nothing compared with conditions in Grand Abergement, where Bellod once again made a record of the weather in his *Livre de raison*:

> December, January, February and March marked a cold so intense that it surpassed the great winter [1709?] by seven degrees. The lake at Nantua was frozen to a depth of seven feet and coaches were able to cross it. This winter there was an outbreak of sickness and malignant, putrid fever and many people died . . .
>
> A man of ninety years had never seen anything like such cold over so long a period nor such a quantity of snow or so many people die.[29]

The estates gathered in March to choose their representatives for Versailles. Still shivering from the cold, the three orders for the Bugey were convened in Belley in the Cathedral of St John the Baptist on 17 March. The assembly for the district was presided over by Louis-Honoré de Montillet, *grand bailli d'épée* (the King's official representative in the district), *maréchal des camps et armées du Roi* (brigadier-general in the King's army), marquis de Rougement and seigneur de Rochefort. Of the 77 eligible nobles, only 47 were present. There were 94 representatives of the clergy, and 368 of the third estate.

The proceedings began with Mass. After the homily, the Bishop, de Quincey, renounced all episcopal privilege on behalf of his order. This magnanimity on the part of the old prelate inspired comte de Seyssel de Sothenod to make a similar gesture on behalf of the nobility, saying that in future the nobility would share with the third estate the payment of all taxes necessary for the upkeep of the state. For the time being, at least, things appeared to be going smoothly.

At this point the orders separated, with Montillet leading off the nobility and de Quincey retiring with his band of clerics. The nobles constituted a committee of seven to draw up their *cahier*. Their deliberations were interrupted by two delegates from the clergy, who asked the nobles if they would consent to a united *cahier* extending to all three orders or, if the third should refuse, to a *cahier* for the nobility and the clergy. The nobles deferred judgement on the clergy's request.

The next day, 18 March, the nobles received a deputation of sixteen members of the third estate. Their spokesman, Etienne Parra, thanked Seyssel for his speech the day before and suggested total fiscal equality between the three orders. But the nobles had begun to have reservations. Parra and, later, Brillat-Savarin made several vain attempts to extract confirmation of the nobles' promise. But the next day the nobles sent word that they would not consent to any change before the meeting of the Estates General. At this 'very reticent' response, the clergy too reneged on their promises and took the same line.[30]

On 20 March the third estate sent another delegation to the nobles. The six-man team was led by Brillat-Savarin who, for the sake of a united front on the part of the people of the Bugey, presented a plea designed formally to commit the nobility and clergy to consent to share the burden of taxes hitherto shouldered by the third estate alone following the meeting of the Estates General, since they refused to commit themselves at this stage.

> *Messieurs* of the nobility are asked to express their declaration and renunciation in the same terms as the third estate [which was] presented recently to *Messieurs* of the order of the clergy, to wit:
>
> [That the nobility] will consent to support their part of the subsidies and contributions to the state following the prescriptions established by the Estates General of the Kingdom, and will pay their part of all public and particular charges for this province, whatever the constitution or regime.[31]

This was bound to be taken amiss by the lords of the second estate, particularly since the talk of legal niceties veiled a deeper allusion to the divisiveness of the nobles, who would not write their *cahier* in conjunction with the clergy and the third estate, as had been done, for example, in Bourg-en-Bresse. But de Montillet was not impressed by the young lawyer's remonstrations. Nor would he receive any more delegations from the third estate.[32]

On 24 March the nobles completed their *cahier* and decided on their deputy: the marquis de Clermont Mont-Saint-Jean. De Clermont was three years older than Brillat, a very distant kinsman of the powerful ducs de Clermont-Tonnerre. His family possessed property not only in the Bugey but also in Bresse and across the border in Savoy. A career officer, de Clermont had by this time achieved the rank of colonel. Later he became a diplomat and general; he emigrated in 1791, joining the armies of the King of Sardinia the following year.[33]

At four that afternoon, the clergy chose Aimé Favre, the priest of Hotonnes in the Haut-Valromey who also acted as arch-priest in the mountainous Abergements. Favre, a Doctor of the Sorbonne, had probably spent more than three years as a tonsured monk at the monastery of Saint-Sulpice where Brillat had eaten so memorably with the Cistercians. Despite that, he was by all reports a conscientious priest much in sympathy with his poor flock.[34]

The first estate's election was not without incident. The Bishop, Cortois de Quincey, at the head of a group which included many of Brillat's friends – Canon Rosset, the artful painter and carpenter from Saint Claude, Canon Césaire Delestra, the walnut-sucking preacher of the Cathedral, Dom Charles Claude, the Abbot of Saint-Sulpice, and Dom Arsène Duhaget, the Prior of Pierre Châtel – was not pleased with the choice. After Favre's supporters left the chamber, de Quincey's men staged a protest at his election. A contemporary witness relates that de Quincey 'lost through his petty intrigues and his obstructive procedures the glory he had acquired by thirty-eight years of success'.[35]

On 26 March it was the turn of the third estate. The first poll produced no clear result and the deputies proceeded to a second election, in which Brillat-Savarin achieved a mighty total of 326 votes from the 345 cast. The next day two more polls were needed to secure the election of Joseph Bernard Delilia de Croze, a 50-year-old lawyer from Nantua. Delilia was a fiery Jacobin, locked in bitter dispute with the comte de Douglas, the local magnate and a descendant of a Scottish family which had lived in France since the sixteenth century.[36]

With Brillat and Delilia elected to serve the third estate of the

Bugey, it was now the moment to determine their brief. As payment they were to receive 12 *livres* a day plus 400 *livres* to cover travel, office work and correspondence. They were issued with instructions for the Assembly at Versailles: they had to acquire the consent of the other orders before proceeding to any major decision; the question of voting by separate orders had to be resolved, and could only be countenanced as a temporary measure; equality of taxation was of paramount importance, and if the clergy or the nobility refused to recognize this then there could be no further co-operation with them; taxation could not be discussed until the public debt had been examined, verified and certified, or before the provincial estates had decided on where the burden of taxes was to fall; no taxation was to be imposed before voluntary contributions had been received, or during the time that the Estates General was not in session; the delegates agreed that no taxes would be paid until January; any taxes the Estates General failed to confirm would be declared null and void.[37]

The *cahiers de doléances* provided each estate with further guidelines, although the estates were by no means wholly in agreement as to the reforms they sought from the Estates General. For the third estate, a 'fixed and unchanging' constitution was a precondition for reform, one which assured the rights of both the King and his people. The nobility were cautious; as they already enjoyed rights which they liked to see as 'constitutional' any attempt to produce a written constitution might lead to 'dangerous innovations'. The nobles also stressed the need for a powerful monarchy.[38]

In convoking the Estates, the King had been clear that the third estate should be represented by twice the number of deputies as the nobility and the clergy. The third estate of the Bugey thought this should be maintained 'in an irrevocable way'. Where the King had been unclear was over the issue of counting the votes. Were they to vote as a whole, thereby giving the advantage to the third estate, or by order, allowing the clergy and nobility united to defeat the commoners? The third estate were obviously in favour of a head count. The nobility was opposed.[39]

The nobles and the third estate also disagreed over the regularity of sessions for the Estates. For the nobles it was enough to give the King counsel and then return to their country seats. The third estate, on the other hand, had sworn not to return to the Bugey before the date of the next session had been decided.[40]

The very nature of noble privilege was touched on by the *cahiers* of the third estate. Where the nobles wanted to retain their monopoly over the higher ranks of the military, the third was against restrictions, demanding an officer class open to talent. The third was also in favour of abolishing the *savonettes à vilain*: the offices which, once purchased, afforded noble status to those rich enough to afford them. *Dérogation*, debasement of nobility as a result of indulging in commercial activities such as trade, agriculture or the arts, was something else the third estate wished to end.[41]

The lawyers of the third estate had their own demands when it came to reforms of the legal system. To protect individuals from the most hated form of arbitrary justice, the *lettres de cachet* by which the Crown could imprison without trial for indefinite periods, the *bugistes* demanded a form of *habeas corpus*. To remove the system whereby lawyers could not charge fees, a general pricing system was advocated. Reforms of both the civil and criminal codes were to be decreed by the Estates General. Finally, all *bailliages* were to be commuted to *présidiaux*, abolishing the intermediate jurisdiction which had existed in Belley, with appeals to be made to sovereign courts; thus Belley would bypass its rival Bourg-en-Bresse, and appeal cases would be heard in Dijon.[42]

As regards religion, the *bugiste* demands showed no radicalism or anticlericalism. The *cahiers* called for the 'continued protection of the Catholic religion, vigilance in the improvement of morals and the maintenance of public instruction.'[43]

There was a desire for the restitution of the region's rights, so many of which had been whittled away by successive Kings of France since the transfer from Savoy. All three estates were united in their call for self-administration.

If there were considerable differences between the nobles and the third estate in the Bugey, there were even greater problems when it came to the Church. Cortois de Quincey was not happy with Favre. On 28 March a group of nineteen priests presented a petition to de Montillet, saying that neither the Bishop nor Canon Rosset would deliver up the *cahier de doléance* for the first estate. De Montillet obtained the document, but the secretary who had taken down the grievances found that it had been tampered with. When the Bishop declared roundly that he had actually substituted a new text for the original, the priests refused to sign the document before them, on the grounds that it did not conform to the text as originally drawn up.[44]

The members of the third estate supported Favre, and de Montillet was obliged to send a member of the assembly to the Bishop to recover the original *cahier*. It was the marquis de Clermont-Mont-Saint-Jean who performed this delicate task, while the third estate threatened to march on the palace. 'This took place at nine o'clock in the evening,' wrote Bellod, 'and all the bells of [the Cathedral of] Saint-Jean were rung. All the members of the third estate were wanting to burn down the palace when the Bishop, to avoid danger and to save his skin, handed over the papers.'[45]

Tranquil, clerical Belley had experienced its first brief murmur of revolutionary violence. It was an omen of things to come. Meanwhile, Brillat packed his bags and set out for Versailles and Paris.

CHAPTER FOUR

In the Limelight

I

IN APRIL 1789 Brillat-Savarin alighted from his coach at Versailles. He found lodgings at No. 43 or 66 rue d'Anjou (or possibly both);[1] almost at once it was apparent how bad the political situation was. His home town had been ready to set fire to the palace of its bishop: the much more volatile people of Paris were uncontrollable. From 26 to 28 April bloody riots broke out in the popular Faubourg Saint-Antoine when it was rumoured that the (essentially liberal) wallpaper manufacturer Réveillon was about to lower the salaries of his employees. Réveillon's house and well-stocked cellar were pillaged during a riot in which more than 300 were killed and 1,000 injured. As Simon Schama has written, 'more blood was shed in the Réveillon riot than at any other *journée* of the Revolution until the great insurrection of 1792 that would bring down the monarchy.'[2]

On 2 May the deputies were presented to the King, dressed in the costumes which distinguished the three orders. As a member of the third estate, Brillat wore a black calf-length coat, black breeches, black stockings, a grey stock and a wide-brimmed black hat turned up fore and aft. The nobility emphasized their superiority with gold trimmings and feathered hats, and the clergy wore their most luxurious weeds.

The differences in dress must have been mortifying to deputies like Brillat-Savarin who had progressed far enough within their own provincial society to believe themselves already a part of the élite. In 1801, then an appeal-court judge, he looked back with an uncharacteristic asperity:

One has seen the disappearance of those pretensions to superiority which were irritating to all our *amours propres*, as well as those self-important airs with which only the rare antediluvian makes an appearance once in a while. We have seen the end of . . . all that embroidery and braid so improper for men. The first rank of society is now pleased to be confused with the others, the same frock-coat covers us all, and even before we had seriously busied ourselves with the question of liberty, the French were already dressed in the garments of a free people.[3]

Brillat-Savarin attended the grand opening procession on 4 May and the first session the following day. After an insipid speech by the King, his popular, reforming minister Jacques Necker reminded them of why they were there: to find the money to eliminate the nation's financial deficit. It was only the next day, 6 May, that the orders separated, and the third estate, calling themselves the *communes* (translating the word from the English House of Commons), got down to business. The issue which most obsessed them was the question of voting by head or voting by order; the more numerous third estate calling for one man, one vote, while the nobility and the clergy held out for voting by order. So far the nobles had proved intransigent, although a number of the clergy, especially the more humble parish priests, seemed prepared to side with the third estate.

Just over a week later, Brillat-Savarin wrote to a friend in Belley giving his impressions:

The Assembly proceeds very slowly, stagnated by the refusal of the clergy and the nobility to act together with us in the verification of their mandates.

. . . I overheard these two statements: a deputy from Vitré said, 'Here everyone is playing their role: the nobles close the door to further discussion, the clerics spend their time plotting, as for us, let's get on with things.'

Another deputy said: 'the nobles have already given us our first slap in the face by separating, let's do the same to the clergy to show them that we adhere to the morality of the Gospels.'

The deputies from Paris have not arrived yet; their election is still very stormy and people are frightened that they will observe only among themselves those rules of honesty which are so vital.

For the rest, we must wait patiently and I have no doubt that once the initial tumult has passed it will be much easier to get on with things.[4]

The 10 a.m. till 4 p.m. sessions of the Assembly did not leave much free time. Until it moved to Paris in October that year, it is unlikely that Brillat had much of a chance to familiarize himself with the attractions of the capital. For the time being he had to make do with Versailles, then a much more bustling place than the middle-class dormitory town it has become in our own time. The presence of the court brought Versailles its share of cafés and inns, and the 1,200 or so deputies to the Estates General were bound to encounter one another from time to time.[5]

The meeting place for the liberal deputies of the Estates General was first and foremost the now-disappeared Café Amaury. Here, it has been suggested, Brillat rubbed shoulders with Mirabeau and Barnave and became friendly with Constantin Volney and Pierre Dupont de Nemours. These last two enjoyed a reputation as liberals under the *ancien régime* which was sonorous enough to have reached as far as Belley. Volney was born Constantin François de Chasseboeuf, the son of an Angevin noble who later decided to award his son the more poetic-sounding family fiefdom of de Boisgirois. Constantin dropped this in favour of Volney: a combination of the first syllable of his idol Voltaire's name and the last syllable of the name of his estate, Ferney.

Volney had achieved fame as an author, and as the founder of a liberal journal, *La Sentinelle*. He had decided to present his candidature to the Estates as a representative of the third estate, and not as a member of the nobility. This did not prevent him from continuing to frequent the better Paris salons, albeit those favoured by the liberal nobility and the *philosophes*.

Dupont de Nemours was an even more important figure. A Calvinist, he was one of the leading physiocrats, those theoreticians of a free market economy who had such a profound effect on the thinking of the Scottish economist, Adam Smith.

The inability of the three orders to communicate with one another continued to be the main stumbling block at Versailles over the ensuing weeks. On 10 June, the third estate decided to take the matter in hand when it proposed to examine the mandates of all three orders gathered in Versailles. All deputies' rights to represent their constituents were subject to verification by the Assembly. Brillat-Savarin and Delilia de Croze were summoned on 12 June, appearing before the President of the Assembly, the astronomer Sylvain Bailly. The verification issue proved a strong card in the battle to bring together the estates and a slow trickle of priests began to leave their own chamber to join the third estate. Encouraged by the third estate's decision, taken on 17 June, to call themselves the National Assembly, the trickle turned into a stream. On 19 June, the clerics put the matter to a vote and a small majority decided in favour of joint verification of powers. Only the nobility still held out for their own chamber and called on the King to safeguard their position. Louis XVI, encouraged by those around him, decided to move against the Commons. The next morning the members of the third estate found the doors to their chamber locked. The deputies assembled in the real tennis court, where they swore on the initiative of Jean-Joseph Mounier, the hero of the Grenoble revolution of the previous year, an oath 'never to separate and to meet whenever the circumstances required until such time as the constitution has been established and consolidated on a solid basis'. Brillat-Savarin, for some unexplained reason, was absent from the proceedings.[6]

II

The Oath of the Tennis Court on 20 June marked a change of tack for the third estate: they went over to the offensive. When the King offered concessions on 23 June, they remained unmoved, unwilling even to disperse at the close of the royal session. When Louis' Master of Ceremonies, the marquis de Dreux-Brézé, heard Mirabeau's famous riposte, 'We will not leave our places until you turf us out on the points of your bayonets', he turned to the King saying 'It's a revolt!' The King replied impotently: *Foutre*! Let them stay.'

Louis' answer to the worsening situation and the drift of liberal nobles (including his cousin, the duc d'Orléans) into the camp of the third estate was to surround Versailles and Paris with troops. In the meantime, while he waited for the completion of his *cordon sanitaire*, he instructed the first two orders to unite with the third. In Paris, the price of bread and a growing nervousness about the possibility of an attack by the army brought the inhabitants to fever pitch; the Swiss and German regiments were particularly distrusted. It seemed increasingly unlikely that the French soldiers would respond to an order to fire on the people.

The fear of a royal *coup* was felt keenly in the National Assembly. On 8 July Mirabeau tabled a motion that the King remove the Swiss and German regiments from the Paris region. The following day the Assembly declared itself to be 'constituent', and thereby empowered to frame laws. On 10 July Louis informed the Assembly that the troops were there for their own protection. At the same time he suggested that for their own safety the deputies should reconvene further from Paris, in Noyon or Soissons. The following day, Saturday, 11 June, acting on the advice of the Queen and his brothers, Louis dismissed the popular minister Necker, replacing him with the baron de Breteuil.

The dismissal of Necker and a rumour that the Assembly was to be disbanded were the signal for further insurrections in Paris. At midday on 12 July, Camille Desmoulins, a provincial lawyer and journalist who had failed in his bid to be elected to the Estates General, leaped on to a table in front of the Café de Foy in the gardens of the duc d'Orléans' town palace, the Palais-Royal:

> Citizens, there is not a moment to lose. I have just come from Versailles. Necker has been banished. His dismissal is the alarm-signal for a new Saint Bartholomew's Day Massacre of the patriots. This evening the Swiss and German battalions will leave their camp on the Champ de Mars to slaughter us. We have only one resource at our disposal and that is to take up arms and to adopt cockades to mark us out . . . What colours would you like? . . . Green, the colour of hope? Or the blue of Cincinnatus,* the liberty of America and democracy?

'The green! The green!' shouted the crowd. The next day, they recalled that green was the colour of the King's hated brother the comte d'Artois, and changed their cockades to red and blue, the colours of the city of Paris.[7] The Swiss regiments did indeed leave their camp that evening, but finding the protesters gone they returned to the Champ de Mars.

In the early hours of the morning of 13 July the mob set fire to the ring of customs posts around the city, hoping to lower the price of grain. Later that morning they sacked the Maison de Saint-Lazare, a prison building in the Faubourg Saint-Denis where, it was rumoured, the government was stocking enormous quantities of grain. The building was certainly used as a commercial depot: the pillagers made off with 25 Gruyère cheeses and a dried ram's head. There was also a considerable quantity of wine. The next day the authorities found a number of rioters still in the building, dead drunk.[8]

Later on the morning of 13 July the electors of Paris (all the city had in

---

*Cincinnatus: the Roman ploughman who delivered his country from danger then returned to his fields. Washington was known as the 'Cincinnatus of the Americans'.

the way of a municipal body) decided to form a 'bourgeois militia' (or civic guard) of 48,000 men. The civil guard, sporting the new red and blue cockades, were issued with antique weapons from the city's depots. Reporting on events to his constituents at the end of that month, Brillat-Savarin voiced some disapprobation of the behaviour of the mob on 13 July; like most of the other deputies, he was not only a bourgeois, but also a man of order:[9]

> everything which they could lay their hands on was taken from the shops of sword- and gunsmiths, while some houses belonging to enemies of the people were attacked and pillaged. It is, however, true to say that the perpetrators of these acts were neither known citizens nor men of property, but rather the mob and that class of men who, having nothing to lose, are always the first to throw in their lot with revolutions.[10]

The governor of the Invalides had refused to hand over any up-to-date weaponry on 13 July, but the rioters (including elements of the regular army) managed to obtain it anyway the next morning. Only powder was now lacking, something it was said might be obtained from the notorious royal prison, the Bastille.

Much has been written about the pathetic group of prisoners liberated by the revolutionaries that day: four forgers, two lunatics and the comte de Solages, an aristocrat incarcerated by order of his family for incorrigible libertinism. One of the lunatics, the Englishman Whyte, was convinced he was the reincarnation of Julius Caesar.[11] Had the crowd taken the prison only ten days before they would have had the doubtful pleasure of freeing the marquis de Sade, also locked up at his family's request. Like most aristocratic inmates of the Bastille, de Sade had been living in comparative luxury, surrounded by his own belongings in the so-called Liberty Tower of the fortress, amusing himself 'by shouting cheerful and indignant obscenities to passers-by'. On 5 July he had been transferred to the lunatic asylum at Charenton.[12]

Brillat-Savarin's account of the taking of the Bastille scrambles the truth:

> At midday the siege of the Bastille began. De Launay [the governor] negotiates, letting 200 of the attackers into the fortress, then fires on them. Sixty are killed . . . *Monsieur* de Launay could expect a justified reprisal; he was massacred by the people.[13]

In fact about a hundred of the besiegers were killed in the firing between the fortress and the crowd. In yielding up the Bastille, the marquis de Launay did his best to avoid a massacre; for his pains he and a number of his guard were butchered in a most repulsive way. The governor was hacked to pieces on the way to the place de Grève.

Later that evening the King, still in ignorance of events, gave orders to withdraw the troops from the capital. This message was taken to Paris by Dupont de Nemours, who on his return was doubtless in a position to inform Brillat of the situation. When the news of the fall of the Bastille began to filter through, the deputies were emboldened to demand the recall of Necker. Brillat describes the appearance of the King before the Assembly at 10 that morning 'clothed in majesty like a father in the midst of his children. He announced the withdrawal of the troops from Paris and suggested, even invited the Assembly, to carry the news to Paris. He filled our eyes with tears by his goodness, his frankness and by the loyal stamp of his discourse.'[14]

The next morning the King made the further concession demanded by the Assembly, recalling Necker and dismissing Breteuil. The demands of the Assembly had been obtained by mob violence, and this set an unhealthy precedent for the future. Brillat may have condoned the acts connected with the taking of the Bastille, but would later himself be the victim of revolutionary justice.

Brillat-Savarin believed at this time in a system of constitutional monarchy. In a letter to his constituents, he dwelt on the popularity of the King's entry into Paris on 17 July, without explaining his abdication of both power and initiative. The King was received by the new mayor, the President of the National Assembly since 2 July, Sylvain Bailly. The crowd, who roared 'Vive la Nation' and not 'Vive le Roi', watched Louis don the new 'national cockade', the blue and red of the city of Paris framing the white of the Bourbon monarchy. The future President of the United States, Thomas Jefferson, described the King's action as 'an apology never before made by a king and one which no people has ever received.'[15]

On 22 July the deputies were given another demonstration of what they could expect from the people of Paris, when the mob strung up Foulon de Doué and his son-in-law, the *intendant* Bertier de Sauvigny, who were accused of wanting to starve the people. Their heads, mouths crammed with straw, were stuck on pikes and carried through the crowd and made to kiss one another: 'baise papa, baise papa'. Brillat does not spare the details; of the unfortunate Bertier, he writes 'his heart was dipped into liqueur and this sinister concoction drunk off with dispatch'.[16]

III

At ten o'clock on the night of 6 August 1789, Claude Garron de La Bevière, a noble deputy from the Bresse, wrote to his wife:

My dear beloved, I have just left the Assembly, which is still sitting. For the past two days sessions have continued into the night. Returning this evening I found your letter of the 1st in which I learn of your departure for Lyon. You did well to flee and not expose yourself to becoming an unhappy witness to the destruction of the former seat of the Lords of Longes. Perhaps if the decrees of the 4th inst. arrive in Bresse soon, our home might escape the flames.

It was on the 4th that the nobility received the *coup de grâce*. Seigneurial justice, the reversion of peasant properties [*mainmorte*], labour service [*corvée*], the exclusive right to hunt and keep dovecotes, are abolished forever. As regards the rights to fixed annual payments or claims to livestock on the death of a serf [*cens et lods*], it is said that they will be purchasable according to rates fixed by the Assembly in any case which does not stem from personal servitude. All of which means that in order to be paid for these rights or indeed to sell them off, there will need to be as many court cases as there are leases, since everyone will make out that they originate in personal servitude. So despite the fact that these rights need to be bought back, they are completely lost to us and so it comes to pass that 20,000 nobles in this kingdom whose entire fortune is to be found in feudal rights are absolutely ruined. Another large part will find their incomes much reduced, and we are of this number. Today we were debating whether we might hang on to our honorary rights: holy water, incense, etc. Several members of the Commons are already talking of abolishing them but the debate has been postponed. Thus we are no more than the greatest peasants of our lands . . . [As regards the Church] ecclesiastical benefices have been limited to one per head and annates* have been abolished . . . For the grandees, pensions have been reduced or abolished. All provinces, cities and corporations have given up their special privileges. Guilds and civic offices have also gone, and all venal offices with them. Justice is to be administered free of charge. It has been declared that any citizen may now aspire to any ecclesiastical, civil or military office, and at the same time a medal is to be struck in memory of this event. The King has been called the Restorer of French Liberty, and a *Te Deum* is to be sung in all cities, towns and villages of the kingdom in recognition of the fact. All these issues were carried with applause and

---

*The monetary payment made to the Vatican during the first year of a bishop's possession of a see.

without any form of debate, between eight in the evening and two in the morning.

It was M. le vicomte de Noailles, who possesses nothing on this earth apart from the King's goodwill, who proposed the abolition of feudal rights. He was cheered and the rights were abolished. The Bishop of Chartres, who does not hunt, proposed the scrapping of the exclusive right to hunting, the Assembly clapped and the motion passed. A priest possessing a stipend demanded the suppression of the tithe and that went too. Another priest who has a benefice worth 4,000 *livres* and another with a value of 30 put forward the project to abolish pluralism, thereby abandoning his 30 *livres*. There were renewed cheers and this was also carried. A noble who is not a member of any legal tribunal put down a motion to suppress venal offices and to make justice free. This too was passed. Just as all the others were, with everyone jostling one another for the honour of making some sacrifice which would be applauded and accepted. In no case was there even the time for the slightest reflection. Carried along by this torrent, the nobility found itself stripped of all its most precious possessions. At the beginning these sacrifices affected only the rich but as time went on it became clear that a good many families were to be reduced to the horrors of indigence and that idea drives one to despair. I have no idea whether the title of noble still remains, but I am ready to make the sacrifice. What will our constituents say? Without a doubt, they have no reason to reproach us, for we predicted all this. In the end if it benefits the common weal I have no regrets. We shall be reduced to enough to live on and our children will have to do the same; we will make a virtue of necessity. Did we deserve persecution of this sort? Or indeed such a rude fate? Without a doubt the answer is no, and it is our sole consolation that they leave us with our lives, for which we must be grateful. You speak of going to Switzerland, you would be well advised to do so if circumstances demand it but you should wait to see the effect of the latest deliberations [of the Assembly]. A letter should break the news in Lyon this evening and I only want it to restore calm to the kingdom and I shall be happy. People tell me that the Swiss don't want our refugees any more. In Lyon you are in a better position to know than I am here. The news which we receive from different ends of the kingdom makes us shiver. Supplies are short both here and in the capital because grain convoys are held up and pillaged; the good weather, however, has brought forward the date of the harvest and that will preserve us from famine, which would be just one more scourge. For his part, M. Neker [*sic*] is busy day and night.

Adieu my dear beloved, my respects to all the family, a kiss for you and all our children; at least you may console one another while I, exiled in this place, I have just my colleague [Joseph Cardon de Sandrans, his fellow noble deputy from the Bresse] and my friend [?] with whom I might discuss this troubling situation. Unhappiness is painted all over our faces and we ought to inspire some pity, but I think that emotions of that sort have been banished from the kingdom.[17]

In December, Garron de La Bevière withdrew from the Assembly.

All over France the news of the fall of the Bastille in Paris led to mayhem. The common people, believing Good King Louis wished to remove all those grievances which troubled their everyday existence, saw in every *château* and in every monastery a Bastille to be stormed. The great incentive to such acts lay in the contents of their archives: the *terriers*, documents which minutely recorded the feudal dues so onerous to the peasantry. While they were there, were not the nobles hoarding grain? Did not their cellars disgorge wine? Added to this was a simple, human delight in destroying an object of hatred. The decisions taken on the nights of 4–6 August must be seen against a background of smoking *châteaux*.

On 19 July the news reached Belley. In the Bugey the reaction was milder than elsewhere in the east of France. In the Bresse, for example, from which Madame Garron de La Bevière had chosen to flee, a scurrilous paper was passed around inciting the people to 'be diligent about wrecking and burning . . . the *châteaux* [of the nobility] and stabbing the traitors who would have us all perish. Nobles, monks and priests are our enemies as are all those members of the third estate who advocate clemency for our foes . . .'.[18]

Inhabitants of the Bugey thought a plot hatched by the Queen had been uncovered when they learned of a letter intercepted in Grenoble which called on the Emperor of Austria, her brother, to provide her with '50,000 men to destroy the third estate'. Another letter circulated in the Valromey, this time supposedly the work of the comte d'Artois and written on 14 July. The letter claimed that Artois, at the head of '30,000 totally dedicated men' was about to slaughter the 200,000 'who are too many' in Paris.[19]

Between 20 July and 6 August, virtually every region of France was touched by the 'Great Fear'; this immense panic was in each case triggered by news that troops of foreign brigands were advancing on a community. As the brigands were deemed to be in the pay of the aristocrats, the village and townsfolk responded by further attacks on the *châteaux*. However, as Garron had hoped, news of the abdication of noble privileges on 4 August helped eventually to bring the Fear to an end.[20]

The first tremors of the Fear were felt in the Valromey and the Bugey on 25 July, when it was rumoured that a troop of 1,000 men was pillaging the district. The reaction of the people of Belley was to order new lamp-posts to illuminate the dark streets. On 31 July, Bishop Cortois de Quincey made a move to have the Royal Étranger regiment, stationed at Seyssel on the borders of Savoy, brought to Belley. His attempt was stopped by the municipality, who were as frightened of the soldiers as they were of the rumoured brigands.[21]

On the same day the inhabitants of Chézery, once defended by Voltaire, decided to have their revenge on the rapacious Cistercians. Breaking down the door of the monastery, they forced the monks to reduce some of their dues in the presence of a notary.[22] On the nights of 6 and 7 August, it was the turn of the Charterhouse of Meyriat, where the peasant bands were led by one Danton, who claimed to have the authority of the third estate of Paris. A gallows was set up in the cloisters and Danton proceeded to threaten the monks with execution. The monks bought the mob off with food and wine. A number of the attackers were themselves hanged a few days later.[23] On 9 August it was the turn of the Benedictines of Nantua. Again the monks' wine cellar proved a panacea.

The Abbey of Saint-Sulpice, where Brillat had enjoyed his musical day in 1782, was next. On 10 August the four monks remaining in the abbey (the Abbot, Dom Charles Claude, and his cellarer, Dom Michel Crochon, were wisely absent) were alarmed to find both their tile kiln and their granaries had been set alight. On 12 August the four clerics found themselves facing an army of five or six hundred peasants from the surrounding villages which owed feudal dues to the abbey. Having seized arms hidden in the abbey they forced open the doors to the apartments of Dom Claude, demanding that the monks yield up the records of their dues and swear that in future the villagers would owe them nothing. Once the monks had made their promises to the crowd, a bonfire was built of the monastery archives which the aptly named Dom Démolire was forced to set alight. These records safely destroyed, the rioters found the keys to Dom Crochon's cellar and 'indulged themselves in the most horrible debauch . . . committing every imaginable excess'.[24]

Next morning the monks found that a gibbet had been erected in their courtyard. The mob spent another day enjoying themselves at the expense of Dom Crochon's cellar, and on 14 August went home, presumably to sleep it off.[25]

Brillat-Savarin now arrived home in Belley, probably during the course of these acts of desecration.[26] He returned to explain the measures taken on the night of 4 August, and for other reasons: Brillat was facing a personal crisis. Moves were being made in Belley to have him struck off the register of the local bar.[27] Back in January 1789 there had been an attempt by the municipality of Belley to stop lawyers representing the third estate at Versailles. The initiative came to nothing and both Bugey deputies were members of the profession, but after they left for Versailles the issue was revived. It was decided, in some quarters at least, that Brillat could not remain a deputy *and* a member of the bar. Brillat's colleague, Delilia de Croze, was also making trouble for him in Belley. Delilia had put it about that Brillat and the deputy for the nobility, Clermont-Mont-Saint-Jean, were conspiring to create higher taxes for the Bugey through their insistence on creating a department of the Bugey with its centre in Belley.

Brillat had returned to Paris when the bar met on 25 August, but argued his innocence by letter. A vote was taken and his name was cleared. Delilia's attacks, however, did not stop there. The heart of the problem was rivalry between Belley and Nantua, which took up considerable time over the coming months.

IV

Brillat-Savarin may have used the coach journey to Versailles to brush up on his *patois*. Claude Bornarel, *curé* of Fitignieu in the Valromey, had recently circulated a long poem commemorating the events of 4 August. Fitignieu is only a few kilometres to the north of Vieu, and the Brillat-Savarin *gentilhommière*. The poem is entitled 'Against the nobles'.

> Éla! pore Dzinti,
> Què vos étès à plindre!
> Vorindré san marci
> On vo forç' à vo rindre.
> Lo deputa dè France,
> A Versaill' assimbla
> I fon dè rèmontrance
> Què vo fon toui trimbla.

. . .

Los Eta-Générau
Dou peupl' arin pedia.
Lo sarvis é lo lo
Sarin toui rètrincia
Broula votre viaou titrè;
La tin passo n'è plu;
Remindos-in lo vitrè;
Pana-vos-in le cu.

Notron Ray bianfesan
Human è caritablo,
A, dinpoué quatorz'an
Affrancia lo taillablo;
Vos in fura fâcia,
Vos in grondira toui;
Mai vo saré forcia
De farè quemin loui.

Sin por d'étré tua
Los anemeu sarvazo
Venon din notro bla
Farè dè gran ravazo;
No leu farin la chasse
Dè la bona façon,
È no ne farin grace
Po mém' à leu pinzon.

É faudra reforma
Lo fainàyan de moino;
É fau èto tapa
Seu lo gro çanoino.
Los incoura utilo
No sarin consarvo;
É lo dzin inutilo
Sarin toui seprima. . . .*[28]

---

*Alas poor nobles,/Now you have something to complain about!/Now without mercy/We're going to force you to yield./The deputies of France,/Assembled in Versailles/Are making their protests there/Which will make you quake . . .

The Estates General/Of the people will have pity./The *cens* and *lods*/Will be scrapped/Burn your old titles;/The old days are gone;/Use them to repair your windows;/Wipe your arses with them.

Our good King/Is human and charitable,/For fourteen years/He has liberated the people from the *taille*/This makes you angry/You all complain;/But you will be forced/To act like him.

Verse by verse Bornarel abolishes the *ancien régime* with the same singularity of purpose as the men of 4 August. Out go titles, salt tax, *intendants* and *parlements*, as the poem makes its way to a eulogy to the King.

Brillat-Savarin arrived at Versailles in time to attend the debate on the Rights of Man.[29] The seventeen articles, later placed at the head of the Constitution of 1791, were modelled on the American Constitution, though the Americans did not actually codify the rights of their own people until September of that year. Given Brillat's absence over the vital period leading up to the vote, he can have played little part in framing the bill, but he had an opportunity to make his feelings known during the drawing up of the body of the constitution.

The National, or from 7 July 1789, the Constituent Assembly was beginning to form into camps, if not into parties as we know them. On the right were absolute monarchists like the abbé Jean Maury, a skilful orator who more than once had to defend himself with his fists against the left in the chamber and Jacques Antoine de Cazalès whose trenchant defence of the King's rights led to his fighting two duels with Antoine Barnave: on one occasion Barnave might have killed his opponent with a bullet in the temple had it not been for Cazalès' hat. Brillat-Savarin remarked wryly, 'M. de Cazalès always liked to joke about the obligation he owed to his hat-maker.'[30]

The baron Malouet and Jean-Joseph Mounier were leaders of the *monarchiens*, a faction which wished to see the establishment of a constitutional monarchy approaching the English model. To the left of these were Mirabeau and the *patriotes*. Mirabeau, however, was making his own private deals which, had he lived, were intended to safeguard the position of the royal family. Finally, on the extreme left the leaders were Jerôme Pétion and a man who was already making an impression in the chamber, Maximilien Robespierre.

Duels in the chamber were by no means unknown, as Brillat-Savarin tells us in a later essay on the subject.[31] One duellist was the marquis de Cussy, with whom Brillat later came into milder conflict over gastronomic issues. Cussy, rudely interrupted while eating a meal at an ordinary (a capital offence to commit against a man who claimed

---

Without fear of being killed/Wild animals/Infest our corn/They create great damage;/Now we will give chase/In the proper way/And will not spare/Your pigeons even.

We will need to reform/Those lazybones monks./We shall also come down hard/On the fat canons./Useful priests/We shall preserve;/And useless folk/Will all be thrown out . . .

to know 365 different ways of cooking a chicken), and not liking the political views of his interlocutor, 'broke his shoulder with a shot from his pistol'.[32]

More important politically was the duel between de Beaumetz, a liberal member of the *noblesse de robe*, and Mirabeau's reactionary brother the vicomte André Boniface, known as Mirabeau-Tonneau because of his girth and his fondness for the bottle. (He was also the equal of his elder brother in libertinage.) Beaumetz opened the vicomte's stomach with his sword. When the orator visited him on his sick-bed, Mirabeau-Tonneau exclaimed, 'You are most welcome, count. Please come closer! You need have no fears – the disease is not contagious; you only catch it when you really want to.'[33]

On the morning of 5 October a group of women, worried by increasing famine and further reports that the King was about to send troops into the capital, assembled before the town hall of Paris. Encouraged by the sinister Stanislas Maillard, one of the great crowd leaders of the Revolution, the women, 6,000 to 7,000 strong, marched on Versailles. They wanted bread, and they also wanted the King to sign the decrees abolishing feudalism. They were received by the King that evening after their 23-kilometre march, and were promised both the signature and the bread.

The following morning some of the women, later reported to be accompanied by men got up in women's clothes, penetrated the *cour de marbre* of Versailles. They were probably admitted by one of the King's bodyguard. They attacked the Queen's apartments and butchered two members of the guard who tried to withstand them; the Queen narrowly escaped, and a detachment of the National Guard arrived in time to prevent further bloodshed. Lafayette induced the King and his family to appear on the balcony of the palace, and turned the humour of the crowd by announcing the King's resolution to confirm the Declaration of the Rights of Man and to live in 'the palace of [his] ancestors', the Tuileries in Paris. At ten o'clock that evening 'the baker, the baker's wife and the little baker's assistant' were installed in the Tuileries, prisoners of the Assembly and the Paris mob.

It took a while longer for the National Assembly to pack its bags. On 19 October, however, it finally moved to Paris, setting up provisionally in the Archbishop's Palace before moving to the *manège* or royal riding school on 9 November. On the day the Assembly opened in Paris, Brillat made his first major speech in the Assembly. The subject was one which stirred him passionately: the future of the Bugey as a province.

In his mania for rationalization, the abbé Sieyès had proposed that France be divided into perfect squares, to make administration (theoretically) easier. The baron Malouet suggested that 40 such departments be created. Mirabeau was for 120. Seeking to protect the integrity of his region, Brillat spoke against a geometrical division. He called it

> Unnecessary, impractical and dangerous: unnecessary because in the present division of France the structure of the population and the basis for taxation are already known: as a result of the differing fertility of the soils, equal division would be prejudicial to equality of representation; impractical because it would require France to be flat and of a regular circumference and, of course, would wholly disregard natural barriers and impediments such as rivers and mountains, history, climate and folklore: these are distinct and have little in common; dangerous because each province would feel they were losing something, they would complain about it, and the only thing which we could say in reply to them would be that all this was necessary to enforce a justified symmetry so that France could be reduced to eighty equal-sized squares. These are therefore the strongest reasons for rejecting the motion and for retaining the division of France into provinces.[34]

'You mustn't believe that the division of provinces is simply a fiction made up by geographers,' said Brillat, warming to his subject, 'nature laughs at arbitrary divisions.'[35]

Brillat had probably discussed his speech with the municipality during his stay in Belley in August. All were convinced that the Bugey should not disappear as an administrative entity, but should survive as a department of the new France. The people of the Bugey feared the consequences of being united with the Bresse. On 18 October de Clermont-Mont-Saint-Jean had written to the Assembly to protest at their refusal to hear his views on the matter: 'The very fear of seeing themselves united with the department of the Bresse has caused the country people a most profound unease.' Assemblies had met with a view to 'acquainting the Constituent with the views of the province and in order to oppose all projects which might lead to the incorporation or dismemberment of Belley's administration'.[36]

In its campaign, the Bugey received little help from its outlying districts. The Pays de Gex saw itself as part of the Jura; and the town of Nantua (represented by Delilia de Croze), while it contested

Belley's claims to be the capital of the Bugey, was none the less united with Belley in its desire to retain local privileges: this was the substance of the region's *cahier*. On 30 October Brillat tabled a motion before the Assembly to retain the Bugey as an administrative assembly.[37]

At the beginning of November Antide de Rubat, the Mayor of Belley, appeared at the bar of the Assembly in Paris to plead the case of the Bugey, a move which incensed the deputies from the Bresse. Antoine Gauthier des Orcières, the radical member from the Bresse, reminded Rubat that as a *suppléant* or substitute deputy who only had right of access to the Assembly in the case of a deputy's resignation or death, he had no voice in the Assembly. It was possibly this ill-advised move which convinced Delilia de Croze, fearful that Belley would dominate a *département* of the Bugey, to lend his support to the creation of a department of the Bresse which would incorporate the whole of the Bugey.[38] Delilia claimed that 47 communes supported him and that there were another 33 which would see the wisdom of having Bourg as their capital. Despite all their efforts, de Clermont's and Brillat's motion was rejected by the Assembly.[39]

De Clermont and Brillat now started a campaign of calumny against Delilia, but to no effect. The Assembly eventually settled upon a France made up of 83 *départements*. There might still have been a chance to retain the name of the Bugey in a 'Département de Bresse et du Bugey', but on 3 November the Assembly decided that the ancient regional names were reminders of the misery of feudalism. A 'Département de l'Ain' was created out of the provinces of Bresse, Bugey, Dombes and the Pays de Gex.[40]

The struggle between Brillat, de Clermont-Mont-Saint-Jean and the curé Favre (who supported them) on one side, and Delilia de Croze on the other, created considerable bad blood in the Bugey, and supporters of the two camps continued to seethe long after the battle was lost and won in Paris. On 6 December Dupuy, Mayor of the small Bugey commune of Lagnieu, wrote home after a meeting with Delilia:

> M. Delilia told me that the city of Belley was in the greatest consternation after the dismemberment of the province, and that faces were very long. Servants were being dismissed, economies were being made in the kitchen, etc. You will not believe this but M. Brillat-Savarin and M. Rubat have tried to prove here that Belley would be a better choice than Bourg as capital of the department, and they have made out that the entirety of the Bugey, including the Bresse, has commercial links with Belley. Of course everyone just laughed.[41]

From this distance the battle seems trivial, but the effect of losing it is more than obvious today. In 1789 Bourg's population was twice that of Belley; today it is nearly six times as populous. Having become the departmental capital, Bourg plays host to the department's institutions – the civil service, the central markets, the criminal courts, police headquarters, even the departmental archives. In this century the Bishop, too, has taken up residence in Bourg.

V

When the Assembly moved to Paris, Brillat lodged first of all at the Hôtel des Arts in the rue du Faubourg-Saint-Martin, in the north of the city. Paris had both advantages and disadvantages for the deputies. The greatest drawback was that the Assembly, like the Crown itself, was increasingly at the mercy of the Paris crowd. The Mayor, Sylvain Bailly, cites in his memoirs an example of their behaviour which occurred soon after the Assembly arrived in the capital. The people were still desperate for bread and were clamouring before the door of the archbishop's palace where the Assembly was meeting while the *manège* was being fitted out for their use. Jean-Joseph Dusaulx, a scholar and translator of Juvenal's satires but not as yet a member of the Assembly, appeared before the crowd exclaiming pompously, '*vous voyez devant vous le traducteur de Juvenal*'. The crowd, never having heard of the Latin poet, believed Dusaulx to be an aristocrat named 'de Juvenal'. 'Who is this de Juvenal?' they cried. 'An aristocrat no doubt! String him up, that M. de Juvenal! String up that man who has just spoken! We need bread – will this de Juvenal give us any?'

Poor Dusaulx' life was saved by Bailly, who came between the mob and its prey. 'Dusaulx is my friend and I have the prior claim.'[42]

The advantages of Paris lay in its fleshpots. We have no evidence that Brillat availed himself of any of the vast population of prostitutes in the Palais-Royal and the city's other chief centres of vice, but given his later, self-confessed preferences it is fair to guess that he did. Nor do we have much contemporary evidence of the gastronomic tastes of the young deputy, but his later writings indicate that he was early an appreciator of good food.

While Brillat and his friend Rubat conspired over local issues they were joined by Rubat's brother-in-law, later the socialist theoretician,

Charles Fourier. Fourier was on his way to Rouen to take up an appointment in a firm there. Brillat and Rubat bore the young political scientist off to the Palais-Royal, to show him the more daring side of the French capital: 'I remained on in Paris for several more days,' Fourier wrote, 'which didn't count for much: the weather was always bad and it was hard to get about: besides, my lodgings were free. I was with M. Rubat and M. Savarin, who were very frank with me and kind . . .'[43] Fourier probably saw much that was new to him in the Palais-Royal.

The gastronomic face of Paris had already been transformed since the 1770s, and the process was considerably accelerated by the Revolution. At the beginning of the eighteenth century the public tables of France were the domain of a bewildering multitude of corporations, all with strictly delimited rights. Sauces were the field of the *vinaigriers-buffetiers-moutardiers-distillateurs*: they alone could provide sauces for public banquets. Cafés were run by *limonadiers*, whose right to sell anything except ices, coffee and drinks was strictly limited. The supply of food to the public tables was in the hands of the *cuisiniers-oyeurs-traiteurs*, who clung jealously to the privilege, and the *rôtisseurs* held a monopoly on roast meats. *Marchands de vin* could sell wine, but only for consumption off the premises. *Taverniers* could sell wine to be consumed in their taverns, but had to purchase their food from the *traiteurs*, the *rôtisseurs* or the *charcutiers*. Below all these were the *regrattiers* who purchased food left unconsumed at the end of a banquet, normally sold to them by the *maîtres d'hôtel* of the great, noble households.[44]

This complex system was blown apart by the antics of a certain Boulanger, sometimes called Chantoiseau. In the mid-1760s Boulanger, the owner of a soup kitchen, hung up a sign above his door emblazoned with the legend *Boulanger débit des restaurants divins* (Boulanger serves heavenly restoratives). Beneath was written in pig-Latin, *Venite ad me omnes qui stomacho laboratis et egos vos restaurabo* (Come unto me all you who have empty stomachs and I will restore you). The word *restaurant* meant at that time a broth, a distillation of meat essences which was thought to have the power to 'restore' energy. Recipes for *restaurants* were not rare, and there was nothing strange or untoward about Boulanger dispensing them. It was his next move which caused the storm: he began to expand his menu. The first dish offered *chez* Boulanger was mutton trotters *à la sauce poulette* (white sauce thickened with an egg yolk). The *traiteurs* were up in arms; Boulanger was impinging on their prerogative.

He was brought before the *parlement* of Paris. The case hinged on whether or not mutton trotters constituted a *ragoût* – the traiteurs held a monopoly on *ragoûts*. The *parlement* decided that it did not; Boulanger had won his case. This caused considerable publicity, all of which was more than welcome to Boulanger, who now added another dish to his list, poultry cooked in rock salt. In 1771 the *Dictionnaire de Trévoux* acknowledged the contribution which Boulanger had made to French (and, in time, to virtually every other language in the world): 'restaurant' had come to mean what it does today.[45]

Until the 1770s, strangers to Paris had very few alternatives when it came to dining. They could eat at an inn, where the food, says Brillat, was 'generally bad', or at an ordinary, one or two of these having been created after the model of an English ordinary. The chief disadvantage here was lack of choice, and the need to arrive at a fixed time if you wanted something to eat.[46]

Food could also be obtained from a *traiteur*, but had to be ordered well in advance, and was sold only in huge quantities, so that it was not worth while except for a large party of people. The control exercised by the corporations prior to Boulanger's victory before the *parlement* was such that 'should you not have the good fortune to be invited to some opulent household [you] left the big city without having experienced its resources or having tasted the delights of Parisian cuisine.'[47]

If Boulanger was the first restaurateur in the proper sense, the first restaurateur of merit was Antoine Beauvilliers. Like so many of the restaurateurs who started their businesses during the Revolution, Beauvilliers was a former *officier de bouche* to an important private household, in his case that of the comte de Provence, the future Louis XVIII. His restaurant opened in the rue de Richelieu around 1782, and immediately became one of the best public tables of Paris. Brillat must soon have discovered his 'elegant salon, well turned out waiters, his carefully chosen cellar and superior cuisine . . .'.[48]

Restaurants such as Beauvilliers' were a rarity until the Revolution, however. The real impetus behind such establishments was the emigration of the aristocracy following the abolition of their privileges, which left any number of competent *cordons bleus* unemployed. Brillat's fellow lawyer, Grimod de La Reynière, was the first man to chart the social progress of the French chef from obscure skivvy to person of note:

In the past the cook's lot was an unassuming one: concentrated in a small number of opulent households, either at court, in high finance or in the world of the judiciary, they exercised their useful talents in obscurity while the number of capable judges of their worth remained small. By reducing the old landlord class to penury, the Revolution threw the best cooks out on to the streets. Since then they have employed their talents by becoming merchants of good cheer with the name of restaurateurs. There were not above a hundred of these before 1789, there are perhaps five times as many now [1803].[49]

Beauvilliers was certainly a person of note. To read Brillat's description of him in his heyday, one might easily mistake him for one of the more self-important chefs of our own day:

Beauvilliers had a prodigious memory. Even after twenty years he was able to recognize and welcome customers who had not eaten more than once or twice in his salons. In certain cases he used a method which was all his own. When he knew that he had a group of rich diners assembled in his restaurant he approached them in an officious manner, kissing hands where necessary and giving them the impression that they had all his attention.

He would show you the dishes to avoid, as well as those which were likely to take time, all the while ordering another which had been on no one's mind. He brought the wine up from a cellar to which he alone possessed the key. He adopted a tone which was at once so friendly and warm that all the extra dishes just appeared to be so many favours on his part. His taking the role of amphitryon, however, lasted a few seconds only. Having fulfilled it he was gone . . .[50]

The first restaurant to gain a reputation to rival that of Beauvilliers' was Méot which rapidly became the favourite haunt of the *indulgents*, revolutionaries like Desmoulins and Danton. In appearance Méot was luxurious to the point of vulgarity, and the former *officier de bouche* to the prince de Condé was not slow to grasp the connection between gourmandise and other physical appetites. Girls were on hand to take care of customers' carnal needs, and it was rumoured that the establishment possessed a huge silver bath in which a man might be bathed in champagne, assisted by suitably undressed nereids.[51]

The third great restaurant of the early years of the French Revolution was Véry, which occupied three arcades of that gastronomic mecca, the Palais-Royal. Its popularity proved so great that Véry later opened a second branch on the esplanade des Tuileries, in the first building ever conceived as a restaurant. It was constructed to resemble the Temple of Herculaneum, but its life was sadly short; it fell a victim to Napoleon's civic improvements, and the site lies beneath the present-day rue de Rivoli.

The Palais-Royal was also the home of the first Provençal restaurant in Paris, the Trois Frères Provençaux, where Parisians for the first time ate *bouillabaisse*, green olives, red mullet, *brandade de morue* and nougat. The introduction of Mediterranean dishes made tomatoes, garlic and olive oil legitimate ingredients in respectable kitchens. The Palais-Royal was also the home of Paris's most popular cafés, like the Café de Foy, the Café Méchanique – where the *limonadière* communicated with the kitchens through a speaking tube – and the Cáfe Février, the scene of the stabbing of the *conventionnel* Lepelletier de Saint Fargeau. So encyclopedic were the pleasures to be procured within the confines of the Palais-Royal that *anglomanes* could even repair to an English tavern, there to drink Burton ale.[52]

VI

While Brillat-Savarin was fighting a rearguard action to preserve the independence of the Bugey, the Assembly continued remodelling the France of the *ancien régime*. On 2 November 1789, as a result of a motion proposed by Talleyrand, Bishop of Autun, the Assembly decreed the nationalization of Church property. From now on the salaries of the clergy would be paid by the state. On 19 December the Assembly decided to sell off Church property, crediting the state with 400 million *assignats* which were to be used to pay off the national debt. The *assignats* were issued in bills of 1,000 at 5 per cent interest. Almost immediately their value began to depreciate against coin. Already in April 1790 they had lost 10 per cent, and by February 1797 an *assignat* was worth 1 per cent of its original face value.

It appears that in December that year Brillat-Savarin may have joined the Club des Jacobins. The club had begun in Versailles as the Club Breton, an organization of radical Breton deputies which met at the Café Amaury. Volney was an enthusiastic member, and Brillat's biographer Thierry Boissel suggests that he was responsible for Brillat's election. If he was a member, Brillat does not appear to have made much of an impression during the debates of the club, which met in the old Dominican friary in the place de Marché-Saint-Honoré.[53]

A 'Jacobin' was the popular name for a member of the Dominican Order.

On 13 February the Assembly decided to suppress religious orders and to forbid monastic vows. The monks of Saint-Sulpice, so rudely disturbed by their village tenants only six months before, were evicted from their princely apartments. Dom Crochon finally lost the keys to his cellar. In Belley the gourmand sisters of the convent of Bons had to abandon their age-long quest for perfection in the art of cooking the freshwater crayfish of the Furens, Madame d'Arestel her pots of chocolate, Dom Duharget his sleepwalking Carthusian monks.

If the future looked grim for Belley's monks and nuns, life was pleasant for members of its 'bourgeois militia' or National Guard, formed on 16 November in the wake of the Great Fear. On 15 March they gave a dinner for their officers and men. The menu for fifty included bread, *vin ordinaire*, sausage, little pâtés, *vol au vents*, tench, salt cod, hake, larded rib of beef, a quarter of veal, a salmon weighing 30 pounds, a stuffed carp, a turkey braised with vegetables, stuffed calves' ears, pigs' ears, brains, ten dishes of roast meats, a pike and a trout both cooked *au bleu*, blanc mangers,* *tartes, tartelettes,* doughnuts ('*bugniets*', i.e., *beignets*), cardoons, cauliflowers, spinach, apple meringue, savoy cake, ham, turkey cock in jelly, pigs' trotters and beans, macaroni, croquettes, freshwater crayfish (now the ladies of Bons had no more use for them), salad, dessert, coffee and 32 bottles of *vin d'entrements* (a superior wine, drunk after the meal). The whole cost 508 *livres* and 10 *sols* – more than two-thirds the average annual stipend of an ordinary parish priest under the *ancien régime*.[54]

Brillat's time was much taken up with local issues. Having lost its battle to retain the name of the Bugey, the municipality was now increasingly concerned with the structure of the subdivisions, or cantons, of the new Department of the Ain. On 12 March they had written to Brillat expressing their concern over a motion proposed by the deputy for the Parisian nobility, Adrien Duport, to limit courts to one between every two departments. Brillat was urged to act.[55] The day after the National Guard's feast, the municipality sent Brillat another letter about the new divisions for the department. The mayor had shown the plan to 'Monsieur *votre père*; he was surprised to see

---

*Not to be confused with modern blancmange. This was an almond milk jelly often containing chicken or meat.

the degree of irregularity in the division of the cantons for the new district of Belley.'[56]

Brillat's father died at some point in the course of the year, 'struck down by apoplexy on the staircase'.[57] The deputy now came into a large part of his inheritance, notably the estate at Vieu in the Valromey. For the time being the Pugieu property passed to Marc-Anthelme's brother Jean-Claude. News from home continued to concentrate on the new cantons,[58] and on the fate of the ecclesiastical properties of the city and region. Housing the now homeless members of the religious orders had become a considerable problem for the town council.[59] On 6 May the Mayor told Brillat of a new sport which was becoming popular in the region, *la chasse aux curés*, or priest-baiting. The country clergymen in the outlying districts were not only being pursued, but also beaten by the village folk: 'it is a form of insubordination we shall have problems controlling,' wrote the Mayor; 'as they don't know how to read, laws mean nothing to them, they apply them when they are to their advantage and either resist or try not to listen when they are not to their taste . . . *O tempora . . .*'[60]

On 13 April 1790 Brillat contributed to a debate before the Assembly on the former peasants' rights to purchase the land they had occupied as vassals of their lords, a problem which had remained largely unsolved since the sweeping magnanimity of 4 August 1789. Brillat drew on his experience of the situation in Savoy:

> It is very easy for me to shed some light on the manner by which feudal rights [i.e., land formerly held under vassalage] are redeemed in Savoy, as I live in a neighbouring province. The King of Sardinia's initial aim was to allow every individual the liberty to redeem their rights. The truth is that the great lords around the throne quickly made him change his mind, and before long they were using troops to buy back the land. Those people who were still paying other dues to their lords had to abandon their attempts to redeem their rights, and the process is still incomplete. I have heard villages quake at the manner in which the redemption was made. The present generation is worse off than the last.[61]

On 22 April Brillat's voice was heard once again. This time the subject was close to his heart: hunting – not priests, but game. Brillat thought it as important to safeguard property as to extend hunting rights to the general public. But like Robespierre, he opposed custodial sentences for crimes occurring during hunts; punishment for trespass in the course of a hunt was to take the form of fines. This time the bill was passed.[62]

On 5 May Brillat opposed the institution of English-style juries in French courts. 'In the opinion even of English authors, their judicial organization is extremely defective,' boomed Brillat across the chamber. 'These much vaunted juries are no more than a judicial superfluity, as they know no other law than their own will and are never accountable for their motives or decisions.' For Brillat, the code instituted by Louis XIV was 'one of the most beautiful monuments ever constructed by the human mind'. It was sufficient to alter the present laws for the better, without establishing a new system for the worse.

In his speech Brillat outlined further reservations: jurors would not have enough experience to come to sensible decisions; the election of judges was quite sufficient to ensure popular justice; the law was by nature difficult to understand, and trials were full of contradictory evidence. Nor were juries without partiality, or immune from pressure. 'I see them . . . surrounded by their relations, friends and allies who have some cause to solicit their favours, I see them won over by promises, frightened by threats, lured on by hopes . . .'. Would jurors be paid, and if so, would that not render justice more expensive? Where, in small towns, would decent jurors be found, since the best, most active citizens would be involved in serving the municipality, and in the National Guard?[63]

The Assembly ordered Brillat's speech to be printed, but it did not turn the tide of opinion, which was in favour of the jury system as tending to democratize justice. Many of Brillat's points would still be relevant in the French assize courts today, the last to retain juries.

On 12 July 1790 the Assembly passed a motion adopting a civil constitution for the clergy. Apart from requiring all priests to swear allegiance to the state, the law reduced the number of bishops from 117 to 83 (one per department) and the number of archbishops from 18 to 10. Bishops and priests were to be elected by 'active' citizens, and so would become civil servants. The question of the oath to the state naturally split the clergy; only a small majority was in favour of the civil constitution. Among the bishops, support for the measure was considerably less: only seven swore the oath at this time.

Once again the measure touched an issue which was extremely delicate in Belley. Most of the deputies from the Ain were opposed to the civil constitution, which they saw as the work of the Protestant element in the chamber. When it came to religion, Brillat was a convinced

Voltairean: religion was useful in its tendency to maintain peace and stability. To force the civil constitution on an unwilling clergy, however, particularly when it did not have the general support of the bishops, would have the opposite tendency.

That summer of 1790 Brillat-Savarin had the attention of the house and the eye of the President in the course of various debates on the restructuring of the judiciary. He was a major contributor to the debate on appeal courts, although it is unlikely that his conduct was motivated by anything higher than the interests of his city and region.

To the majority of deputies, the solution seemed simple: there should be one court of appeal for each of France's 83 new departments. Brillat was against this. With the ancient enmity towards Bourg clearly uppermost in his mind, he cunningly pointed out the long journeys such a plan would necessitate, the inconvenience it would cause and the fact that it would benefit the rich and not the poor.[64] But he failed to sway the Assembly.

In the following days he intervened three times in the debate. Finally he crossed swords with Robespierre.

Under discussion that day was an attempt to introduce another idea culled from English law: public prosecution. Once again, Brillat was opposed. The debate had delved into the ethics of prosecution, with the deputies of the left predictably crying 'tyranny' at the notion of the Crown pursuing an individual before the courts. Brillat reminded the Assembly of the danger of the tyranny of public opinion:

When the social order is threatened the executive, empowered to maintain and protect order, has the right to pursue those who upset it, as in such cases prosecution is nothing more than carrying out the law. In their desire to see the introduction of public prosecution people quote the Greeks and the Romans but they have forgotten to tell you that both Aristides and Scipio were victims of the system. One is assured that it is in the highest interests of the nation not to relinquish this right, but one could say as much about all the parts of government presently delegated to the Crown. Public prosecution placed in the hands of the Crown prosecution, but tempered by juries, presents no danger: the inconveniences are exaggerated, the number of difficulties have been multiplied. You must reflect on the most frightening inconvenience of them all: that of placing in your constitution an executive power which has nothing to execute, as impotent to oppose evil as it is to co-operate with good.

Robespierre rose to his feet: it was a prophetic clash between Brillat and the dark force which would make of him an émigré.

> Public prosecution is a measure for the common good. All crime which attacks society attacks the nation; it is therefore for the nation alone to prosecute it and to seek vengeance, or to prosecute together with the injured party. The executive power has no power to act until these two other powers have decided on a course of action. Reflect therefore on the danger, which is by no means imaginary, of conferring on ministers or their agents a terrible weapon with which they might endlessly strike the true friends of liberty.[65]

VII

Earlier in July the diversity of France had received another blow, when the abbé Grégoire set out to gauge the extent to which *patois* and dialect were spoken in France. This was the prelude to an attempt to force the people of France to discard local variations in language for the greater convenience of administration. It was all part of the process of reducing France to 'that flat surface which facilitates the use of power'.[66] In the case of the Bugey, the responses to Grégoire's questionnaire reveal the dialect there to be softer than in the neighbouring plain; also that French had begun to make incursions into the local patois from the time of the construction of the royal roads earlier in the century.[67]

Brillat remained preoccupied with local affairs. Niggling problems concerning the new administrative divisions for the Bugey brought him into conflict with his fellow deputy for the third estate, Delilia de Croze. Belley having failed to become the capital of the new department, other towns in the Bugey now disputed even its right to headship of the canton. If Brillat was not particularly successful in maintaining the prestige of Belley, its citizens were none the less appreciative of his efforts: on 2 October the Mayor wrote, 'It gives me great pleasure to inform you that all the commune were unanimously in favour of the choice of yourself as colonel of the city's National Guard.'[68]

The following month, Brillat-Savarin moved from the north of Paris to lodgings at 14 rue des Bons-Enfants. His new home was close to the rue Saint-Honoré (where Robespierre, among others, lived) and within easy walking distance of the Assembly in the royal *manège*. On 12 November Brillat was peripherally involved in what was possibly the most famous duel of the Constituent (National) Assembly, fought between two liberal nobles, Charles de Lameth and the duc de Castries.

Both Lameth and Castries were veterans of the American War of Independence and well-known for their radical ideas. After 1 May 1789, however, Castries realized that the future existence of a nobility in France depended on safeguarding the privileges of the Crown. In his defence of royal privilege he came into conflict with Lafayette and, through him, with Lameth. The duel resulted in Castries wounding Lameth in the chest. Lameth was popular with the Paris mob and a crowd, learning the news, ran to Castries' Paris *hôtel* with the intention of wrecking it. The police stood by, making no attempt to intervene. The Assembly, unlike the police, behaved wisely, as Brillat recounts:

> The Assembly sent a delegation of twelve members to put an end to . . . [the pillage]; I was one of them. We arrived too late: an ugly little fellow, lame and hunch-backed, was making a frightful mess with his crutch. I picked him up by the scruff of his neck and thrust him into the hands of the guard. Nobody tried to stop me.[69]

Brillat was strongly built, with lungs to match: not for nothing did Balzac later refer to him as the 'Drum-major of the Appeal Court'.[70]

Although Brillat was unsuccessful in his wider aims for Belley and the Bugey, he was at least responsible for ensuring that the departmental seminary and the seat of the Bishop of the Ain remained in Belley.

Crisis loomed in November 1790 when Bishop Cortois de Quincey refused to swear the oath to the state. A recalcitrant bishop was now part of the manoeuverings to prevent the see being transferred to the new department's capital, Bourg-en-Bresse, and the town council turned to Brillat for help. His negotiations with de Quincey culminated in a letter of flattery and admonishment which ended:

> Reflect, sir; the new constitution has already been founded on a pedestal of brass, should it come up against this obstacle it would certainly sweep it aside.
> Reflect that the oath that we have asked you to swear contains nothing which you have not sworn already.
> Reflect that resistance to the law does not bring honour to anybody and that the names of refractory bishops will go down in history

coloured by the hatred of their century, while the nation will recognize the memory of those who had the courage to obey.

Sir, it is up to you to give your colleagues a great example. A life so pure and free of blemish gives you the right. It is for you to remind them that submission to the law was always the teaching of the Divine Legislator and that all scruple must give way before the general will; all argument must cease when the nation speaks, all self interest must be crushed to ensure the happiness of the people.

By obeying [i.e., swearing the oath to the state] you will teach [your colleagues] that the nation only asks of its children that which it has the right to demand, and that a bishop worthy of his office cannot be a bad citizen.

It is unlikely that Gabriel Cortois de Quincey had a chance to read this hectoring letter, dated from Paris, 6 January 1790. He died on the night of 14 January.

On 18 January the electors of Belley were summoned to the polls to choose a new bishop. The choice was between the incumbent of Chavannes-sur-Suran, Claude-François Rousselet, and the radical Jean-Baptiste Royer, whose suggested reforms for the Church had made him unacceptable as a representative of the clergy in the Estates. Brillat knew him well, and described him as 'an excellent man, an enlightened patriot whose principles are neither extreme nor compromised'.[72]

Royer's election was confirmed on 9 February, but it presented problems: he had evinced a desire to live in Bourg, where the magnificent church of Brou would have made an admirable cathedral and where the adjacent Augustinian priory, empty since the departure of the monks, might have been fitted up as a suitable episcopal palace.

To retain the see at Belley, Brillat had to overcome a more powerful adversary than Delilia de Croze, in Gauthier des Orcières, the radical member for the Bresse who had clashed with Rubat over the future of the Bugey. Obviously the municipality were anxious that Brillat should win: on 24 February they wrote to their deputy, 'Please take all possible pains concerning this important goal and waste no time. Your province has been impoverished by the continuous suppression and it does not desire to have to make further sacrifices.'[73] Fortunately, there were precedents for the cathedrals of new departments to be situated other than in the departmental capital. In the Saône-et-Loire, for example, the see was Talleyrand's Autun and not Mâcon. This time

Brillat was able to sway the authorities: the cathedral remained in Belley.

Brillat's next problem was the site of the seminary. The Assembly had limited the number of seminaries to one per department. Naturally Belley wanted the seminary, as it would be another source of income for the city; urged on by his municipality, Brillat was again triumphant. The institution was set up in the Convent of Bons, vacated by the 'Sisters of the Crayfish',[74] and its presence in turn helped defeat renewed arguments for dislodging the see.

VIII

In the middle of December 1790 Brillat returned from his brief annual visit to Belley. Not long after he had settled back into the routine of life at the Assembly and at 14 rue des Bons-Enfants he received a visit from his brother Frédéric, who was serving in the National Guard in Belley before joining the regular army. Frédéric Brillat-Savarin was 19 years old and, one assumes, built on the same scale as his brother the deputy.

While he was in the capital Frédéric went to the opera, which after a fire had destroyed that at the Palais-Royal was situated from 1781 to 1794 in the boulevard Saint-Martin. Brillat tells us that his brother Frédéric arrived at the opera wearing an enormous wig 'which had gone out of fashion years before'; this provoked a foppish gentleman behind him to indulge in repeated drolleries at the expense of an undoubted provincial. The mirth of his neighbours eventually awakened Frédéric, 'not much of a wag', to what was going on:

> He turned round and gave him a slap which could be heard throughout the length and breadth of the auditorium.
> 'So, *Monsieur*, can you see more clearly now?'
> 'No,' replied the Parisian, dizzy from his blow, 'and I will have satisfaction'.

But when the ballet was over, Frédéric's antagonist had disappeared: 'He had taken advantage of the applause . . . to plunge into the waves of the *parterre* and he has still not re-emerged.'[75]

On 3 February 1791 the Assembly took the decision to outlaw duelling, the proposer, M. Chevalier, stressing the danger of 'thugs' abusing honest citizens. The measure was, predictably, contested on the right of the chamber.[76]

Brillat continued his role as one of the minor figures of the Assembly. Compared with many of the deputies he was, indeed, positively loquacious, and this may perhaps be put down to the power of his lungs, since for many deputies the greatest problem was to be heard during the debates. In the chamber that spring Brillat was privileged to hear the last speeches of another man with powerful lungs, Mirabeau. Mirabeau saw the writing on the wall. Referring to new taxes, he boomed:

> the people have been promised more than can be promised; they have been given hopes that it will be impossible to realize; they have been allowed to shake off a yoke which it will be impossible to restore, and even if there should be fine retrenchments and economies . . . the expenses of the new regime will actually be heavier than the old, and in the last analysis the people will judge the revolution by this fact alone – does it take more or less money? Are they better off? Do they have more work? And is that work better paid?[77]

On 28 February Mirabeau protested against a 'barbaric' measure which the Assembly had introduced, to regulate the movement of suspected *émigrés*. He rightly foresaw in it the beginnings of that 'police state' which arrived with the National Convention. But on 2 April Mirabeau died, in the arms of his friend and physician, Pierre Jean Georges Cabanis; his death removed from the scene the one man who might have managed to avert the Terror. At Versailles Jean-François Coste, friend of Brillat's father and for the past year mayor of the city, spoke:

> Let them weep for Mirabeau! The people for whom he was the greatest friend; the people whose name he restored and dignified, to whom he was attached; may they preserve forever that dignity by remembering the rights of man without ever forgetting the duties of a citizen.[78]

Little more than a year later the September Massacres revealed to just what extent these pious hopes were rooted in reality.

On 16 May, as a result of a motion proposed by Robespierre, the Assembly decided that members of the National Assembly would not be eligible for re-election to the Legislative Assembly which was to succeed it. The following day Brillat wrote to his constituents:

> the majority of the Assembly, are looking forward to the moment when their already tired hands may lay down the immense power with which they were entrusted, and set an example of obedience to the law . . .[79]

On 31 May Brillat was heard again in one of the major debates of the National Assembly, concerning the abolition of the death penalty. Brillat followed Jérôme Pétion, one of the darlings of the left, an abolitionist who might have benefited from abolition. Brillat countered Pétion's arguments for the sanctity of human life by saying that it was precisely to preserve life that the state must possess the ultimate sanction:

> My duties have often brought me to those asylums where crime awaits its punishment; there I have seen how the death penalty is superior to all others. I have seen guilty parties congratulating one another for being sentenced only to the galleys. But do men become better in these prisons? On the contrary, between themselves they form a sort of school for crime, they give mutual instruction on the manner of performing the most artful tricks, on the means of avoiding conviction . . .[80]

On Tuesday, 21 June 1791, at ten past midnight, the royal family, with the King got up as a *valet de chambre*, climbed into their coach and set off to Varennes. The royal coach stopped at five to eight that evening outside the inn in the town of Sainte-Menehould in Champagne. According to Camille Desmoulins, the King could not resist a dish of pigs' trotters cooked *à la sainte-menehould*; and so his gluttony was responsible for his arrest. Whether this is true or not the postmaster, Drouet, was able to compare the face of this so-called *valet* with the King's effigy on a crown coin. Alerted by Drouet the *procureur* for Varennes, a grocer named Sauce, forced the royal family to leave the coach.

As the humiliated captives rode back into Paris accompanied by the deputies Jérôme Pétion and Antoine Barnave, the rest of the Assembly was in a state of shock. The Flight swayed some deputies to favour republicanism; even those on the centre right began to revise their ideas. Louis had lost most of his appeal for the moderates. For the time being Brillat remained a *monarchien*, a partisan of constitutional monarchy. After the King's return he wrote to the citizens of Belley to inform them of the Assembly's decisions relative to the flight: 'Yesterday an almost unanimous Assembly decreed that those guilty of abetting the King's flight should be brought to justice, but added that the King himself could not be indicted.'[81] Brillat listed the reasons: the monarchy was inviolable, this being 'one of the true founding principles of the monarchy';[82] efforts had to be made to prevent the monarchy from splitting into two camps; the King was not a citizen and could not be tried as one, nor was he breaking the law by going to Varennes or even to Montmédy (his real destination), as there were no foreign troops there.

> this decree is perhaps one of the most important that we have passed for some time. There were scarcely twenty voices against the motion in the house; on the other hand, the most inflammatory, the most republican pamphlets have been circulated, particularly to the people most avid for change. It is certainly true that it required some courage on the part of the Assembly to stick to its principles and not to give in to these opinions, which are not those of the general public, even if they are at present fashionable.
>
> M. Barnave has surpassed himself in this business: he has grasped the essential point, namely that we are not at the start of a new revolution, but in the process of completing the old one, that we are proceeding along a path from which we should not waver; that what was planted on the night of 4 August has come to fruition; and that the only aristocracy which exists today is that of property . . .[83]

There can be few clearer statements of Brillat's views: he was a man of order, an upholder of private property, a supporter of a limited revolution which passed over the reins of the state from the old nobility to the *haute bourgeoisie*. Sadly for Brillat and his friends, they allowed power to slip into the hands of the more active and vociferous elements on the left, who were not content to let the Revolution stop.[84]

The split was aggravated by the events of 17 July. The radical Cordeliers club, with Danton at their head, laid a petition for signature at the 'altar of the nation' which had been erected in the old military parade ground of the Champ de Mars. Six thousand signatures were obtained. The crowd took no notice of an order to disperse, sent by the Assembly and followed up by a declaration of martial law by the Mayor. Lafayette's National Guard fired into the crowd; several were killed or wounded, more were trodden underfoot in the ensuing panic.

On 23 July 1791 the Assembly put martial law to the vote. Brillat rose to declare that it was expedient in the circumstances, even if it represented a certain infringement of the liberty of citizens. He called for those responsible for the riot to be swiftly brought to justice. Once again his intervention was followed by a speech from the furious Robespierre: 'Never do I believe I have had so much right to be heard . . .'.[85]

The deputies of the right had played no active part in the Assembly since the capture of the King. Though Brillat's own political force was spent, in the course of July he continued to act in the interests of the municipality of Belley. The town had fallen on hard times, and they asked Brillat to exchange an *assignat* on their behalf.[86]

On 3 September the Assembly wound up its debate on the constitution. The Constitutional Act was finally voted on 8 September, Brillat-Savarin was designated one of the sixty deputies to present it to a king restored to his position following the suspension which had been imposed following his flight. On 14 September, the King swore an oath of loyalty to the Constitution. On 30 September, their huge labours at an end, the deputies returned whence they came. The institutions of the *ancien régime* had been wound up, and a new France erected in their place.

Brillat had distinguished himself on a minor plane, both as a defender of his native region and as one of the legal experts of the house (with so many lawyer-deputies, this must be seen as an achievement). On his return to Belley, there was dancing in the streets. In addition to his honorary colonelcy of the National Guard, Brillat became president of the civil tribunal of Belley.

He had, however, essentially failed. Like all the elements of the centre and the right, he had been unable or unwilling to stop what was, in ideological terms, the victory of Rousseau over Voltaire. The abbé Maury knew this when he wrote:

> It is too easy to enthrone the general will in the place of legitimate authority and soon afterwards to substitute oneself for this pretended general will, while claiming to be its agent. No one can define popular sovereignty for us precisely since no one dares to admit that this pretended sovereignty is merely the right of the strongest. Remember that we are, in actual fact, representatives of the French nation and not Jean-Jacques Rousseau's plenipotentiaries; we have not submitted the *Social Contract* to the verdict of the electorate, as the measure of our power and the title of our mission.[87]

Brillat-Savarin realized too late what dangerous forces he had been party to bringing into play.

CHAPTER FIVE

Fortunes High and Low

I

A FTER A NIGHT of dancing and illuminations, Jean-Anthelme Brillat-Savarin settled down to his new jobs and his old ways. It seems he had consented to sit on the bench in Bourg as well as taking office in the smaller court in Belley. He was also elected substitute judge on the new national appeal court, the *Tribunal de cassation*. This court was made up of a single judge from each department, with a substitute to take his place in case of resignation or death. From the Ain, the judge was one Martinon, an advocate from Bourg-en-Bresse. Strictly speaking Brillat should have replaced Martinon after his death on 28 June 1792, but in the turmoil of the times and the erratic history of the first years of what became the *Cour de cassation*, no one seems to have informed him of the fact.[1]

In Bourg, Brillat was a judge in the civil court until 20 January 1792, and from then on lived permanently in Belley until his flight on 12 Frimaire of the year II (2 December 1793). We do not know why he abandoned his position in the departmental court; perhaps he simply preferred to live in Belley, and Belley was a long, hard ride from Bourg.[2]

The distance was not, however, enough to prevent Brillat from returning to Belley from time to time during his stay in Bourg to see his old friends or to go out with the guns in the woods of the Valromey or on the slopes of the Grand Colombier. One legal family well known to Brillat were the Sibuets, a talented trio of brothers the eldest of whom, Georges, enjoyed a career which at many points echoed Brillat's own.* The most distinguished of the three was Benoît Prosper Sibuet, who became a general and a baron d'Empire, and fell at the crossing of the river Bober following the retreat from Moscow.[3]

Many years later, Brillat recalled with admiration a feat of gourmandise performed by the 18-year-old Prosper Sibuet in the autumn of 1791. It happened in the weeks immediately following the vintage when the old men of the town would gather at Genin's inn to eat chestnuts and drink the still-fermenting wine called *vin bourru*.[4]

Autumn is not merely a time to relax after the vintage; it is also the shooting season, when appetites are at their keenest. A few moments before Sibuet entered the inn, the innkeeper had taken from the spit 'a magnificent turkey-cock . . . golden and cooked to a turn, the aromas of which would have proved too much even for a saint.'[5] The unsaintly regulars, we are told, were not much interested in the turkey, but Sibuet's mouth began to water, and he wagered he could eat it by himself. '*Sez vosu mezé, z'u payo*', replied the portly farmer Bouvier du Bouchet, who was there at the time, '*è sez voscaca en rotaz, i-zet vo ket pairé et may ket mezerai la restaz*' ('If you eat it all, I will pay for it, but if you give up half way, you will pay, and I will eat the leftovers.') Sibuet munched his way through most of the bird with no difficulty and was about to tackle the last leg when the unfortunate farmer cried out with a doleful wail, '*Hai! ze vaie praou qu'izet fotu; m'ez, monche Chibouet, poez kaet zu daive paiet, lessé m'en a m'en mesiet on mocho*' ('Alas! I can see I'm licked; but M. Sibuet, as it is me that has to cough up, please leave me just a little bit').[6]

That summer the economy began to feel the pinch caused by the inflationary effect of the *assignats*, the revolutionary paper money. A year before, Brillat had accurately predicted the dangers of this paper money:

> With coin you may perform any transaction for which you might employ an *assignat*, but with an *assignat* you don't have the same flexibility that you enjoy with coin. The effect of issuing them will be to cause the despair of all those people who are not the state's creditors, that is to say, all the most faithful friends of the constitution.[7]

Preventing the steady decline in the value of the *assignat* may well have been in the minds of the new deputies who made their

---

*The youngest brother, Marin Sibuet, was elected Mayor of Belley in 1835. A. Chagny, *Le Général Sibuet* (Le Bugey, 1934).

way to Paris for the opening of the Legislative Assembly (which replaced the National or Constituent Assembly) that autumn. All six from the Ain were connected with the law: the notary Étienne Deydier, and the advocates Jean-Baptiste-Marie Girod, Grégoire-Marie Jagot, Jacques Regnier, Thomas Riboud, and Brillat's friend, Antide de Rubat.[8] Their legal talents, however, were not sufficient to rescue France from the effects of inflation on a massive scale.

Brillat was not the only 'Parisian' to return to the Bugey that year. A Monsieur Briguet, from Tallisieu on the Grand Colombier, returned to his native village with his wife. Both had done well in Paris. Starting out as a coachman, Monsieur Briguet had turned to horse trading, and made his fortune; his wife, cook to a celebrated courtesan, had known how to profit from her work, and with their nest-egg the Briguets were able to buy a small estate in Talissieu.

The last months of 1791 were the calm before the storm as far as the village clergy of France were concerned. As yet persecution of the Church had largely been restricted to the monks, now evicted from their cloisters. In each administrative canton of the Church the local priests would hold a meeting once a month to discuss ecclesiastical matters, preceded by High Mass and followed by dinner. Local incumbents took it in turns to play host to this ambulant synod. When it was his turn, one of his parishioners generously provided the parish priest of Talissieu with an eel, more than three feet long, which he had fished out of the 'limpid waters of the [river] Séran. Worried lest his own cook should prove unequal to the task of preparing this magnificent eel, the priest ran to Madame Briguet, begging her to provide him with a recipe which would 'do honour to an archbishop'. The *parisienne* was not only happy to comply, but went so far as to lend the priest a little box of seasonings which she had used when cooking for her former mistress. Brillat tells how 'The dish of eel was prepared carefully and served with distinction. . . . Once it had been sampled by the company . . . It disappeared, body and sauce, right down to the last particle.' By the time dessert came round, however, 'these venerable gentlemen found themselves roused in an unaccustomed manner.' The conversation turned to sex.

> Certain priests retailed stories of their adventures at the seminary, while others chided their neighbours about one or two reported scandalous episodes; in short, the conversation settled on, and remained fixed on, the most delectable of the seven deadly sins. What is more

remarkable is that the assembly had no sense of the sin they were committing, so much were they in the power of the devil.

The next day the priests, ashamed of their licence the night before, and looking for an explanation of their conduct attributed it to the influence of the eel, which they concluded it would be wiser not to eat again.

Brillat was anxious to discover the detail of a recipe which had had such an aphrodisiac effect. The most he could learn from Madame Briguet was that it involved a highly spiced *coulis* of freshwater crayfish, 'but I think it can be said with certainty that she was not telling the whole story'.[9]*

II

For the first half of 1792 at least Brillat's life remained, if anything, calmer and more provincial than it had been in the last years of the *ancien régime*; rarely did he appear in the limelight, even in his native Belley. Perhaps after his experience of Paris during the Constituent Assembly, he valued a quiet life away from from the city and politics.

On 4 January 1792 the municipality of Belley opened a new list of 'active citizens', or electors, to replace that of 22 July 1790. Brillat's name figures low down, at No 349 out of a total of 620.[10] That same month Brillat started a slate with a *cafétier* of Belley called Narcisse Beaucamp. Beaucamp provided the meals for the judge's *garçonnière* in the Grand'Rue, and when Brillat fled at Christmas 1793, his account remained unsettled.[11]

On 26 March, as President of the Court of Belley, Brillat delivered a speech fiercely critical of the clergy and the nobility to a meeting of the electors of the new *juges de paix*. In bellicose vein, it cried out for war, for the blood of those neighbours of France who played host to French royalist elements.

In vain will our common enemies roar from the borders; they will tremble when they reflect on the warlike phalanges which our fertile land has been able to raise up in an instant . . . Even more vainly still

---

*There is possibly a connection between the idea of aphrodisiac cooking expressed here and the preparations of the cook Asie in Balzac's *Splendeurs et misères des courtisanes* of 1842. For Balzac's views on Brillat, see his article on the judge in Michaud, *Biographie universelle* and *Variétés gourmandes, suivies d'une traité des excitans modernes* (1838).

will the enemy within plot and intrigue; the law will grind them into dust. Fanaticism, that old enemy of our fathers, has dropped its dagger before the banner of reason. The titles which the Constitution has outlawed are beginning to look ridiculous; soon they will be used as insults, and after sixty centuries of error that first wish of nature, that we should all be equal, will at last be accomplished.[12]

On 8 June Brillat came into the family property in Belley. His mother, possibly believing that she should apportion her share of her husband's estate, or perhaps turning her mind to emigration (the goods of *émigrés* were liable to confiscation under a decree of 9 February), turned them over to her eldest son, now 37. He became the owner of the house in the Grand'Rue, and other property in the cathedral city, to a value of 17,000 *livres*. The fate of *la Belle Aurore* is not clear. Perhaps she retired to Vieu or Pugieu, to leave her son as master under his own roof.[13]

France had declared war on Austria on 20 April 1792, when Austria refused to banish French *émigrés* from her territory. This war continued, virtually without a break, until 1815. With it came a new paranoia, a perpetual fear of enemies without and within, which later contributed to the Terror. On 8 July the citizens of Belley were required to deposit their weapons with the National Guard. Brillat's name is notably absent from the list of citizens who complied, but he was later compelled at least to register the arms he kept under his roof: the list includes one National Guard issue rifle and two guns of his own, a pistol, a sabre and a pound of powder.[14]

On 10 August 1792 the King and Queen were attacked in the Tuileries. The *coup d'état* was largely the work of the Paris Sections (district councils), who controlled the volatile crowds of the capital. Danton, who had achieved a position of power at their head, was elected Minister of Justice. New elections were ordered, designed to produce a more democratic 'Convention' on the American model. On 14 August Antide de Rubat reported back to the people of Belley, 'Calm is beginning to be re-established in the capital.' The day before, the King and Queen had been imprisoned in the Temple keep, at the centre of a collection of chiefly medieval buildings once the home of the Templars.[15]

On 17 August Danton created a new *Tribunal criminel extraordinaire*, thereby institutionalizing revolutionary justice and initiating (possibly unwittingly) the Reign of Terror. Danton made it clear that his aim was to sweep the conservatives from the provincial benches.

He wrote to the magistrates, 'You can still win back the goodwill of the nation . . . turn against traitors and enemies of the public weal the sword of justice that [the monarchy] tried to turn, in your hands, against the apostle of liberty. Let the justice of the courts begin and the justice of the people will stop.'[16]

New judges were elected and Brillat lost his job.[17] The fall of the monarchy had brought a new assembly with its own brand of justice. Under the Constitution of the year I all courts, whether civil or criminal, were to be staffed by elected magistrates. In civil actions, justice was to be administered by elected *juges de paix*.[18]

From 2 to 5 September, a new wave of mob violence erupted in Paris. Encouraged by the writings of Marat and Fréron, crowds of armed men forced their way into the prisons and asylums of the city, which had been filled to bursting point with men and women arrested as 'suspects' after the Prussians laid siege to Verdun on 30 August. Those hacked to death in four days of unfettered violence (Danton, the Minister of Justice, made no attempt to stop the blood-letting) were chiefly members of the Church and nobles opposed to the drift of the Revolution. Rubat, who was in Paris as a member of the Legislative Assembly, wrote to the citizens of Belley 'in a state of great consternation . . . Since this morning Paris has offered a display of horror and carnage such that history can so far offer no precedent at no time and in no place'.[19]

Copycat September Massacres occurred along the Rhône valley and in Provence, claiming nearly 300 victims to add to the 1,400 or so dead in Paris. It cannot have escaped Rubat and Brillat, men of order, that they and the other moderates had failed to limit the Revolution as they had wanted. In Belley, Bishop Royer was having endless problems with priests who refused to swear the oath to the State.[20]

That very month measures against suspects were issued in the Ain: orders were to disarm 'former' nobles, 'former' members of the religious orders, refractory priests, priests refusing to swear a new oath which required them to accept 'liberty and equality', and the mothers and fathers of *émigrés*.[21]

Brillat and his friends must at least have derived some comfort from the success of French arms in the rout of the Prussian army at Valmy on 20 September. In their border province the *bugistes* were particularly vulnerable to invasion scares. The day after Valmy news arrived from the village of Céyzerieu, in the marshes below Culoz, that the Savoyard army, part of the anti-French coalition, had crossed the frontier. This false report caused predictable panic in Belley. Two days later the army of the French under General de Montesquiou-Fézensac entered Savoy, thereby putting an end to the crisis. The transalpine provinces of Savoy which thus came under French control were eventually incorporated into the Republic as the Department of Mont-Blanc.[22]

The tide of the war had turned. On 29 September volunteers from the Ain were among those who took the city of Speier on the left bank of the Rhine. Victories such as this were offset by the increasingly menacing tone of the National Convention, the successor to the Constituent Assembly, which began sitting the day after Valmy. In Belley the political situation was bound to be the subject of endless speculation and discussion, especially among the former 'notables'. Having been a deputy at the Constituent Assembly, Brillat doubtless excelled himself in analyses of what was happening. In mid-December 1792 he was unanimously elected mayor of the city.[23]

III

The National Convention did not radically alter the political representation of the department of the Ain. The rule disbarring deputies to the National Assembly from election to the Legislative Assembly had been dropped, and the left-wing Gauthier des Orcières, a former Constituent, was elected to the Convention, as was Bishop Royer on the right. Two Legislative deputies, Etienne Deydier and Grégoire-Marie Jagot, were also returned by the electorate. Two new men were the lawyers Jean-Marie François Merlino and Jean-Luc Anthelme Mollet. Mollet withdrew from the Convention in August 1793 leaving his seat to Anthelme Ferrand, another lawyer who practised in Belley.[24]

In November 1792 the Convention began the process of indicting Louis XVI, and by January had decided that the *conventionnels* themselves should decide the fate of the man they now called 'Louis Capet'. The deputies from the Ain were split between the left and the right.

It is tempting to speculate on how Brillat would have voted had he been a member of the Convention. Most former *monarchiens* who had neither gone into exile nor fallen victim to the September Massacres had either withdrawn from politics, like Brillat, or altered their sympathies in the light of the King's intransigence, also like Brillat. By 1793 he was no longer a *monarchien*; he had shifted his allegiance to the Gironde (so-called because of its preponderance of members from the Bordeaux area), which sought to increase the power of the provinces and so counter the influence of the Paris mob, which supported the more radical Jacobins. The Girondins, to some extent bourgeois lawyers and merchants, were anxious because of their interests and growing wealth to bring the Revolution to a halt before the enormous amounts of property brought on to the market by the sale of Church and feudal lands could filter further down the line into the hands of the peasants. As France became embroiled in wars with her neighbours, the Girondins' advocacy of a limited federalism came to be seen as nationally divisive, and therefore treacherous. The Girondin leadership was divided on the issue of the King's sentence, and since Brillat appears to have made no public utterance on the subject, we do not know which way he would have cast his vote.

In the second half of 1792 political clubs had begun to spring up in the smallest towns, and even in villages. After the September Massacres, the Clubs or *Sociétés des amis de la Constitution* began to split into Jacobin and Girondin camps, often as a result of local interests or the attitudes of the towns' deputies. This was true of Belley, which possessed two clubs in 1793. The 'Club du Temple' was affiliated with the Jacobins in Paris. Following the September Massacres it changed its name to the *Société des amis de la Liberté et de l'Egalité* and embraced more moderate ideas tending to the Girondin side. It met in the old Cistercian monastery of Belley under the presidency of Brillat-Savarin himself. In the summer of 1793 the Jacobin party activists or *sans-culottes* of the city founded their own club to oppose federalism and press the Jacobin line. This became known as the *Société des sans-culottes*.[25]

The growing power of the left-wing Jacobins, the 'Montagne' as they were termed because of their fondness for the upper benches of the chamber, was not felt in the provinces until the arrival of the *représentants en mission* after 9 March 1793. These emissaries of the Convention had been given a brief to visit all the departments of France and observe to what degree the laws were being enforced. Two each were assigned to a pair of departments. In addition to 'instructing their fellow citizens on the dangers threatening the country', Jean-Marie François Merlino and Jean-Pierre André Amar, sent to the Ain and the Saône-et-Loire, were empowered to take whatever measures they thought necessary.[26]

Amar and Merlino reached Belley on 22 March, to find the local

administration in the midst of a furious uproar. A denunciation had
been lodged against the local *procureur*, one Vettard-Piot, for having
profited from the sale of the belongings of the *émigré* and former
grand-bailli, Louis-Honoré de Montillet. Vettard-Piot was arrested
and sent for trial. By 7 April Amar and Merlino had left Belley;
although they must have spoken at length with the Mayor, Brillat-
Savarin, nothing of their conversation has come down to us.[27]

April 1793 was dominated by a renewed threat of invasion from
Switzerland and Savoy. Shots were exchanged with the Savoyards at
the border fortress of Pierre Châtel on the Rhône, and in nearby
Belley the people became increasingly aware that their city would
receive the full force of any attack. The local administration decided
to provide reinforcements for the frontier, but they were hampered by
a shortage of rifles and cannon. While the enemies of France formed a
coalition to depose the revolutionary government, the Convention
replied by calling for more volunteers: 3,000 from the Ain alone.
Belley sent 23.[28]

IV

On 1 April 1793 the Girondin General Dumouriez went over to the
Austrians, taking with him the marquis de Beurnonville, the Minister
of War, and four representatives of the Convention who had been sent
to arrest him. Dumouriez' act of treason ultimately brought about the
fall of the Girondins.

For the next two months the battle between the Montagne and the
Gironde grew fiercer on the benches of the Convention. Robespierre,
speaking for the Montagne, did not hesitate to tell Pierre Vergniaud
and all those he believed to have been implicated in Dumouriez' flight
that 'Liberty will triumph when all those vile scoundrels whom I
denounce will be lying in their tombs.'[29]

The Gironde counter-attacked by having Marat sent for trial, but
the darling of the Paris crowd emerged victorious from the Revolutionary Tribunal, and the Paris Sections descended on the chamber
to demand the banishment of the 22 leaders of the Gironde. The
Girondins could not enforce their will on the Montagne since they
lacked sufficiently powerful support in Paris. In their frustration they
issued threats against the capital. Marguerite Élie Guadet from Saint-
Emilion called for the Convention to be moved from Paris to Bourges,

out of the way of the revolutionary Paris Sections.[30] In Girondin-controlled provinces, including the Ain, a call went out for the formation of a Girondin army to march on Paris.

On 24 May the Ain administration decided to send an armed force to accompany a delegation to Bourges. That same day Maximin Isnard, a fiery orator from Grasse in Provence, stood up in the Convention to declare that if the Montagne 'struck out at the representatives of the nation . . .', Paris would be obliterated: 'soon people would search the banks of the Seine for the place where the city had once existed.'[31] Isnard's speech gave the Jacobins their pretext. Urged on by the rioting of the Paris mob outside the chamber and by the actions of Marat within, the Convention voted on 2 June to suspend the leaders of the Gironde.

On the evening of 10 June Brillat was in the chair at the Club du Temple when his cousin, a cathedral preacher by the name of Louis-François Savarin, made a breathless and inflammatory speech enthusiastically supporting the reaction in Lyon, Marseille and Bordeaux against the fall of the Gironde. He continued:

> Finally Paris will rise up, not in anarchy but to crush with her victorious foot all that impious scum which has made outrageous and unchecked threats to slaughter the representatives of the people. . . . these bawling cannibals [led by] the foul, unspeakable Marat who never cease to hound the representatives of the nation.[32]

If it was not risky enough for Brillat to be present during this violent diatribe against Marat and the Montagne, he followed it up on 13 June with a discourse of his own. But Brillat was more prudent and guarded:

> Citizens! For the past three years you have tasted all the benefits of the new laws; agriculture has prospered and your houses are now filled with plenty . . . yet civil war has now broken out in several departments, the fields have been ravaged; husbands and fathers have perished in battle, French blood has been shed by French armies.
>
> If you have not been prey to these terrible scourges, citizens, you owe it to the good minds who have governed this district; you owe it also to the magistrates whom you have chosen. They have watched over you with an indefatigable zeal in confounding the plots of aristocrats and fanatics, of faction and those for whom the prosperity of the public is a torture. In these critical times, they will redouble their vigilance; it is their duty and they will fulfil it in all its magnitude.[33]

On 23 June Brillat was present at a meeting of the Club du Temple at which addresses were read out from the federalists of Lyon and Marseille. His presence at such an assembly was another example of uncharacteristic carelessness. But three days later there were no allusions to either the Montagne or the Girondins in a speech he delivered to the massed citizens of Belley. This was the prudent, public image of Brillat. On 26 June, he officially opened the Temple of Liberty in Belley. The mayors of all French communes had been called upon to take over a local church and dedicate it to the cult of Liberty. Brillat took the opportunity to make a speech, from which it appears he had decidedly altered his view of the dangerous nature of public opinion since speaking against its tyranny before the Constituent Assembly. However, while he was keen to speak up for Liberty, it is clear that his ideas on property and law were still far removed from those of the Montagne and the *sans-culottes*:

> Citizens, Liberty has a daughter called Equality, and she is her constant companion and principal support.
>
> But don't imagine that by equality is meant the perfectly equal distribution of property, wealth, physical and moral qualities; such equality is not to be found in nature. The Author of all that exists was content to share out his gifts in unequal portions, and all of us carry at birth the germ of passions and virtues which will ultimately result in different quantities of strength or weakness, obscurity or glory, unhappiness or prosperity.
>
> True equality is the equality of rights and duties.

Equality before the law and the Constitution was the message of Brillat's speech, cloaked though it was in fashionable slogans abjuring egotism and fanaticism. The warnings were all too clear: obey the law and defend morality, though that morality might owe little to the teachings of the Catholic Church.[34]

Brillat was playing a careful game. On 16 July the new constitution was published, replacing that which Brillat had been privileged to present to his now-dead monarch in 1791. Brillat welcomed it: 'May it become the constitution of the whole human race,' he said, 'everywhere recalling the reign of law and happiness'.[35] Was this perhaps inspired by a glance across the frontiers of France to where the armies of the nation were carrying with them the Revolution and its creed? It was certainly a call for the re-establishment of law within the ancient boundaries of France. 'The vile, unspeakable Marat' had been stabbed to death on 13 July. The day before, Kellerman's armies had been ordered to proceed against the rebels of Lyon. Brillat must have felt keenly the need for prudence.

Notwithstanding the widespread sympathy for the federalists of Lyon in both Belley and Bourg, the Convention required both cities to provide troops for the suppression of the revolt. Brillat's views on the tyranny of the Montagne had not changed but, no doubt from motives of prudence, he undertook to accompany the 146 men of Belley to Bourg in person. To concentrate his mind further, one of them was his own brother Frédéric.[36]

Brillat had supported the Girondin call for war against France's neighbours; war was now raging on all fronts. He could derive satisfaction for the time being from the success of the French armies and from the valour displayed by people from Belley and the Valromey. In the battle for Puigcerda in the Pyrenees, for example, the young lieutenant Prosper Sibuet was blooded; for his valour in protecting French soil from the Spanish, the Convention awarded him the Sword of Honour.[37]

On 19 August the administration in Belley received a letter from the citizens of Chambéry (annexed with the rest of Savoy in November 1792) asking for assistance. It was believed that troops of the Duke of Savoy (King of Sardinia since 1720) had crossed into the new French department of Mont Blanc (formerly part of Savoy) and were threatening the city.[38] Two days later the Convention decided to send a detachment of the National Guard to help.[39] Gauthier des Orcières, who was organizing this defence, wrote to the citizens of Belley: 'You have promised to assist your brothers in Mont Blanc. This help is now more necessary than ever. Fulfil your promise as best you can by sending armed volunteers . . .'[40]

Panic was reported at Seyssel on the Rhône, where refugees had fled fearing reprisals from Sardinian troops in Annecy. The administration in Belley appealed to Bourg: 'The Piedmontese and the Austrians are making considerable progress in Mont Blanc.' The path to Belley lay open, defended only by the *invalides* or army pensioners manning the fort at Pierre Châtel.[41]

Brillat had returned from Bourg-en-Bresse. At six o'clock on the morning of 22 August, he spoke in the Place de la Liberté (the former Place des Terreaux) in the centre of Belley. Having read out the letters from the directory of the department and from Gauthier in Chambéry, 'he then asked volunteers to write their names in a register opened for that purpose, to go to the assistance of our brothers in

Chambéry, and to re-establish order in that city' until Kellerman could get his regular troops there.[42]

Belley's little army of 80 men, under Brillat's command, set off on 22 August in the direction of Chambéry. Brillat was surrounded by friends and relations: the inflammatory cathedral preacher Louis François Savarin, François-Xavier his brother, Tendrets and Rouxs. That night they slept at Yenne by Pierre Châtel, and arrived in Chambéry the following day.[43]

Brillat had made a wise move. With the *sans-culottes* of the city itching to have him removed for his anti-Montagnard views, the excursion to Chambéry was a good way to clear his name. Even before his squad reached Chambéry, the administration of that city had sent off a tribute to the men of Belley:

> Dear friends and brothers, from the instant that you learned of the dangers we faced, you rushed to send us help. We recognize our true friends and brothers in this resolution of yours . . . The presence of the Citizen-Mayor of your city, who is said to be at the head of your force, adds to our transports of joy and gratitude . . .[44]

Wallowing in glory, the detachment refused to heed instructions received from Belley on 24 August to retreat, and regroup at the Rhône. They would not, they informed all concerned, desert the people of Chambéry until the arrival of Kellerman's army.[45]

> Citizens [Brillat wrote to the administration in Belley], the detachment which was entrusted to me arrived in Chambéry on Friday the 23rd inst. On their arrival, the municipality provided refreshment and lodgings, even though all that was necessary were subsistence rations. When the officers visited the city, they were allowed into the town hall where they were embraced by the councillors . . .
>
> We also received the news that the person responsible for the troubles in Annecy had been guillotined; that the Piedmontese were still far away from it and that our troops were strengthening their position daily.[46]

The administration clearly thought Brillat's little army would be better employed in defending their home town; justifying the recall in a letter to Gauthier and the Alpine Army, they pointed out that order had been re-established in Chambéry by the generous sacrifice of 'Young men, married men, even public office holders'.[47] Brillat's squad bade farewell to a grateful town council in Chambéry and returned to Belley. The recall was not, however, popular with General Kellerman, who replied curtly that the squad should return to

Chambéry on pain of disciplinary action. They did not; Brillat had had his moment of glory.

V

On 23 August the Convention ordered a *levée en masse* to cope with the dangers on France's frontiers:

> From this moment, until such time as the enemy has been chased from the territories of the Republic, all Frenchmen will be permanently in demand for the services of our armies. Young men will go to war; married men will make arms and transport supplies; women will manufacture tents and uniforms and serve in hospitals; children will transform old linen into bandages; the old will be taken to public places where they will excite the courage of our warriors, preaching hatred for kings and love for the Republic.[48]

The crisis on the frontiers threw the civil conflict into a new perspective: men like Brillat had to choose between the Girondin resistance to the Jacobins, and the need to devote the full forces of the nation to vanquishing her enemies. Family problems complicated the issues confronting him. Frédéric Brillat-Savarin was now an adjutant-major in the National Guard, due to leave shortly for the front (in fact, he was after all dispatched to help besiege Lyon). Like other Girondins, Brillat increasingly determined to bury the ardour of the June days. On 15 September his name topped a bill posted in the streets of Belley, addressed to the young citizens called to arms.

> The law calls you first into the fray. Young citizens, who more than you deserves that honour, you who will one day reap the full benefits of the Revolution, you who are destined one day to raise the generations of the free, you for whom the *ancien régime* was merely a sinister dream which has been dispelled by the awakening of Liberty?
>
> ... A few moments more and the universe will proclaim you its salvation; a few moments more and the human race will be free. You will take precedence in this; but if victory should require our lives also, we will heed the call and we will set an example to other citizens, teaching them that the judges of a free people prefer death to slavery: THIS WE SWEAR.[49]

But patriotism was not enough to placate the *sans-culottes*: that month they produced a poster of their own, sparing no one, least of all a 'bourgeois aristocrat' like Brillat:

. . . Bouillé, La Fayette, Rochambeau, Montesquiou, Dumourriez, Custine and all our generals have betrayed us . . .

. . . in the National Convention cowardly plotters, vile toads from the Swamp, monsters from the Plain,* are selling their votes to the highest bidder; . . .

The administrators are as perfidious as they are barbarous in the departments of the Jura, Rhône-et-Loire, Ain and the Midi . . . [and] Lyon, that city of scoundrels and ingratitude . . .

The gold of foreign powers† is being passed around the country.

Former nobles and bourgeois aristocrats are the secret agents who shell out this money in order to devalue the *assignats*; to burn down our fortresses; to hoard, and encourage the hoarding, of all our goods.

The time has come to put a stop to all this treason . . .

Let all the primary and communal assemblies assist us in our task; yes; all . . . May all ardent republicans in every commune bring over their stout fellow citizens.[50]

Then the *sans-culottes* dwelt on Brillat and his sort:

those fat bourgeois . . . to whom modest artisans and good villagers never dared speak without doffing their caps, they only want to govern in the place of the nobles. They don't like equality: the word alone frightens them out of their wits . . .

As for those former advocates and prosecutors [lawyers and administrators], the new constitution has done away with all that chicanery, it was despicable to call them 'masters'‡ of that infernal art: they made everything look difficult in order to show how talented they were.

The recall was demanded of all ex-noble generals, officers and men; immediate arrest was proposed for ex-nobles and ex-bourgeois who 'gave themselves noble airs by adding the names of fiefs or *métairies* [stock-jobbing farms] to their names', all persons were to be disarmed and arrested if they had been denounced by ten known patriots; all civil servants were to be arrested if they had, since 31 May, 'raised their shields against Paris'; all fanatics [i.e. priests] were to be restricted to

---

Marais and *plaine*: those moderate elements in the Convention, opposed to the radical Montagne.

†'Pitt's gold': the money with which the British were allegedly buying off moderate *coventionnels* to stop radical laws being enacted.

‡As a token of respect, lawyers were and still are addressed as *maître* or master.

the commune on pain of fine; the treason of the former generals was to be made the responsibility of the former nobles; weapons were to be seized in the interests of creating a truly Republican army; the property of federalists was to be seized; ten commissioners from each commune were to oversee these new edicts; and all those found delaying their enactment were to be fined. Finally there was a call for a 'French eruption' – six weeks of concentrated effort to stamp out the coalition of brigands and tyrants.[51] Fear of this sort of action was what Brillat had had in mind during his exchange with Robespierre in the Assembly on 9 August 1790.

Behind the attacks on Brillat and his friends was one Antoine Bonnet who, ironically enough, had made his name in the food business, starting out as a sweetmaker, and eventually becoming a *limonadier* or café owner. When Jacobin principles began to filter down to town and village assemblies he made rapid progress, being elected to the administration and acquiring the offices of director of Belley's post office, military agent, elector, major in the National Guard, operator of the franchise on the *fours banaux* (public ovens in the villages) and, last and most importantly, secretary to the town's Watch Committee.[52]

Bonnet was typical of the village revolutionaries. He delivered his views to the *sans-culottes* on 9 September:

> Citizens, we need *sans-culottes* in all positions . . . men with more common sense than education, virtuous, sensitive, humane; men outraged by the slightest whisper of injustice; intrepid, energetic men who desire the common good, Liberty, Equality or death: in short, those abused, persecuted individuals who are so cordially detested by the former nobles, federalists and bourgeois aristocrats that they calumny them with the names *incendiers, enragés, Maratists* because they despair of ever succeeding in corrupting them or seducing them . . .[53]

Louis-Marie Dubost, imprisoned for 75 days by the *sans-culottes* of Bourg and Belley, thought otherwise:

> [Bonnet was] . . . the perfect complement to Robespierre and Collot [d'Herbois – actor and terrorist]. These men and their toadies exercised such power over public opinion that they were the very soul of *sans-culottisme*. They persecuted anyone who was honest, or who had talent or virtue . . .[54]

In August, Bonnet had been caught tampering with the mail of the commander of the National Guard, Peysson. Peysson reported

Bonnet to the Mayor: Brillat had to remind Bonnet that even in those denunciation-crazy days, the director of the post office was not authorized to read other people's letters without the permission of the town council. While they were debating Bonnet's crime, the council discovered (clearly to their joy and relief) that it was unconstitutional to hold two municipal offices at the same time. As Bonnet was acting as both director of the post office and a member of the directory, Brillat and his friends had him denounced to the Minister of the Interior, Jean-François Paré. Bonnet responded in kind; accompanied by another *sans-culotte* called Carrier he travelled to Dôle in the Jura to see Claude-Charles Prost, who was the central government's *représentant en mission* in the Jura, the Ain, Mont Terrible, Côte d'Or and Saône-et-Loire.[55]

On 8 October Antoine Bonnet was able to score a success in his war against the Mayor and the 'bourgeois aristocracy' of Belley. Backed up by two representatives of the Convention, the defrocked priest Jean Bassal and the Robespierrist lawyer Antoine-André Bernard de Saintes, Bonnet was authorized by the Convention to institute changes in the administration of Belley. Two civic officers were sacked and the *procureur* Dumoulin was replaced by the nail-maker, Charvin.[56]

On 13 October, Bonnet's campaign achieved another success: this time he was authorized to replace the entire administration from the Mayor downwards. This order came directly from Prost, who had replaced Bassal and Bernard as the authority of the Convention in the district. The directory was replaced as the municipal authority by the Watch Committee, composed of an innkeeper, a bootmaker, a cabinet-maker and a nail-maker. A Monsieur Barquet became mayor. The *sans-culottes* were finally in the saddle.[57]

Later that month Louis-Marie Dubost was transferred from his prison in Bourg-en-Bresse to the fortress at Pierre Châtel. In his account of his imprisonment, he gives some impression of the atmosphere in Belley during this period:

> During the time we were crossing Belley, no one dared show their face at the windows. On the other hand, triumphant *sans-culottes* occupied the place des Terreaux. Some of them together with their wives shouted the cruellest abuse at us, for example that 'it would be much more efficient to bludgeon us to death there and then, thereby avoiding the trouble of stringing us up later!' We thought it prudent to pretend not to hear.[58]

Bonnet and his fellow-members of the Watch Committee longed to denounce Brillat and other 'bourgeois aristocrats'. They obtained access to the register of correspondence and speeches of the Club du Temple, and used these as the basis of a lengthy decree:

On the evidence of the different writings . . . contained [in the register] we are convinced that [the Club du Temple] had promised the city of Belley to the rebel coalition.

It is clear that the principal members of the club occupied positions in the district and municipality, in which they had been set by a cabal of the wealthy.

Bearing in mind the fact that the nation demands rapid and strong measures to unravel and confound their malevolent plots;

It is decreed as a measure of General Security that all those members attached to the Club du Temple de la Liberté will have their registers sealed and are hereby declared suspect. An exception will be made in the cases of those who, in the course of the next month, come and reveal before the Watch Committee the names of the main orators and leaders of the treacherous club.

. . . The names of the members who frequented the aforesaid club, and who did not leave it before it was too late, will be printed and listed after this decree . . .

Brillat's name headed the list.[59]

But he was not finished yet. He saddled his favourite horse *La joie* and rode off to the sunny slopes of the Jura. He intended to search out Prost and obtain a safe-conduct to protect himself from arrest pending news from Paris regarding his own denunciation of Bonnet. He travelled north, probably via Nantua, Oyonnax and Lons-le-Saunier, to Mont-sous-Vaudrey, a journey of three days or more. Arriving at lunchtime in Mont-sous-Vaudrey, Brillat was troubled by a rumbling stomach. His hunger was increased by what he saw at the inn:

Before a fierce, bright fire turned a spit, wonderfully garnished with quails, king quails and those fat little green-toed corncrakes. This choice of game was shedding its last drops on to a huge slice of bread. The workmanship pointed to the hand of a huntsman. Alongside this one could see, already cooked, one of those round-flanked leverets; game unknown to Parisians but with a redolence which would fill a church.

'My dear fellow,' Brillat asked the innkeeper, Monsieur Tramu, 'what do you have that's good, for my dinner?' 'Nothing but good things,' replied Tramu: 'good boiled beef, good potato soup, good

105

shoulder of mutton and good beans.' Brillat was not thrilled by this rustic menu. 'So who's going to eat all this lovely-looking game, then?' The game was for some magistrates who had been lodged in the inn while they tried a celebrated case.[60]

Brillat does not mention the case in *La Physiologie du goût*, but it was something of a *cause-célèbre* in its day. Even the *conventionnel* Prost had been involved, and had let his views be known before returning to Dôle. Stephanie-Louise de Bourbon-Conti was suing her husband, a local justice of the peace called Billet, for divorce and for the return of her 20,000-*livre* dowry.[61] But Stephanie-Louise was less than she made herself out to be. The supposed natural daughter of the prince de Bourbon-Conti and the duchesse de Mazarin was in reality a *fille de joie* who had been intimately connected with a number of high-ranking aristocrats at court. Taking her earnings with her, Anne-Louise-Françoise (her real name) had married Billet even though (according to her memoirs)[62] he was 'old and repulsive'. The divorce of a Bourbon married to a local member of the third estate would naturally cause a certain stir in the region; as a supposed member of the royal family Anne-Louise-Françoise had chosen a bad moment to fight her case. Perhaps for this reason, she was not successful in recovering her dowry. She fled to Paris where she died in poverty in 1825, a year before Brillat himself. This story was well known at the time, and later inspired Goethe's tragedy *Die natürliche Tochter* (*The Natural Daughter*), completed in 1803.[63]

Brillat's appetite was in no way affected by his misfortunes: the sight of the magistrates' game was too much for him; his dignity overwhelmed by the aroma of the little birds, he sent Tramu into the judges' room to inform them that a 'well brought-up gentleman' would like to share their meal, adding that he would be more than happy to pay his share of the reckoning. After sending in a spy to size him up, the judges invited him to eat at their table. More than thirty years later Brillat had still not forgotten that meal, the *fricassé* of chicken crammed full of truffles, then the game, followed by vanilla cream, cheese and fruit. Nor did the wines escape his attention: a light *vin ordinaire* the colour of garnet,* some Hermitage† and after that some *vin de paille*.‡

---

*Jura wines rarely achieve any depth of colour; Brillat's was exceptional.
†The abbé Fromond contends that this was the 'Ermitage d'Arbois' rather than the more famous Hermitage of the Rhône valley. This is unlikely; Brillat expresses his fondness for Hermitage elsewhere in *La Physiologie du goût* (see the episode of the Chevalier de Langeac).

Brillat paid for his lunch by singing some verses of his own creation. The magistrates were so enchanted that they asked him to stay for dinner; he was unhappy to have to decline, but the object of his mission was Prost. He had missed the *conventionnel* in Mont-sous-Vaudrey, so he saddled his horse and continued his journey to Dôle.[65]

It is possible that the ex-deputy and the *conventionnel* had been university contemporaries at Dijon.[66] However that may be, Prost had already taken sides against him; he prepared to use his charm. He had a useful ally in the mayor of Dôle, Anathoile Amondru or Amaudra; they certainly had studied law together. Amondru was able to prevail on Prost to dine with them while Brillat pleaded his cause.[67] Prost remained unmoved, but Brillat found he had much in common with Madame Prost: for the second time his musicality came to his aid. Madame Prost had something of a reputation as a singer in Dôle, and had sung a solo at the unveiling in 1783 of a statue to Louis XVI, once one of the principal ornaments of the town.[68] From the moment she learned of Brillat's musical talents, their 'hearts vibrated in unison'.*[69]

> She talked to me about treatises on composition – I knew them all; she spoke of the more fashionable operas – I knew them by heart; she produced the names of the most famous composers – virtually all of them I had seen in the flesh. She talked non-stop because it had been so long since she had had the opportunity to talk about such things. She spoke like an amateur, although I later learned that she had worked as a singing teacher.
>
> After dinner she sent a servant to fetch some scores; she sang, I sang, we sang together; never have I performed with so much ardour, never have I derived so much pleasure from song . . .[70]

Prost himself lost patience with this performance, and several times tried to break up the soirée. Finally Brillat was asked to leave. At the door Madame Prost whispered to her new friend:

> Citizen, when someone like you cultivates the arts, he does not betray his country. I know you have come here to obtain something from my husband. You will have it! You have my word for that.[71]

---

‡The sweet *vin de paille* was (and occasionally still is) made by leaving overripe Poulsard grapes on straw mats (hence the name) until the liquid content has been considerably reduced. The grapes are then pressed and the juice fermented.

*It is a tradition in the Valromey that Brillat's relations with Madame Prost did not stop at singing duets. According to M. Perrin of Vieu, local legend has it that she bore him a child.

The next morning Brillat received his safe-conduct and passport:

Laissez-passer for Jean-Anthelme Brillat-Savarin, French citizen resident in Belley, by profession property owner and farmer, aged 37, five feet seven and a half inches tall,* blond hair and eyebrows, receding hairline, eyes grey, turned-up nose, mouth medium, large chin, face scarred by small-pox. He is travelling to the interior of the Republic and is to be afforded help and assistance whenever needed.[72]

He rode back to Belley in triumph.

Madame Prost was able to secure more from her husband: the minutes of a meeting of Belley's council on 1 November 1793 record Prost's decision that, while Brillat was still deprived of his office as mayor, he 'should temporarily enjoy total liberty until such time as we have received information either as a result of our own investigation or as a result of those undertaken by appointed commissioners.'[73]

Bonnet and his *sans-culottes* were still in control of the city. The abolition of the ordinary courts and the new elections to the bench of *juges de paix* had introduced a form of popular justice which was quite unable to maintain order. Everywhere the peasants were seizing the estates of *émigrés* without waiting for official sanction. Now that the squires and monks had lost their rights to the forests, peasants laid waste to the land in an orgy of tree-felling.[74]

On Sunday, 17 November, Brillat received the news he had been waiting for. His friend Dor returned from the Convention in Paris armed with a decree dated 6 November: Brillat was to be temporarily reinstated as mayor, pending investigation. He spoke generously before the assembled council; it was minuted that his replacement, Barquet, was satisfied with the authenticity of the decree, and Brillat once again signed the register as mayor of his home town.[75]

He lost no time in locking up the troublesome *sans-culottes* and reversing the decisions taken in his absence. The *sans-culottes* in Bourg-en-Bresse, learning the fate of their fellows, were outraged. This was rank treachery! Protests from the *sans-culottes* once again reached Paris and the Convention. Brillat later described the actions of his enemies, and their dramatic result, in his petition of October 1794 to the Convention:

---

*Five foot ten and a half inches in modern British or American measurements.

[The *sans-culottes* first of all] . . . adopted a system of vague defamation, which is always successful in the long term, and which is quite irrefutable in the case of a man in public office who, wholly absorbed by his duties, cannot or will not condescend to root out the slanders from the obscure corners where they exude their poison.

Strong in his own conscience . . . [Brillat-Savarin] hoped at first that his enemies would destroy themselves but soon, as a result of utterly scandalous intrigues, they managed to have themselves elected to the Committee of General Security of the city and he learned that while the members [of the committee] prepared his arrest, two of their number had gone to Paris to spread their falsehoods.

. . . seeing little or no chance of having himself proved innocent before a Revolutionary Tribunal which was in the pay of Robertspierre's [*sic*] faction, and seeing that the Public Prosecutor* was a personal enemy . . . he was obliged to flee.[76]

Brillat's version of events is the only one that has come down to us; from Prost he had bought time, but he must have known that once the Committee of Public Safety took an interest in his case he would be in danger of being sent to Paris to answer to the capital charge of federalism. As he got back into harness at the town hall, the *sans-culottes* representatives were busy in Paris. At the beginning of December, when Brillat had been back in office for less than a month, he received word that a *représentant en mission* was on his way to Belley to investigate the matter on behalf of the Convention. On 10 or 11 December, the Mayor vanished.

---

*Antoine Quentin Fouquier, known as Fouquier-Tinville, was named Public Prosecutor on 13 March 1793 and continued in office until after the fall of Robespierre on 9 Thermidor (27 July 1794). During that time he sent to the scaffold in their thousands the victims of the Committees of Public Safety and General Security. Despite a spirited defence of his conduct, Fouquier-Tinville was himself executed, on 7 May 1795. Brillat gives no reason in his petition for saying that Fouquier-Tinville was a personal enemy, but at a time when all Paris was crying out for his execution it was certainly a politic assertion.

CHAPTER SIX

'French Leave'

I

ON 26 FRIMAIRE of the Year II of the United, Indivisible Republic (16 December 1793, elsewhere), the town hall in Belley was honoured by a visit from *la Belle Aurore* Brillat-Savarin. The minutes record the purpose of her visit.

> [She] . . . informed us that she had learned from gossip circulating in the city that there existed a denunciation against her son Anthelme Brillat-Savarin, Mayor of this Commune, inscribed in the registers of the ~~société populaire~~ [crossed out: i.e., the *sans-culottes*] of the municipality, and relating to his disappearance. She visited us to make it clear that there was nothing in his absence that should give rise to the slightest suspicion towards her son. She assures us that he has been gone only since the 11 or 12 Frimaire, at which time he was obliged to leave in order to deal with some very pressing business, and that he had in his possession a passport which had been issued to him last October (old style) and that she expected his return at any time.[1]

Brillat's mother signed the minutes in an unsteady hand. Later, Brillat's brothers left a statement at the town hall that they had ridden far and wide in search of him, but so far had found no trace.[2]

The Convention's *représentant*, Benoît Gouly, had been born in Bourg-en-Bresse. For some years he had been surgeon to the army on the Île de France* where with the benefit of the governor's friendship he had acquired a plantation, and later the Cross of St Michel. At the

---

*Now Mauritius: it was invaded by the British in 1806 and became a British colony in 1814.

beginning of the Revolution he was one of the leading notables of the Île de France.

On the Île de France the elections to the National Convention took place only in February 1793. Gouly, known to be 'hotly in favour' of the new ideas of the French Revolution, was the favourite candidate in the election. Anxious to reach the Convention as quickly as possible, Gouly loaded a ship with commodities to sell in France and set off. The British, who had entered the war against France, captured the vessel, and Gouly spent four frustrating months in captivity.

On 2 or 3 October he arrived, penniless, in Paris, to present his credentials at the bar of the Convention. One of his first actions was to add his signature to those condemning Louis Capet to death, though Louis had in fact been executed even prior to Gouly's election. Because of his connections with the region, Gouly agreed to represent the Convention in the department of the Ain.[3]

He arrived in Bourg-en-Bresse on 12 December and rapidly established control there, steering a middle course between moderates and Jacobins. But he made clear his view that 'the Republic must pursue to the utmost limit the selfishness of the rich as well as the sophisms and rapine of lawyers and *procureurs*'. 'The former courts of justice' he also condemned, as 'no more than a gathering of people who lived by the sweat of others, principally that of the farm worker.' And his scorn was directed as well at the *juges de paix*, 'supporters of the rich, and the evil doer.'[4]

On 18 December Gouly arrived in Belley, which he described as being on the verge of civil war. At first he showed scant sympathy for either moderates or *sans-culottes*. Establishing authority with a small army of 400 men, he set to work to stamp out 'moderatism, fanaticism and superstition'. The day following his arrival he ordered the arrest of all former nobles, priests and unmarried ex-priests within 24 hours, and the same day wrote triumphantly back to the Committee of Public Safety in Paris: 'The famous Belley affair has been wound up this day. I'm going to appoint good *sans-culottes* to all the offices to replace all that vermin from the bar which wanted to push them down, and thereby hang on to their appointments in the courts and other public offices.'[5]

On 21 December Gouly turned his thoughts to the missing Mayor.

given that the Mayor of Belley abandoned his office more than a month ago and that he is at present a fugitive and that there exist several serious denunciations against him, such as having woven a plot against the Nation in order to take up arms against it; such as having been at the head of a popular club which allowed a speech to be made from the tribune which was both liberticide and insulting to Marat, the friend of the people, a club which passed motions and wrote letters which were insidious and federalist: it is hereby decreed that the Mayor of Belley, named Brillat-Savarin, is dismissed from his functions. He will be apprehended and transferred to the prison in Bourg. The seals will be placed on his papers and all his goods sequestered.[6]

By Christmas Eve of 1793 Gouly had either been told more, or had gone into the accusations against Brillat in more detail. The result was a certain sentence of death:

In the name of the French people, the Representative of the People in the Department of the Ain . . . is satisfied . . . [that] the said Brillat-Savarin is responsible for corrupting the majority of the citizens [and] promoting federalism, and . . . finally that he was assisted by the ex-cathedral preacher, citizen Savarin who . . . had the impudence to deliver a speech of the most liberticide nature, insulting the memory of Marat, the people's friend.

. . . decrees: that the citizens Brillat-Savarin, ex-Constituent and Mayor of the commune of Belley, and Savarin, ex-cathedral preacher, shall be seized, arrested and transferred to Paris where they will be arraigned before the Revolutionary Tribunal.[7]

Gouly liberated Bonnet, who had been languishing in prison since Brillat's resumption of the office of mayor, which Barquet resumed in his turn.[8] Later Gouly returned to Paris, where he denounced Brillat before the Convention.[9]

Gouly's successor in the Ain was Antoine Louis Albitte ('Albitte la Terreur'), who can claim to have executed the Kings of England, Prussia, Spain and Sardinia, plus the Emperor of Austria, the Pope and the British Prime Minister Pitt, all on 12 January 1794 – and all in effigy. It was this fanatic anti-clerical who demolished the church towers in virtually every commune in the department of the Ain.[10]

II

Where was Brillat-Savarin? He had saddled his horse and ridden north to the Haut-Bugey. Avoiding Nantua and the steep land-mass of the Grand Colombier, he must have followed the gorges below the lac de

Sylans, which join the Rhône near Bellegarde-sur-Valserine. Reaching the Rhône near Collonges, he crossed into Switzerland.

Geneva was the obvious first stop, but Brillat did not linger there. He had made an arrangement to meet a friend in Lausanne: Jean-Antoine de Rostaing, a native of the Valromey born, in Talissieu, in 1764 and thus eight years Brillat's junior. He was the son of the marquis Just-Antoine de Rostaing, like Lafayette a hero of the French forces who fought in the American War of Independence. After the battle of York-town the marquis had been promoted *maréchal de camp*, or brigadier. In the heady days of the Convention, however, such a history meant nothing. Rostaing was merely the son of an aristocrat, now, and so had his own problems.

Lausanne had been a magnet for exiles for many years, even before the Revolution rendered France so dangerous for many of its sons and daughters. Its connection with Edward Gibbon is well known, and it was in Lausanne that Brillat's contemporary, the founding father of gastronomic writing, Grimod de La Reynière, had his first taste of liberty. Most of the *émigrés* prior to 1794 were embittered nobles and priests, to a great extent the victims of men like Brillat who had profited from the troubles of the Church and nobility.

Naturally, perhaps, the *émigrés* of the first stage of the Revolution and those of the second stage did not trust one another. In October 1794 Brillat wrote in a petition to the Consul in New York that in Lausanne 'he could not abide being confused with *émigrés* whose intentions and sentiments were so different from his own'. The petition was, of course, written for the eyes of the Thermidorian Convention, but there is no reason to doubt that Brillat would have been uneasy with the people whose downfall he had in a sense helped to bring about.[11]

In *La Physiologie du goût* Brillat gives a picture of existence in Lausanne. For the time being he was not short of money. One can assume that his flight had been planned well enough in advance that he was able to fill some bags with coin before making off into the night. In Lausanne Brillat and Rostaing lodged at the Hôtel du Lion d'Or; there, for a modest sum, they were able to procure three-course dinners which included the best game from the nearby mountains – chamois and boar as well as *gibier à plume* – and the fish of Lake Geneva, very similar to those of Lake Bourget. All these delicacies were helped down with unstinted quantities of white wine 'as limpid as spring water and enough to tempt the most fanatical revolutionary'.[12]

Not all the *émigrés* Brillat and Rostaing met in Lausanne were so fortunate. A Lyonnais they encountered ate just twice a week, when a kind wholesale tradesman provided him with a sumptuous meal. Brillat tells us that on such days this man 'stuffed himself to the oesophagus', and never neglected to carry off some item from the table, such as a hunk of bread. For the rest of the week he took to his bed. During their brief acquaintance Brillat, too, provided the Lyonnais with some square meals, but he was not impressed by his sloth. He intended to work for his own bread, when necessary.[13]

Brillat and Rostaing left Lausanne and travelled up to Moudon in the canton of Berne. Here lived the family of Brillat's maternal grandparents, the Triollets.* By 1825 the Triollet family was extinct, Brillat informs us, no male heirs having been produced after his mother's generation. But when Brillat visited them they occupied the position of *baillis* or hereditary magistrates to the town. The family was old, 'one of the most ancient in the neighbourhood'. Among their papers Brillat found something to treasure: a recipe for *fondue*.†

His own profitable use of the years of emigration was a pet theme of Brillat's. He was not one to spend his time moping; he was also too compromised to mix easily with the exiled nobility now dotted throughout Europe and the New World, and in any case could not relive with them their days of glory. In *La Physiologie du goût* he expresses his admiration for a certain noble Chevalier d'Aubignac or d'Albignac who earned a decent living in London by teaching the English how to dress a salad. D'Albignac eventually made a fortune of 80,000 francs, and with it bought himself a *gentilhommière* in the Limousin when he was able to return to France. Sadly, the art of salad-making survived no more than a generation on the English side of the Channel.[14]

While the two were enjoying the hospitality of Brillat's relations, Rostaing first put forward the idea of sailing to the United States. For Rostaing the United States represented an ideal, a cause inherited from his father. The United States was the country of political liberty, and was not at war with France. Neither man had any desire to fight the Montagnard regime in Paris; neither had been effective in his attempt to counter the fanatics of the Committee of Public Safety. But Brillat and Rostaing awaited only a propitious moment

---

*Brillat's aunt, Claudine Triollet, was also his godmother.

†In modern French Brillat's *fondue* would be called *oeufs brouillés au gruyère* or scrambled eggs with Gruyère cheese.

to return to France; they had no quarrel with the broad lines of the Revolution.

In Switzerland Brillat obtained a passport under the name of Benoît Sattner. For the next few months, while the Terror raged in France, the two friends travelled up through Germany to Holland. They must have spent some time there before they found a suitable ship, and a captain willing to take on board yet more Frenchmen. Brillat met a rich schnapps merchant from Danzig who, clearly making a handsome profit from his business, was an expert in the various stages of progressive alcoholism, beginning with a morning tot and ending in total addiction. Brillat also encountered a sailor who had had the misfortune to be taken prisoner by Algerian corsairs. The pirates had cut out his tongue, and Brillat was anxious to know whether he retained the ability to taste. The Algerians, it seemed, had left enough tongue for that, although acidic foods caused pain.[15]

III

On 24 Messidor of the Year II (12 July 1794) Brillat and Rostaing set sail for the United States of America.[16] Only fifteen days later, on 9 Thermidor (27 July), Robespierre and his leading henchmen fell from grace. They were executed the next day. The so-called Thermidorian Convention which followed was still not purged of all elements of the extreme left, nor had all leading Terrorists been banished from its ranks. So even if Brillat had waited a further two weeks before sailing, there are no grounds for thinking that he and Rostaing would have been safe in France: Gouly's petition was by no means a dead letter, and Gouly himself remained a member of the Convention.

The two Frenchmen sailed on the brig *Friendship*, commanded by Captain Labangardner. The journey from Rotterdam to New York lasted 80 days, the ship docking at Manhattan on 30 September.[17] The federal government of the United States had migrated from New York to Philadelphia in 1790 but New York, with over 33,000 inhabitants, remained the largest city in the Union. Disembarked, Brillat must have seen a city with none of the elegance of the European centres he had known: two fires had destroyed it in the last few years, and there were many temporary structures, pending the erection of permanent replacements in stone. As he sailed into the harbour, he may have noticed the repair work taking place around the old fortifications first constructed by the Dutch. On his first walks he must have seen the spanking new City Hall, and also the City Hotel which was just nearing completion on Broadway. Elsewhere there were a few relics of Dutch building, still a few houses with crow-stepped gables like those of Rotterdam and Amsterdam.[18]

Brillat's first stop was the French Consulate. To ensure his ultimate return to his native shore he had to maintain that he had left France, not by choice, but as a result of persecution. The news he received of Robespierre's fall must have heartened him. From Belley, too, Brillat had got wind of the fact that some of his tormenters (including Bonnet) had been arrested on the orders of the new Committee of Public Safety, but the mere fact that he had left France without a legitimate cause 'erected an impregnable barrier against his return' for the time being. His views are enshrined in his petition of 15 October 1794. Brillat told his story to the Assistant Consul, Claude Jean Baptiste Bussi, who seems to have written down exactly what his visitor wished him to write:

> the petitioner hopes that days of gentleness and clemency will follow those days of severity and that the Convention will know how to distinguish those Frenchmen who left their country only because they wished to escape persecution and for whom the danger was only too obvious, from those who wished to take up arms against it . . .

Rostaing prevailed upon the Consul to give him a job. His father's war record may not have impressed his detractors in Bourg, but in New York it was invaluable.[19]

Brillat took lodgings at 67 Pearl Street. Money was now presumably short, and he earned a living as best he could. He could teach Americans French,[20] but he could also put another talent to use: he played principal fiddle in the John Street Theater. This ugly wooden clapboard building, painted red, was the only theatre in the city, and its orchestra the only one of its type in New York; from all accounts, the standard of playing was not high.[21]

Despite their enthusiasm for things French, most Americans had little knowledge of either the nation or its people. In 1780 Nathaniel Tracey received a delegation of officers from the French navy at a dinner to celebrate their participation in the War of Independence. The astonished French sailors were each served a bowl of soup with a fat green frog wallowing in the middle.[22] Most of the émigrés stuck together, finding American life little to their taste. Talleyrand, in

particular, came to dislike a country which boasted 'thirty-two religions and only one dish', and where he could find 'no one who was
ready to sell him his dog'.[23] Brillat, on the other hand, not part of the
émigré circle, enjoyed both the food and the life of the new nation.
After his death his friend Henri Roux recalled that 'it was on that
hospitable, foreign soil that . . . he had spent some of the best days of
his life'.[24] Brillat himself says as much in *La Physiologie du goût*:

> I spoke like them, I dressed like them, I was careful not to give the
> impression of being cleverer than they were, I found everything they
> did good; thereby repaying their hospitality by a consideration which I
> believe necessary and which I counsel to all those people who find
> themselves in a similar position.[25]

Sadly, we have little evidence of Brillat's activities in the United
States besides what we learn from *La Physiologie du goût*. In New
York he seems to have spent much of his time in and around the city's
main street, Broadway, where he met the vast 'Edward', an idle American who spent his days looking on to the pavement from a chair 'the
legs of which would have held up a church'. Edward was there all day,
every day, with a correspondingly Brobdingnagian jug of beer at his
hand – a hand, Brillat tells us, with

> fingers like those of the Roman emperor who wore women's necklaces
> as rings; his legs and arms were cylindrical and each as broad as a
> middle-sized man. He had the feet of an elephant, covered by the fat
> hanging from his legs. The weight of fat on his face had pulled away his
> lower eyelids so that they yawned at you; but what made him particu-
> larly grotesque were his three spherical chins, which hung down for a
> foot on to his chest so that his face resembled a capital on top of a
> column in the form of a torso.

Not surprisingly, Edward had become a tourist attraction, but
gawpers were discouraged with deep, sepulchral oaths. Brillat, however, was occasionally allowed to stop for a chat, in the course of
which he learned something of Edward's apparently remarkable inner
contentment.[26]

For the time being Brillat had the company of his friend and compatriot Rostaing. He also met a banker, Étienne Delessert, who
having quit Paris as a result of his royalist leanings, had opened a
branch of his family's bank in New York.[27] Étienne, the eldest son
of an enlightened Protestant financier from Lyon, had been sent to
Edinburgh to study under Adam Smith and Dugald Stewart, and then

on to Birmingham to visit the inventor James Watt. When Delessert fell victim to the yellow fever which ravaged New England, his younger brother Benjamin took over the family firm, and in later years he, too, became a friend of Brillat's.[28] Doubtless friendship with Delessert was helpful in dealing with some of the pecuniary inconveniences of Brillat's exile, but his assets remained frozen in France for the time being, and teaching and fiddling must have been a strong necessity.

Two other New York friends of Brillat's, encountered in the pages of *La Physiologie du goût*, were the vicomte de La Massue, and Jean-Rudolphe Fehr who, despite his Alsatian-sounding name, was a broker from the port of Marseille. Brillat was in the habit of meeting these two in Little Michael's tavern on Broadway. After checking to see that Edward was in his accustomed place, the trio would lunch off turtle soup or dine on welsh rabbit moistened with cider and ale, the cider reputed to be the best in the United States.[29] Between the pear and the toasted cheese, the *émigrés* 'talked softly of their sadness, their happiness and their hopes'.[30]

It was in the same tavern that Brillat and his friends met a planter from Jamaica by the name of Wilkinson, who was generally attended by another character, described by Brillat as 'one of the most extraordinary men . . . he had ever met'. Brillat never learned his name, and rarely heard him speak. He did, however, hear him laugh.

> He had a square face with twinkling eyes which seemed to examine everything attentively, but he never spoke and his features were as immobile as those of a blind man. Only, when he heard a joke or some witty remark his face fell and, while his eyes closed, his mouth opened as wide as the bell of a trumpet. He then let out a long sound which combined a laugh with a sort of whinnying noise, a bit like a horse. When this performance had come to an end he would pull himself together and relapse into his usual taciturnity![31]

The planter challenged the Frenchmen to a drinking bout. Although Brillat accepted the challenge, he was not naturally disposed to such orgies. He was confident of his own success as he was younger, fitter and, above all, bigger than the opposition. But he was worried about the rest of his team, and called Fehr and de La Massue to his lodgings in Pearl Street, to give them a lecture on tactics. He recommended drinking in small sips, pouring away drink on the sly where possible; and, most important, eating slowly to retain appetite for as long as possible, as eating tempered the effect of drink. Before they set out they ate a dish of bitter almonds, as Brillat had heard that these too allayed the effects of wine.[32]

The three Frenchmen repaired to Little Michael's, where instead of the frugal welsh rabbit to which Brillat usually treated his friends (neither played a musical instrument, one presumes), Wilkinson and his creature had laid on a huge joint of roast beef, a braised turkey-cock, boiled root vegetables called 'plenty', a raw cabbage salad, and a jam tart.

> We drank in the French fashion, which is to say that the wine was served from the beginning of the meal. It was excellent claret which at that time was cheaper [in America] than it was in France; there had been a succession of shipments recently, and the last ones had sold very badly.

Brillat's countrymen played their parts well: de La Massue, normally of gargantuan appetite, ate like a fussy girl, while Fehr contrived to pour his drinks into a beer jug at the end of the table. Brillat himself did not indulge in this chicanery, but stood his ground against the planters.

After the claret came the port; after the port, madeira. The dessert consisted of butter, cheese, coco and hickory nuts. With the port were the toasts: to the power of kings, the liberty of peoples; to the beauty of women, and to Wilkinson's daughter Mariah, the most beautiful woman in all the island of Jamaica, they were told.

Fortified wines gave way to spirits and liqueurs: rum, brandy, gin and raspberry liqueur. Brillat thought this would lead to trouble and asked for a bowl of punch instead. Little Michael himself brought in the bowl, big enough for four; 'in France we don't have bowls of those dimensions', writes Brillat.[33]

Having lined his stomach with five or six slices of toast and butter Brillat felt confident of his capacity for the punch, especially when he saw that his own team, quietly shelling hickory nuts, were in far better shape than the planters. Wilkinson's face had turned crimson; he was flagging, and clearly having trouble seeing straight. As for his friend, his 'head was smoking like a boiling cauldron while his vast mouth had turned the shape of the backside of a hen.' Wilkinson rose to his feet to sing *Rule Britannia* but collapsed, slid under the table and passed out. His friend gave one of his loudest guffaws and rose to pick him up, but bending over he too fell to the ground where he settled next to Wilkinson.

The Frenchmen were more than satisfied with their victory. Little Michael was called and while they drank a valedictory glass of punch in honour of their comatose companions the innkeeper gave orders that the planters be carried home. Wilkinson was still vainly trying to form the words of *Rule Britannia*, while his strange companion maintained a paralytic silence. According to Brillat, every newspaper in the Union printed the story.[34]

IV

In France, life was gradually returning to normal. In March 1795 a shift in the Convention away from the extreme left was marked by the arrest of three of the most bloodthirsty Terrorists, Jean-Marie Collot d'Herbois, Jacques-Nicolas Billaud-Varenne and Bertrand Barère. The following month they were banished to Guyana. The relaxation of Jacobin rule led to the White Terror, the murder of former Jacobins, generally in their prison cells. On 20 May an insurrection in Paris demanding a return to the Constitution of 1793 was put down by the regular army. At the end of the month the Convention alloted fifty days for former public servants to return to the country and take up their jobs. It was at this stage that Aurore Brillat-Savarin decided to act.[35]

Noting that Brillat was too far away to appear in Belley, she demanded that 'the name of her son be crossed off the list of *émigrés* and that he be re-established in his profession and restored to his property'.[36] On 20 August her petition to the Department explained her son's flight: Brillat was 'persecuted by the terrorist hordes [and] was obliged to take to his heels to escape the daggers of those vile assassins.' Her son was 'a passionate friend of liberty [i.e., a supporter of the Revolution] and had always demonstrated his love [of it].' Because of the actions of the Jacobins, 'he sought asylum in the United States while he waited for some happy change which would allow him to return to his country.'[37]

While the Department was evidently sympathetic, Brillat had still to clear his name of the charges against it. Above all, he had to explain his conduct in the late spring of 1793 and his leadership of the federalists in Belley. The action of the Girondins in fomenting civil war was still not forgiven. Gouly's decree was still in force. However, the sale of Brillat's property was suspended until such time as he should have explained his conduct before the legislative committee of the Convention.[38]

Fortunately for Brillat, his family had proved cunning in hanging on to their missing brother's estate. They had managed to retain seven-eighths of the price fetched by Brillat's coach, which had been sold by the Commune, claiming that it was their property too. They also managed to perform the same trick with Brillat's house in Belley, though as it was definitely his property, having been made over to him alone by his mother, the ploy must have involved some chicanery. They were, however, unable to save Brillat's cherished vineyard at Machuraz in Cheignieu-la-Balme, facing his property at Pugieu.[39]

On 2 June 1795, probably alerted to their change of heart by his mother, Brillat wrote to the town council of Belley requesting a good word.

The Mayor and the town council obliged with the 'most flattering testimonials', as well as extracts from the registers of the town hall attesting to Brillat's revolutionary vigilance when the Savoyard army was thought to be at the gates. The Mayor wrote that Brillat's letter had 'dispelled the terrible uncertainty which we were in as regards the fate of one of our dearest [fellow] citizens . . . who had fled a persecution of which we were all nearly victims.' After the 'doleful trials' of those months, 'we will count among the finest days produced by the revolution of 9 Thermidor that on which you receive the fraternal embraces of your fellow citizens, who have remained sincerely attached to you.'[40]

V

On 26 May 1795 Jean-Antoine de Rostaing decided he had had as much of America as he could bear. On that day, as an officer in the French army he obtained permission to sail on the French frigate *La Sémillante* with a passport for Lorient in Brittany.[41] With Rostaing's departure Brillat lost his best friend in the United States.

Just at the time Aurore Brillat-Savarin had succeeded in obtaining an order suspending Brillat from the list of *émigrés*, an epidemic of yellow fever broke out in New York, New Haven and Norfolk, and continued to rage until November that year.

Brillat and de La Massue had left New York, and by October were in Hartford, Connecticut. Brillat sent Rostaing news of the epidemic.

This summer the most frightful calamity has struck the American continent, cutting a terrible swathe through the sons of Columbus; these last two months yellow fever has ravaged in New Heaven [*sic* – Connecticut], Norfolk [Virginia] and most particularly in New York. . . .

All provisions have been locked up in the warehouses for these last two months, business has been suspended and the ships are laid up with their merchandise still on board. The shops are closed. All one sees are people wandering with pale faces, scrawny figures shunning one another in the streets so as to avoid passing on the infection . . .

On average more than thirty people have died every day from a total of 8,000 obliged to remain in the city.[42]

Yellow fever carried off several of Brillat's friends, including Delessert. The John Street Theater Orchestra took up residence in Boston. *En route*, a Mr Bulow invited Brillat to shoot on his land, which was near Meriden, or Berlin, in the Blue Mountains (now called the Hanging Hills). Brillat travelled up with an Irishman called King.[43]

The Bulow farmstead was thirty miles from Hartford, 'in very high mountain country and thick forests as yet untouched by the European axe. There I observed the different ages of trees from the moment they pierce the soil until their decline, decrepitude and death, an interesting spectacle and one unknown in our corrupt old world.'[44] As they dismounted from their hired horses, Bulow and his family were there to meet them. Brillat took a particular interest in the daughters, four 'buxom lasses'* aged from 16 to 20, 'exuding freshness and health . . . they had such simplicity, grace and such a relaxed air that the most straightforward action was sufficient to make them endlessly charming.'[45]

Bulow served a stout meal to his visitors: corned beef, stewed goose, 'a magnificent leg of mutton' and root vegetables of all types. To drink with this feast Bulow had put out two enormous pots of excellent cider.[46]

Bulow did not join Brillat and King on their shoot, but indicated areas where game might be found: squirrels, grey partridges and wild turkeys. Earlier that day he had seen wild turkeys fly over the house, and thought there might be a chance of bagging one. The first victims

---

*In English in Brillat's original description.

were a number of 'plump and tender' partridges, after which six or seven grey squirrels were shot. It was only after this that the party chanced on a group of seven wild turkeys. King fired first, but failed to kill his bird. The turkey ran off, its two wings broken, with King in hot pursuit; as Brillat told Rostaing, 'my mouth began to water'.[47]

At that moment, amid the cackling hubbub of the alarmed turkeys, 'the laziest bird' flew into the Brillat's range. Brillat shot into the clearing and the bird fell to the earth, dead. 'He was handsome, fat, heavy, and of a most attractive appearance.'[48] Filled with pride in his *coup*, Brillat heard King cry out to him for help. 'I ran over to discover that he needed my help to find a turkey-cock, which he purported to have killed, but which had none the less disappeared.'[49]

Walking back they nearly lost their way in the woods, but were guided home by Bulow and his silver-tongued daughters who had come out to look for them. The four girls were dressed to kill: 'dresses freshly put on, new belts, pretty hats and polished shoes, which pointed to the fact that they had gone to some trouble on our behalf.' Brillat took the arm of one of the girls, 'with a proprietary air more appropriate to one's wife.'[50]

The next day, as King and Brillat prepared to leave, Bulow expounded an early rendition of the American dream. His stockings knitted by his daughters, his shoes and coat made from the hides of his cows, the food from his garden and farmyard, were as much objects of his pride as the fact that there was no lock to his door. Taxes were low and the prices paid for his produce high. Since the end of the war there had been no troops in the land. Everyone in Connecticut slept soundly in peace, wealth and security.[51]

On the ride back to Hartford, Brillat's mind was absorbed by the question of how he would cook his turkey in a manner which would do it justice.[52] He determined to have it stuffed with onions, garlic, mushrooms and anchovies.[53] The partridges would be served in little pastry packets, while the squirrels were to be stewed in madeira.

VI

Although Brillat appears to have found the Bulow girls attractive, the ageing bachelor did not waver from his path. He was now 40 years old, and had so far shown not the slightest inclination to marry. Possibly his domineering mother stood behind him, figuratively if not always literally, measuring his candidates with a cruel, dismissive scrutiny; possibly he had become used to frequenting prostitutes. No adequate explanation has ever been deduced. Other writers on the subject have, however, concluded that his contacts with the opposite sex were 'undoubtedly numerous'.[54]

Brillat and de La Massue arrived on foot in Boston at the end of October 1795. Brillat liked Boston, and *its* womenfolk, too:

> Both Boston and its seaport are charming little cities* . . . whatever you have heard of the sociability, the affability or the politeness of the Bostonians, is not exaggerated. I have received unimaginable kindnesses from them, and for these last three months have lived [in] a perpetual whirlpool of parties and banquets, some of which would not have been outshone by the most opulent households of Paris. The women are extremely pretty and one day a while ago I found myself in a theatre box that was occupied by so many heavenly faces and adorable bodies that I was driven mad with desire just by looking at them . . . I am living in a furnished room on half-board only: it provides me with lunch, but I have to make my own arrangements for dinner and breakfast.[55]

One of the establishments where Brillat was able to procure the dinner not provided by his landlord was Julien's Restorator, 'one of the most famous restaurants in America'.[56] Between 1794 and 1824 Julien's was to be found on the corner of Milk Street and Congress Street. The old building with gables and overhangs was actually the first of its kind in America, a derivative of the new restaurants Brillat had encountered in Paris. It now drew gourmands from all over the United States.[57]

Julien, known in Boston as the Prince of Soups, was an *émigré* from Bordeaux, where he had been *cordon bleu* to Champion de Cicé, the radical archbishop. Brillat knew Julien and even went so far as to give him his recipe for *fondue* which, Brillat recalled later, was an instant success with the Bostonians. 'This dish, which was entirely new to the Americans, was so popular that [Julien] felt obliged to thank me by sending me the hindquarters of one of those pretty little deer which one shoots during the winter in Canada.'[58]

Although Brillat's name remained on the master-list of *émigrés* in Paris, it was crossed off the departmental list in Bourg on 21 October 1795.[59] On the same day, French electors returned a largely right-wing

---

*Boston was the United States' third biggest city, with 25,000 inhabitants.

assembly to replace the Convention. One of the outgoing assembly's last acts before dissolution was to vote a general amnesty for all – except those on the list of *émigrés*. Brillat might hope for better things from the Directory which came to power on 31 October.

The news of the elections in France must have reached Brillat before he visited the French Consul in Boston, Jean-Louis Dorival, on 20 November.

There he signed a fresh petition, and included with it a certified copy of his tribute from the town councillors of Belley.[60]

The epidemic of yellow fever which had driven the John Street Theater Orchestra from New York to Boston came to an end in the winter of 1795–6. Brillat returned to New York with the rest of the troupe some time before March. On 2 March he played in Jean-Jacques Rousseau's opera *Pygmalion* when it was staged at the theatre. At about this time he acquired a New York mistress, but sadly the prudishness of later generations of Brillats has robbed us of details about her. On 16 March he wrote a final letter to Rostaing. Exceptionally, the letter is written in English, and in view of Brillat's claims to have been a prodigious linguist it is worth reprinting 'warts and all'.

The Beaver [*sic*] of this, my dear Joe, is M. Philip des Bassins from isle de France, with whose acquaintance I wish favour you in token of our sworn friendschip.

If we ever meet again, you will thank me for that [,] he being a most amiable and sympathising young man, though somewhat too fond of pettycoats, what I forgive him.

If the devil who is incessantly playing some of his tricks upon me didn't swallow up the many letters I have directed to you, you must be acquainted with the whole of my history. – If not know that [I] have been successively in Hartford, Boston, Providence, New London etc, – that I live still on my musical skill, – that I am hearthy high spirited and lusty, – that Levieillard and Bruno are dead, – Malibrand going to France, – that I killed a wild turkey in blue mountains – and finally that I am stubbornly determined to not go in Europe, till I have received some precise answece to the letter I sent thiter.[61]

Brillat had not received any such answer, and he was beginning to lose patience with the Directory for not replying to his letters. From New York he sent off yet another petition, this time couched in rather stronger and less supplicatory language.

Citizen deputies, it is not enough to have rescued liberty from the hands of criminal factions, you still need to save those whom they sought to immolate through their criminal acts. You need to cure the ills done to France by instituting a government of reconciliation.

It was during those sanguinary and convulsive days that I was obliged to quit my country. They came when, after five years of working for the revolution and ten years of satisfying work for the good of the people, my whole life which had been dedicated to good works was to be set at naught owing to the fact that there was not a single citizen who was not in fear of his life and because truth dared not let its voice be heard under the reign of terror. In the end I was obliged to flee to escape the clutches of a small band of scoundrels who would have willingly combined the functions of prosecutors, judges and executioners.

It was this alone which made me bend before the storm, and while the most rigorous application of justice has ever been the object of my desires, I cannot tolerate the thought that I should be banded with traitors,* be sentenced without trial, and perish the victim of an arbitrary power . . .

Almost as soon as I arrived in a neutral country I hurried to see the minister of the Republic and to put on record my true sentiments and sincere remonstrances, for I never doubted that the stormy days would give way to brighter, clearer days when all true friends of liberty would be reunited in virtue, and when their insuperable cohesion would present astonished despots with the novel spectacle of a nation as formidable abroad as calm within.

These days have now arrived: the unscrupulous power-seekers have disappeared and everywhere victory has crowned a righteous cause: it is the duty of a triumphant France, nay the obligation rather, to summon to her bosom all those who have loved liberty; who have sustained it and fought for it and who, apart from preferring a necessary flight to a useless death, have committed no other crime than to have been liberty's partisan.

I therefore request, citizen deputies, that having examined the facts set down in my petition of 24 Vendemaire [15 October 1794] made at the Consulate in New York you declare my absence to be involuntary, and that you grant me permission to return to France without further ado so that I may be judged according to the law, should there remain any denunciation against me. [62]

Brillat-Savarin's position was doubtless aggravated by a new worry which prevented him from enjoying life in New York to the full (and the company of female New Yorkers in particular): he was broke. On

---

*Emigrés of the noble and clerical sorts: opponents of the Revolution.

17 June the Consul wrote to the Ministry of Foreign Affairs to say that Brillat had not been able to pay his return fare to France, and that he had had to lend him the money.[63] That same day, Brillat embarked from Philadelphia on board the *Seaflower*.[64]

VII

Despite the prudence expressed in his letter to Rostaing, Brillat's difficulties drove him to leave the United States before he had received assurances that he would not face trial. His impassioned letter may have had some effect, as Benoît Gouly consented to withdraw his charges against the former Mayor of Belley sometime in June or July.[65] Some detect the hand of Brillat's cousin Jacques Rose Récamier at work here. The banker was a friend of Barras, and his wife Juliette was reputed to be capable of obtaining any favours he might desire.[66]

In *La Physiologie du goût* Brillat describes the beginning of his journey by packet-boat down the coast from New York to Philadelphia, and the brawl which took place between the French and the Americans on board. Possibly the French were all in the same situation as Brillat, uncertain as to their future; he boarded the packet, his mind on the mistress he was leaving behind. Only after a while did he notice that the boat was late in setting off, as two Americans had failed to come on board. The boat might now miss the tide, thereby doubling the time necessary to get to Philadelphia. The French were becoming very cross.

The distracted Brillat hardly noticed: 'I had a heavy heart and I was thinking of what fate had in store for me in France, so much so that I did not know what was going on. Soon, however, I heard a loud noise and looking round I saw that it had been caused by Gauthier's having administered a slap to the cheek of an American which might have knocked out a rhinoceros.'[67]

Gauthier's aggression sparked a fight. There were eight Frenchmen to eleven Americans, and the latter were set to throw all the former into the sea, Brillat included.

> My appearance revealed that of all those on board I was likely to put up the most vigorous resistance to *transbordation* [sic], for I am well built and I was aged thirty-nine at the time [actually he was 41]. This, no doubt, was why they pitted against me their most dangerous champion, who advanced towards me with hostile mien.

He was as tall as a church tower and scarcely less solid, but when I fixed him with a glare which would have shrivelled an even bigger man, I rapidly discovered that he had a puffy face, dead eyes, a tiny head and the legs of a woman.

This is word for word what I said: 'Do you believe to bully me?* You damned rogue. By God! It will not be so . . . and I'll overboard you like a dead cat . . . If I find you too heavy, I'll cling to you with hands, legs, teeth, nails, everything, and if I cannot do better, we will sink together to the bottom; my life is nothing to send such a dog to hell. Now, just now . . .'

At these words, with which my whole person was in harmony (for I felt as strong as Hercules), I saw my man grow shorter by an inch, his arms dropped to his sides, his cheeks deflated and, in a word, he showed obvious signs of fear. This was no doubt noticed by the man who had sent him over, for he came across as if to interpose. He did well, because I was ready to act, and the inhabitant of the New World was about to experience the fact that those who bathe in the Furens have nerves of steel.

On the other side of the boat, however, some words of peace could be heard and the arrival of the latecomer created a further diversion. The sail had to be hoisted so while I was still in the attitude of a wrestler, the tumult came to a sudden halt.

Things came to an even more satisfactory conclusion, for when calm had returned and I had gone to seek out Gauthier to upbraid him for his quick temper, I found the man who had been slapped seated at this same table in the company of a ham and a pitcher of beer a cubit in height.[68]

Philadelphia was the United States' second city, with a population of 30,000 inhabiting its neat, red-brick squares.[69] There was a flourishing French community, centred on the bookshop and press of the creole Médéric Louis Élie Moreau de Saint-Méry, on the corner of Walnut Street and Front Street.[70] Here gathered Talleyrand, Beaumetz, the vicomte de Noailles, Volney, Omer Talon and the duc de Liancourt – all of whom had, like Brillat, been members of the Constituent Assembly – as well as the marquis de Blacons and Louis de La Colombe.[71] Grumbling about life in the United States was the chief conversation among this exalted group. It was not the sort of talk which appealed to Brillat.

Not one of the published memoirs of the *habitués* of Moreau's shop

---

*This speech is reproduced in Brillat's curious English in the text of *La Physiologie du goût*.

alludes to a meeting with Brillat-Savarin,[72] but this is not really surprising: he was no royalist, he seems to have been short-tempered all the time, and no doubt his thoughts were concentrated on his uncertain future. Probably he lived quietly while he was in Philadelphia, and did not stay long.

CHAPTER SEVEN

Position Vacant

I

I T WAS SOMETIME between the middle and the end of August 1796
that Brillat-Savarin again glimpsed the shores of his native land: he
had been absent for the best part of three years. The *Seaflower* probably docked at Le Havre, giving Brillat a two-day coach-journey to
endure before he reached the city he had left, covered in glory, in
September 1791.[1]

He found lodgings in the Hôtel de Portugal in the rue du Mail. The
choice of street may not have been wholly accidental: at that time,
No. 12 was the home of his cousin, the financier Jacques-Rose
Récamier, whose good relations with the Director Barras Brillat may
have found useful. He already had a slight acquaintance with
Récamier's wife Juliette, one of the most celebrated beauties of the
age.[2]

Politically France was now tending to the moderates. In place of the
Thermidorian Convention, the country was ruled by five Directors
chosen by the two houses of the chamber, the Five Hundred (named
after the number of deputies elected to it) and the *Conseil des Anciens*,
the latter composed of 250 deputies aged 40 years and over. The
winding up of the Convention had removed much of the power of the
Jacobins, but France was far from stable, and the Directory had to
reckon with constant attempts to unseat it, both from the left and the
right.

First and foremost, Brillat had to ensure that his name was removed
from the list of *émigrés*. His first important visit was to his former

fellow-Constituent, the moderate Jacobin Gauthier des Orcières. Brillat had initially enlisted Gauthier's support in November 1795, when the deputy from Bourg was a member of the purged Committee of Public Safety. Despite their past differences, Gauthier seems to have been quite ready to help.[3]

The next day Brillat expressed some of his preoccupations in a letter to Rostaing:

> My chief business is to get myself crossed off the list of *émigrés* and although I have no reason to fear any major objections, it will take a good deal of tiresome pledges and muttered obscenities in view of the great number of officers there are to visit; many secretaries to greet, and undertakings to make: I shall soon long for the time when I had nothing more to do than to rosin my bow and cuddle my mistress . . .[4]

On 12 September Brillat sent off a new petition to the Directors, this time also asking for permission to take up the seat on the bench of the *Tribunal de cassation* which had been his by right since the death of the lawyer Martinon in December 1791. Brillat explained how he had 'worked by his hands while he awaited permission to return to France', how he had travelled back on the *Seaflower* through the good offices of the Consul in New York, and so on. Then he made known his decision to return to Belley:

> The law forbids me to remain in this city . . . having sent in my petition, I could remain here [while I waited for an answer] but my former colleagues have made me aware of the difficulties. Since the Directory requires submission above all else, I am leaving immediately . . .[5]

But he did not leave at once. On 9 September there had been an insurrection at the military camp of Grenelle when a Jacobin element called for the restoration of the Constitution of the year I. Two were shot by soldiers loyal to the Directors. In a letter to Rostaing on 13 September, Brillat over-enthusiastically predicted that the rest (132) would also be shot; in fact, only 45 were executed. 'What really worries me is that they only arrest and punish the Jacobin rabble, while the leaders have gone into hiding and will be difficult to winkle out . . .'[6]

Two days later, in another letter to Rostaing, he revelled in the fate of those who had forced him from the country three years before: 'The house-to-house searches continue; more and more Jacobins have been arrested. It is said that Drouet* is hiding somewhere around here: I hope they nab him.'[7]

Brillat's letter then turned to his *liaisons amoureuses* in America. 'When I'm back in the Bugey I shall send you the final instalments of my American existence. It is the most interesting bit as, being able to speak the language and flirt with women, I was able to reap the richest rewards.'[8]

The promised letter, describing his adventures, was sent to Rostaing in Lyon while Brillat was stopping over in Bourg-en-Bresse, as we know from a subsequent letter to Rostaing. But it has disappeared, the fate of any papers which related to his sex life: subsequent generations clearly decided they would only sully his reputation in other spheres.

II

It seems likely that Brillat arrived back in Belley sometime in the last week of September. It must have been a great moment, for despite his persecution by the local *sans-culottes*, he had retained a passionate love of his home town. He must have seen some of his former tormentors walking freely through the streets of the small city, but he showed no desire for revenge, and in Belley at least he refrained from revelling in the fate of the fallen Jacobins. All bitterness was subsumed in the 'transports of joy' he experienced seeing the city, the countryside, his family and friends once again. His mother, who had done so much to rescue his property, was there, as were his unmarried sisters. (Thelmette had married Marc Carrel in April 1794.) At least one of his brothers – François-Xavier – was probably also on hand.[9]

Brillat probably also had an opportunity of seeing his godson, Anthelme Richerand, who had been only 14 when Brillat fled. Richerand was about to begin his studies in surgery, of which he later became one of the most famous practitioners in France. In 1808 he had the singular honour of treating the novelist Stendhal for syphilis.[10]

However, Brillat sadly missed Rostaing, who was at that moment travelling from Lyon to Paris. After an unsuccessful love affair, Rostaing was about to join Hoche's army as Chief Commissioner for War; Hoche was putting together forces for an invasion of Ireland.

---

*Jean-Baptiste Drouet, one of the Revolution's great survivors. For his role at Varennes see Chapter 3. His fame ensured him a permanent position on the left of the house.

They sailed on 15 December; but like the Invincible Armada, their ships were scattered by a severe storm. The British squadrons were not even required to engage.

Brillat was successful in quashing the sale of his property. While his petition was being handled in Paris, the council thought it fair not to sell off any more of his effects.[11] On 10 November he again wrote to Gauthier. Papers were missing from his dossier:

> The chaos which reigns in the archives of our former district prevents me from laying my hands on the warrants for my arrest which were made out by Gouly. Instead I am sending you his report.[12]

In the wake of Thermidor there had doubtless been a rush to destroy incriminating evidence. Brillat thought that the original orders for his arrest had taken the form of hand-bills. Could Gauthier possibly ask Gouly? Gouly was still in the chamber as one of the 500 deputies of the Directory.[13]

It is safe to assume that, in his more relaxed moments back in Belley, Brillat was able to take a gun and some dogs out into the valleys and hills of the Valromey in pursuit of autumnal game. Here were no wild turkeys, nor any enchanting American women, but Brillat was content to take aim at a partridge or a pheasant or, when the occasion arose, a boar or a chamois. The Directory knew where he was; if need be they could contact him in Belley.

Brillat must have returned to Paris at some point that winter. Changes were taking place in the *Tribunal de cassation*, and Brillat had to be on hand should his name be called. On 12 June 1796, prior to his return to France, the Five Hundred (the lower house of the Directory) had heard a report on the state of this court.

Since the original elections of 1791, when Brillat became substitute (or 'understudy judge') for the Ain, several judges on the bench had died. The Constitution of the year I had changed the selection procedure: new judges were to be named by the Convention. A dozen or so had been chosen in this way, including Brillat's compatriot, Georges Sibuet.[14] The Constitution of the year III (22 August 1795) had returned to the idea of judges elected at the beginning of each government. So far only a few elections had taken place. The court required a bench of 50; only 40 of the 1791 judges remained, plus those named by the Convention.

The report of 12 June advocated that the *conventionnel* judges be replaced by substitute judges wherever possible, either those (like

Brillat) elected in 1791 or, in the case of some departments, those chosen in the year IV. There was a problem, however, in that those elected in 1791 had only eight months of their term still to run; in this case the report advocated re-eligibility.[15]

On 5 January some of the reforms proposed for the *Tribunal de cassation* were voted in. Brillat judged the moment when he might take up his place on the bench to be close at hand.[16] On 4 February the *Conseil des Anciens* finally passed the decree which would restore Brillat to the position of substitute on the bench; Sibuet was held to have been falsely nominated in his place. Sibuet thoughtfully tendered his resignation, giving as his reason that as he was not yet 30, his place on the bench was unconstitutional.[17]

The same day, the *Conseil des Anciens* restored Brillat to all his sequestered property, including those effects sold off as the property of the nation. Even so, Brillat was never able to wrest his vineyard at Machuraz from the hands of the canny peasant who had bought it.[18]

The Terror was a period the survivors hastened to put behind them. As the civil servant handling Brillat's case expressed it, his story touched on 'events the memory of which every good Frenchman seeks to forget.'[19] Brillat could congratulate himself. His earlier federalism was glossed over; who, after all, could claim that their hands had been constantly clean in the years between 1791 and 1795? It is particularly significant that he was able to enlist the support of Gauthier, who was so often his enemy during the years of the Constituent Assembly, and who later served the Convention as a *représentant en mission*. As a later member of Brillat's profession put it, writing soon after the end of the Second World War, Brillat 'always knew how to adapt himself to events with skill and diplomacy, indeed, with an admirable ingenuity which recalls the memorable acrobatics of certain of our fellow citizens during a period closer to our own.'[20]

III

Now that Brillat had regained his place, he could relax and enjoy the charms of the Paris of the Directory, the days 'which followed the time of Robespierre'.[21] Politically prudish, and still covering up the horrors of the recent past with an omnipresent censorship, Paris had nevertheless become a carnal paradise. Nothing and nowhere could have suited the tastes of our hero better. If the famous Beauvilliers remained closed for crimes of *lèse-liberté*, there were many other restaurants with their printed cards, where a fortune could be squandered in one night of pleasure, and where more prudent men 'tapped their waistcoat pockets to find out if [they] really had enough to pay for the meal'.[22] Famine still tortured the common people, and restaurant portions decreased daily in size so that the politician and publicist Sébastian Mercier was driven to ask himself whether cows had not, perhaps, shrunk to the size of turkey-cocks.

> You ask for a chunk of eel *à la tartare* and it is brought to you; but this chunk is only an inch and a half long. Be careful to note from the menu how many inches you are entitled to, or you will get no more than a slice. It is the same for every other dish; each is the most scanty of delicacies. They look like samples of some future meal. Hey! Citizen-restaurateurs, I've not come here to taste the food, I've come for a meal![23]

Chez Méot, the grandest restaurant in Paris, the absence of flesh on the plate was compensated for by the availability of female flesh in the salons. Here all the *nouveaux riches* assembled in the huge rooms: arms dealers, speculators, administrators of lotteries, crooks, and so on.

> On certain days you can find here all the rich eccentricity which characterized the *cena trimalchionis*.* At a given signal, the ceiling opens and from the heavens Venuses descend in chariots drawn by doves. Sometimes it's Aurora, sometimes Diana who is looking for her dear Endymion. They are all dressed as goddesses. The spectators make their choice and the divinities, who hail not *de caelis* but *ex-machina*, then couple with the mortals.[24]

Mercier found the mixture of gluttony and Republican virtue comic, and the terminology of the kitchen particularly so. The Revolution was rarely innovatory in the kitchen, its claim to fame being the development of the restaurant; the dishes themselves were all survivors from the gentle days of Louis XV.

> You hear a waiter call out to some sort of *maître d'hôtel*, bring a soup *à la ci-devant reine* [in the former queen's style] with two kidneys on a skewer; bring a soup *à la ci-devant Condé* [in the style of the former Prince of Condé] with a jugged hare. Here we eat Condé's soup, the

---

*From Petronius, *The Satyricon*. The *nouveau riche* Trimalchio invites his friends to a vulgar, lavish feast or *cena*.

man who fled so quickly and so far: his name rings out down the tables, and it means no more than a soup; a soup he'll never eat again.[25]

In the grand boulevards to the north of Brillat's lodgings, he could sample the famous ices of Garchy and Velloni; strolling down the rue de Richelieu he would reach that 'disgusting cesspit', the Palais-Égalité, the former Palais-Royal, the palace of the duc d'Orléans. Here Brillat could obtain sustenance for both his passions.

> you can see, one after the other, shops full of girls holding cold lunches and dinners. People go in and out without speaking, they are served on presentation of an *assignat*. Here you find the brokers, jobbers and speculators, smoking, chewing and drinking in these silent dens, no one speaks, and the most prodigious orgies are carried on in silence.
>
> Nearby run streams of urine; the avenues are gloomy and frigid, Lord knows what icy form libertinage takes here, it seems to have a style all of its own.[26]

For the super-rich like Récamier, there were shops in the Palais-Égalité filled with partridge pâtés, fresh peas, wild boar brawn, and other delicacies, which Brillat surely tasted at the Récamier table, even if he could not afford to buy them himself. Elsewhere there was a show where a bogus savage made love to a woman of his own race, and spectators paid 24 *sols* for the privilege of watching. They could see wigmakers beautifying prostitutes among the hanging hams and tripe sausages for nothing.

Frenetic balls had now become a feature of the capital. Mercier tells us there were 23 theatres and 1,800 public dance-halls. Dancing made people forget some of the horrors of the last few years. There were the *bals des victimes*, which were only open to those who had lost a close relation to the guillotine; dances at the Carmelite monastery where one of the worst of the September Massacres had taken place; dances at the Jesuit Noviciate, in the Seminary of Saint-Sulpice, the *alma mater* of Talleyrand; and dances in any number of half-demolished churches.

Voyeurism may have sent Brillat to some of these balls, where the women went almost naked. At the Hôtel de Richelieu he would have encountered the most lavish display.

> an ark filled with transparent dresses, of hats overburdened with lace, gold, diamonds and chiffon and muffled chins! Only people of suffi-cient wealth may enter. In this enchanted place you meet a hundred goddesses scented with rare essences, crowned with roses, floating in

their Athenian robes, damning and encouraging by turns the stares of the *incroyables* with their wild locks, Turkish slippers, etc. . . .

Here the women are nymphs, sultanas, or savages, Minerva or Juno, Diana or Eucharis. All the women dress in white, and white suits all women. Their arms and breasts are bare.[27]

The Directory was a period of eccentric clubs, like the Dîner des Mystificateurs or hoaxers' dining club; or the Société des Gobe-Mouches or flycatchers' club, over which presided one of the September Massacres' most eloquent escapees, Journiac de Saint Méard.[28] Many of them numbered Grimod de La Reynière among their membership. Brillat-Savarin, in contrast, was not the most clubbable of men. He was naturally cautious; those who met him rarely remembered anything positive from his conversation.

But Brillat's prudence didn't help him in the long run: there was another turn in the tide of French political life. On 4 April the monarchists, or pseudo-monarchical 'Clichyens'* made sweeping gains in the elections of the year V. Of the 216 *conventionnels* who stood, only 11 were returned. The Republican Directors, Barras, Reubell and La Revellière-Lépeaux, were faced with a hostile legislature they could neither dissolve nor adjourn and there were rumours of a monarchist plot. The monarchists were, however, too disunited to form an effective opposition, and were thrown into further disharmony by the machinations of the three Republican Directors.

Barras persuaded General Hoche to head for Paris with a force of 12,000 men, but he failed to support the General when he was hauled before the Directory to account for his having brought troops within the proscribed distance from Paris. Hoche retired from the scene and took no further part in events.

The Republicans then turned to Bonaparte, General of the Army of Italy, who sent Augereau to Paris where he arrived on 7 August 1797. It may be that as the son of a servant and a greengrocer Augereau felt a special interest in protecting the Republic. Barras, whose own origins were impeccably aristocratic, has left a portrait of Augereau at this time:

Augereau's language was wholly in keeping with his rebarbative appearance. He exclaimed, without the least embarrassment and at the

---

*Named after the Club de Clichy established after the closure of the Jacobin Club following Thermidor. Its members were largely ex-Constituents who had been imprisoned during the Terror. Given Brillat's experiences, it seems highly unlikely that he would have had anything to do with such a club.

top of his voice, 'I have come to kill the royalists. Our purity and courage will save the Republic from the terrible fate reserved for it by the agents of the throne and the altar.'[29]

He was shortly to cross Brillat's path. On 2 September General Jean-Charles Pichegru again tried to launch a monarchist *coup d'état*. Two days later, on 4 September (18 Fructidor), Barras and the other Directors moved into action, arresting the leaders of the conspiracy. Augereau, having prepared himself with champagne (wrote Barras later), as he often did before a battle,[30] advanced on the Tuileries with 1,000 men, meeting no opposition. By the law of 19 Fructidor the elections of 49 departments were annulled, and 177 deputies were banished. More than 60 right-wing politicians were deported to Guyana. Fructidor also saw a renewal of persecution of the Church and of the *émigrés* who had returned from abroad. Added to this, all the 1791 elections to the *Tribunal de cassation* were declared null and void. All of Brillat's efforts went for naught: after Fructidor he lost his job.[31]

IV

In the next few days 150,000 *émigrés* had to leave Paris. Brillat may have fled to Belley, but he wrote to Rostaing first. Rostaing was on good terms with Hoche, the Commander in Chief of the Army of the Rhine and Moselle, who was his chief, and arranged for Brillat to be offered a job with the army as secretary to the General Staff. But Hoche died of tuberculosis, aged only 29, on 19 September. By one of those unhappy twists of fate in Brillat's life, his replacement was the irascible Augereau.

Augereau did not reach the army headquarters, at Offenburg in the Black Forest, until 20 October. The meeting between the Man of Fructidor and the newly fructidorisé Brillat-Savarin was probably not a happy one. Brillat wrote to Rostaing:

> I would not advise any of you, nor anyone whose interests you represent, to apply for a position in our army; this would be tantamount to committing the same error as I have done . . . I shouldn't complain of my lot; [it is not too bad] if one looks upon it as a stable where one is given food; and General C[hérin] is really very kind and familiar with me, being just as fond of chasing the girls and sleeping with whores as I am. But no money, and no hope of any! My friendship with the boss is

bound to excite the jealousy of all the top brass milling about me here, so much so that come what may, I'll be damned if I spend another fortnight in this job. None the less it is not without pleasure that I have observed the conduct of a great army . . . All that I know of German is perfectly useless in this area, at least for the basic needs of life. I have already directed my batteries against two German women; the forward positions have been taken and tonight one of them may expect a full frontal assault from your friend . . .[32]

Once Augereau had settled in, life became even more intolerable. Augereau had retained the manners of a corporal, drinking himself under the table every night of the week, raising bumpers of schnapps with cries of 'toujours l'amour'. The Germans around the table were highly confused by these shouts from the drunken French general, believing that he was calling for more schnapps. Thereafter the servants were convinced that 'le schour l'amour' was the French name for their national spirit.[33]

The problem was not so much that Augereau was a drunk, but that he was a violent drunk. He was also invariably bad-tempered while he digested his food. For an hour or so after he had finished his lunch, Brillat tells us, he would have killed anyone, 'friend or foe'.

> I once heard him say that there were in the army two people whom he intended to have shot: the head of ordnance and the chief of the General Staff. Both were present at the time; General Chérin [Brillat's whoring friend] replied, calming him, and not without wit; the ordnance chief said not a word, but he was probably thinking about it all the same.[34]

Brillat's place was always laid at the General's table but he rarely availed himself of the privilege of sitting down with him; 'in a word, I was frightened he would send me off to digest in prison.'[35]

Instead, he looked for a means to escape from the army. By 23 November he was beginning to believe he might find himself a job at the Congress of Rastatt, convened to settle the territorial claims of dispossessed German and Italian princes. One of the French plenipotentiaries was Jean-Baptiste Treilhard, whom Brillat had known at the Constituent Assembly. He wrote to Rostaing:

> Much is said here about Rastatt. Everyone is getting ready to go, and me too, if I can find a way. Treilhard is there, one of my former colleagues, and I think he would receive me with open arms . . . If I could get myself some work there, I think I would be even happier.[36]

Brillat was also able to send Rostaing some good news from Paris, where the Directory had clearly been informed that Brillat was not among the more dangerous former *émigrés*:

> I have just received news that on the 18th of last month the Directory appointed me President of the Criminal Court in Bourg. That's just as well, I've had it with the army, but I have an ample stock of military stories to tell, each more extraordinary than the last . . .

Still, life was not always gloomy. In *La Physiologie du goût* Brillat tells of one of his great successes as secretary to the General Staff. The officers were complaining that they had neither game nor fish to eat at their table.

> This complaint was founded on a maxim of public law, that the victor should eat well at the expense of the vanquished. That very day I wrote to the chief forester an extremely polite letter which diagnosed the disease and prescribed the remedy.[37]
>
> The chief forester was a tall, lean, dark-skinned old nobleman who couldn't stand the sight of us, and who doubtless treated us with scant regard in the hope that we wouldn't stay long on his territory. His response was therefore almost totally negative and little better than an attempt to wriggle out of his duty: the foresters had fled from fear of our troops, the fishermen no longer obeyed orders, the water was rough just at this moment, etc., etc. These reasons were so cogent that I didn't even bother to reply; I merely dispatched ten grenadiers to his door with orders that he should lodge and feed them until further notice.
>
> The medicine had an effect: two days later, at the very end of the morning, we received a cart richly laden; without a doubt the foresters had returned, and the fishermen had been disciplined, for we had been brought enough game and fish to keep us for a week and more: venison, woodcock, carp and pike. A real blessing!
>
> Upon receipt of this expiatory offering, I relieved the miserable chief forester of his house-guests.[38]

On 1 October the Armies of the Sambre-et-Meuse and of the Rhine had been united, under Augereau's command, as the Army of Germany. Increasingly, however, Augereau's progress was exciting opposition from Bonaparte, who thought the General was spying on him. Brillat comments on the growing quarrel between Bonaparte and Augereau in a letter to Rostaing on 5 December:

> Bonaparte passed through without so much as calling on Augereau. I realized that they had fallen out, but I had no idea that things had got

to this point. The theory is that the quarrel stems from something Augereau said to the effect that all Bonaparte's glory is due to him, which is certainly not the truth. For the rest, Bonaparte is more than his match . . .[39]

Brillat believed the Corsican had designs on Hanover, whose Elector was none other than George III of England. Hanover had, however, been promised to Prussia, as a prize for her neutrality in the European wars.

A special courier has just arrived with orders to mount an expedition against Hanover. The preparations, however, have been kept secret for as long as possible as the attack could concern the King of Prussia and things have not yet been properly settled with him. That's why Bonaparte has gone to Paris.

I hope to be able to visit Rastatt, the place where we had such a terrible fright four years ago;* however, since meeting Bonaparte, though it was only for a minute, my enthusiasm has somewhat waned.[40]

For once Brillat was lucky; he failed to get the job, but Rastatt ended in disaster. When the Conference broke up the following April, Austrian hussars attacked the French plenipotentiaries on their way back to Alsace, and two of them were killed.

In Paris, Bonaparte successfully intrigued to have the status of Augereau's army reduced. It was now to be known simply as the Army of the Upper Rhine. (In February 1798 Augereau was removed from its command and posted to the backwater of Perpignan.) The scaling-down of operations convinced Brillat that the time was right to take up his appointment at the court in Bourg. By 13 December his mind was finally made up. To Rostaing again:

My friend, in five or six days I shall leave for Paris where I hope to hear some of your news . . . You are no doubt aware that I am the President of the Criminal Court of the Ain Department. I have been weighing up for ages whether to go or not . . . what has really decided things is that the German army is finished. It is to be divided into two, with one part to be called the Mainz Army, under the command of General Hatry, while the other, to be called the Rhine Army, will continue under the command of Augereau . . . These changes have been brought about by intrigues so complicated that it would take too long to explain them to

*Perhaps Brillat and Rostaing had a brush with Hoche's army as they crossed the Black Forest on their way to Holland and the United States.

you. It is sufficient to tell you that it is as a result of the all-powerful Bonaparte, with whom Augereau is in open conflict . . .'[41]

V

After Christmas in Paris with his friends there, Brillat took up his new appointment in Bourg-en-Bresse at the beginning of Pluviôse of the year VI (the third week of January).[42] Bourg was not entirely without its attractions for the sensual Brillat: the food, then as now, was as good as any in France. To the north of the city lay the Bresse region, famous for its red, white and blue chickens. The Dombes was famous for its game and for the fish and wildlife of its lakes. Decent wine could be had from the Mâconnais and the Beaujolais on the far side of the Saône. As Brillat told Rostaing, 'I think I can amuse myself well enough here: the food is good and there are some quite pretty women.'[43]

By St Valentine's Day 1798 he had 'already one session under his belt'. As the head of the criminal division, Brillat had not only to judge the terrorists of the city (work he enjoyed), but also to sentence members of the *Compagnies de Jéhu*. The *Compagnies de Jéhu* emerged after the fall of Robespierre as part of the White Terror and its members sought to avenge God, or the executed king, or families who had fallen victim to the Jacobins. Bands of the *Compagnies* existed throughout the Lyonnais region. In Bourg, their most famous exploit was the slaughter at Challes of the leading Terrorists as they were transferred from the city to Lons-le-Saulnier in the Jura. Frilet, the one Terrorist to escape being bludgeoned to death with clubs and stones, was later slaughtered in prison in Lons.

Most of the massacres occurred between January and June 1795, but renewed outbreaks, thought to be the work of refractory priests, nobles and young men of good family, led to an order from the Direc-tory of 18 January 1798 which stipulated the death penalty for all members of assassination squads.[44] Brillat describes to Rostaing a long trial involving either terrorists or *Compagnons*: 'I've had the devil of a problem over these last six days, which had the disagreeable consequence of my having to acquit three murderers . . .'[45]

This work did not last for long. On 3 May he was appointed 'com-missaire exécutif près le tribunal civil de la ville de Versailles', or State Prosecutor for the Department of Seine-et-Oise. It was an important position: at that time there was no appellate jurisdiction for the department, and Brillat, as the Directory's commissioner, had to hear all appeals.[46] With 575,000 inhabitants, the Seine-et-Oise was one of the most populous departments in the Republic, and despite the departure of the King's court Versailles was still a bustling city.[47]

Brillat found an apartment at 6 rue Homère (today occupied by rue Maurepas and rue Galliéni); his office at the court was nearby in the rue des Reservoirs. Such an important court as Versailles had a correspondingly large bench of magistrates: 22 judges and two substitutes.

> The departmental court was a bizarre gathering of political opinions of the most disparate sort, comprising former Terrorists like Pierre Denis-Dufour, a former lawyer and Mayor of Rambouillet; moderates like Jacques Vincent de La Croix, a former advocate at the *Parlement* and brilliant polemicist; Brière, a former notary from Saint-Chéron and President of the Court of Rambouillet, who, during the Revolution, had known how to run with the hare and hunt with the hounds.[48]

In the more innocent days of the Revolution, Vincent de La Croix had delivered public lectures on law near the Palais-Royal, his dissertations on the constitutions of Europe and the United States embroidered with couplets on the political events of the day. The execution of Louis XVI marked a turning point for de La Croix. At the end of 1794 he attacked the *Convention Thérmidorienne*, demanding that a plebiscite should be held and the monarchy brought back. He was sent before the Revolutionary Tribunal, but was acquitted. Brillat met de La Croix for the first time in his chambers on 27 May.[49] Later he described him as 'a man of letters as kind as he was prolific'. At the time de La Croix was obsessed with sugar, which as a result of the British naval blockade had become a considerable luxury, costing more than five francs a pound.

> 'Ah,' he said, in his gentle tender voice, 'were the price of sugar ever to go back down to thirty *sous*, I would never again drink water unsugared.' His wishes have been fulfilled; he is still alive, I hope he has kept his word.'*[50]

The Clerk to the Justices, Laperte, was a man with an unlimited appetite for oysters, who confided to Brillat he had never once managed 'to eat his fill'.

---

*Jacques Vincent de La Croix outlived Brillat by five years. It is doubtful whether sugaring his water added in any way to his longevity.

I resolved to allow him just that satisfaction, and for that reason I invited him to lunch with me the next day.

He came and I kept him company until the third dozen appeared, after which I let him go on by himself. Whereupon he consumed [another] thirty-two . . . I stopped my guest just as he was beginning to pick up speed: 'My dear fellow,' I said, 'it is not your destiny today to "eat your fill" of oysters, let's have lunch.' We had lunch, and he performed with the vigour and address of a man who has been on a diet.[51]

A third friend of Brillat's at Versailles was Étienne Montucla, who lived in the former Hôtel des Inspecteurs in the rue du Potager. Montucla, the author of a history of mathematics and an essay on the squaring of the circle, lived on a 'meagre pension' as a member of the examining jury of the École Centrale of the Seine-et-Oise; eccentrically, he had refused to take up a seat as a member of the Academy of Sciences. When Brillat made his acquaintance, Montucla lived in a limited circle composed of his daughter and son-in-law, Monsieur and Madame Corbez de La Tour, and the de La Croix.

Brillat discovered he had much in common with Montucla, who was not only proficient in five modern languages, but was also planning a dictionary of gourmand geography, though only a few passages had so far been written. Possibly Montucla's notes gave Brillat the idea for *La Physiologie du goût*. If so, he is singularly honoured by a footnote in the famous book: Brillat's other major sources were in no way acknowledged. He was present when Montucla died, in 1799.[52]

Brillat was sworn in as State Prosecutor by the clerk Laperte on 27 May, declaring solemnly that he had never signed a seditious or illegal document, and that he was not related to any *émigrés*.[53] The two sections of the court proper were staffed by seven and six judges respectively; the other judges served as circuit judges in the courts of Versailles, Étampes, Saint-Germain-en-Laye, Mantes and Pontoise. The courts sat for nine days of the ten-day revolutionary week, from nine or ten o'clock in the morning, reconvening after lunch at two. With such a regime, Brillat can have had little time to travel to Paris, and his social life must have centred on his few good friends in Versailles.[54]

A local historian in the 1920s examined the records of Brillat's Versailles judgments. Though they give the impression that the author of *La Physiologie du goût* was a conscientious magistrate, they do not make thrilling reading: a ruling on the stamp act; the suppression of a district court in Dourdan; the settlement of a bitter marital dispute between the marquis de Soyécourt and his German wife; or the ticking-off of a judge in Mantes who had failed to appear in court properly dressed, and who had demonstrated an insufficiently 'republican' attitude.[55]

Brillat was at pains to look after the well-being of his court staff. During the bitter winter of 1799, he complained that the court was too cold, and threatened to terminate proceedings unless more money was provided to heat it. He also petitioned for more money for his staff, based on the size and population of his jurisdiction, the fact that the court met twice a day, and the expense of produce in Versailles, where it was no cheaper than in the capital.[56]

Despite his busy schedule in Versailles, Brillat found the time to dash off a letter to Rostaing at the end of August.

> We are all griefstricken at the death of General Joubert.* Now only Moreau knows how to wield a great army;† . . . Without [Joubert], everything would have been lost and the army would have been scuppered. Leaving Paris, he said that in two months either he or Souvorov‡ would be dead. Sadly, he was only too right . . . Poor Joubert had only slept one night with his wife, but managed to eke it out from nine o'clock in the evening till one o'clock the following afternoon. I hope he had time to make a little citizen out of it . . .[57]

On 9 August Brillat had managed to reclaim some particularly valuable items which had been sold off after his flight. It is easy to imagine how much joy this success brought a man of Brillat's proclivities: fifty pounds of tin in plates and serving dishes; four chandeliers in copper plated with silver; two cauldrons, one small, one large; two copper-plated frying pans; three casserole dishes with their covers; two fish kettles, one having two legs, the other three; one tin basin; the instruments (including a spit) for three chimneys; an iron grill; a tin jug, napkins, and so on.[58] Now Brillat was ready to entertain again!

---

*Brillat had a great admiration for Barthelémy Joubert, who was born at Pont de Vaux in the Ain, and like Brillat himself studied law at Dijon. There the similarities ended. Joubert was killed at the battle of Novi. At this time his popularity rivalled that of Bonaparte.

†General Jean Victor Moreau took over command after Joubert's death at Novi. Later Brillat was involved in his trial for treason.

‡Alexandre Souvorov, Russian general. The real victor of Novi.

Later that year, on 8 December, Brillat also managed to get his library back. The collection consisted of two sets of shelves, one entirely filled with legal works and books inherited from his father, the other with books of his own. Brillat had inherited an eighth share of his father's books; his own acquisitions were distinguished by the letters 'BSP', for Brillat-Savarin *puiné* (Brillat-Savarin the younger).[59]

VI

On 21 April 1799 Brillat wrote an uncharacteristically skittish letter to the Minister of the Interior, François de Neufchâteau. Perhaps Brillat knew the minister was possessed of a sense of humour.

Despite a justified reputation for hostility to the Church, Neufchâteau was nevertheless upset by the general indifference to the idea of celebrating the *décadi*, the revolutionary sabbath. The ministry sent out numerous circulars, including war reports and government notices, to the *temples décadaires* (deconsecrated churches made over to the Cult of Virtue), but they failed to lure the people in. Brillat suggested a solution, based on the current enthusiasm for all things Classical:

> What made Greek feast days really interesting was above all the great numbers of beautiful women who came from far and wide in search of lovers and husbands. In this respect we become more like the Ancients daily, as in Paris all people do is chase pretty women, and they are only happy when they believe they have found one.
>
> Taking these facts into consideration, would it not be possible to introduce into the celebrations for [the anniversary of the founding of the Republic on 23 September] some system compelling the attendance of one beautiful woman elected in each department?
>
> I calculate that this would cost 120,000 *livres* to cover transport. I think one could recover the money through indirect taxation and from the thousands of foreigners which this unusual occasion would attract to Paris. I seem to recall having read somewhere that the chief minister of one of our kings had a talent for collecting money even from the costly festivities which this prince gave at his court.
>
> Could one not also alter the exhibition arcades on the Champ de Mars in such a way that one could be given over to each Department, thus making the exhibition into a sort of map of industrial

geography?* Citizen minister, these are the ideas which I offer in homage, to demonstrate my appreciation of what you are doing for the prosperity of our common land.

I hope that you will do me the justice of believing that I should have been quite prepared to submit two memoranda of some length. But if you are not going to adopt my ideas, this would obviously be a waste of my time. If you do intend to make use of my project, I should not wish to intrude upon the right of your own staff to work out the scheme according to their own lights.

The minister minuted, laconically, 'Bon'.[60]

If Brillat could be frivolous here, as he was in *La Physiologie du goût*, none the less he had not forgotten his experience of politics, or his still-strong republicanism. On 26 October the members of the bench of the Seine-et-Oise were required to swear a new oath to the Constitution then being prepared by the Directors. This gave Brillat an opportunity to analyse publicly the three revolutionary constitutions which had been enacted since the fall of the Bastille, including that of 1791 in whose drafting he himself had played a role.

After saluting the architects of the new Constitution of the Directory, Brillat's speech reviewed the laws of 1791. These, he said, 'taught the people what they were, showed them the meaning of liberty and laid the bases of the social contract, but it perished because no one wanted to enact it . . .' Naturally the Constitution of the year I did not receive such fulsome praise. Brillat described it as 'an explosion of passions and an unleashing of vice . . . What is extreme is never lasting.' In its wake the people had been plagued by elections and at the same time had been made victims of the 'furies of intrigue and the errors of beginners'.

For the present constitution Brillat expressed nothing but praise (as was wise). 'We have been built by experience . . . the science of political mechanism is now perfected and we live in hope that the wise men now working, backed up by the intelligence of all the good citizens they call loftily to their aid, will grant us a charter which will finally be as close to perfection as a work can be which is written by men for men.'[61]

The new constitution, however, was not fated to be the Directory's

---

*Neufchâteau had been behind the first ever exhibition of French industrial products. Brillat's ideas perhaps owe something to Montucla, though for the time being it is sex and not food which interests him.

crowning achievement. Bonaparte was already conspiring to take over the reins of government, and on 18 Brumaire (9 November) he launched his *coup d'état*. The following day his guard removed the protesting deputies from their session in the orangery of the Château de Saint-Cloud. Bonaparte was now master of France.

By a stroke of luck, Brillat-Savarin was a witness to the occasion; he wrote of it somewhat uninformatively to his friend Rostaing on 8 November:

> I saw what happened from close up. You'll be astonished to hear that I was actually in Saint-Cloud on the 19th and in the chamber itself. We'll have a chat about it as soon as we meet, that is, if we have not forgotten all about it by then . . . You're going to see some big changes . . . All the troops are swearing the new oath and all civil servants and officers of the courts will do the same. People believe that Masséna* will be recalled. Championnet† already has been. Moreau is to be given a new command. We are assured that our men have reached Milan and that every day brings reverse after reverse to the Russian and Austrian armies.[62]

Although Brillat is discreet in his letter, he was undoubtedly pleased by the events of Brumaire. He had had enough of the Jacobins in the government. He wanted stability at home and victory abroad. Joubert was now dead, and Moreau's star had been eclipsed. Bonaparte was the man of the moment.

On 19 November, the judges of Versailles met in Brillat's office. Together they drew up an address, congratulating General Bonaparte on his *coup*. There was only one dissenter, Denis-Dufour, a Jacobin who had been a friend of Robespierre's.[63]

Napoleon Bonaparte's triumph led to a further reorganization of the courts, which once again affected Brillat-Savarin's position. Courts were being re-established in each *arrondissement*, which meant that the job of the *procureur* for the Seine-et-Oise would be wound up. Moreover, the new Consulate was intending to create department appeal courts, and this would remove the major part of Brillat's role within the legal system.[64]

On 19 January Brillat petitioned to be restored to his place on the

---

*André Masséna rose from a cabin boy to become one of Napoleon's marshals and prince d'Essling.

†Jean-Etienne Championnet, a former cook in Barcelona, was named commander of the Army of Italy in 1800; he died in an epidemic later that year.

Tribunal de cassation. The *coup d'état* of Fructidor (September 1797) had failed to establish the *Tribunal de cassation* as a National appeal court. The five judges purged in June 1796 (to make way for Brillat and others) had been restored to their positions on the bench after Fructidor; among them was Brillat's compatriot Sibuet.[65] The bench, however, was still understaffed, and it was decided to ask the electoral colleges of the departments to choose new judges, the ordinary electorate being deemed too untrustworthy.[66]

The anomaly of judges who also sat as members of the Five Hundred or the *Conseil des Anciens* was brought up in debate on 15 May 1798.[67] Later that year Pierre Jean Marraud, a judge on the bench, was sacked after being denounced for his former attachment to federalism. Brillat must have observed his fate with interest: he was wise to maintain his habitual caution.[68]

Napoleon's military dictatorship was bound to seek an accommodation with the moderate elements in the state; Brillat's tormentors, the remaining Jacobins, were the chief victims of Brumaire. Brillat was right in thinking that his application would be smiled upon after Napoleon's *coup*: it was.

On 8 April 1800, Brillat-Savarin was officially reappointed to the bench.[69]

CHAPTER EIGHT

Establishment

I

TWELVE DAYS AFTER Brillat's reappointment to the bench the comte André Joseph d'Abrial,* Minister of Justice, spoke before the assembled magistrates of the *Tribunal de cassation*. The minister summed up the problems which had dogged the court in the first nine years of its existence: too many elections too close together, and arbitrary decisions rather than solid jurisprudence.

However, there was some unequivocally good news in the minister's speech: 'You will escape from these irritations *by unlimited tenure*'. Brillat could breathe a sigh of relief; he was secure for life. The minister carried on in flattering vein:

> Where is the citizen who would not be inspired with respect seeing the kind of men sitting in your ranks, some grown old in glory in a career at the bar; others well-known for the wisdom of their opinions in divers legislative assemblies; all exemplary in their morals, their patriotism and in the distinguished reputation which goes before them?
>
> Where is the magistrate who would not, from now on, cast his gaze towards the *Tribunal de cassation* as the focal point of his hopes, the model to follow in all things, the most glorious reward for his labours! Here, all at once, is the temple of justice, virtue, talent and honour.[1]

Under the Consulate the seeds were finally sown which made the *Tribunal*, now *Cour, de cassation* the body it is today.

Brillat's entry into the *Tribunal* once again pushed his compatriot

---

*Minister of Justice after 18 Brumaire. Transferred to the Senate in 1802.

Georges Sibuet out; he took up a new post in the Appeal Court in Brussels. There was no bitterness between them. Brillat stayed with Sibuet in the country, and Sibuet read one of the speeches at Brillat's funeral.[2]

If Sibuet had had to make way for him, there were plenty of familiar faces still on the bench, including a number of regicides. One newcomer was the Counsellor Pierre-Paul-Nicolas Henrion de Pansey, a man Brillat held in high esteem. For the past ten years this Lorrainer had served in Champagne. Once Napoleon asked him the origin of the well-known *champenois* expression, 'ninety-nine sheep and one *champenois* makes a hundred animals'.

Sire: Your Majesty is aware that princes are always short of money. Thibault IV, Count of Champagne, was no different from the rest. He therefore imposed a tax on all flocks of one hundred sheep and above. The *champenois*, in order to escape the levy, reduced their flocks to ninety-nine sheep; but when the Count was informed of this subtlety, he interpreted his edict in these terms: the shepherd of the flock counts as a sheep, and the tax will be levied.[3]

Napoleon must have liked Henrion de Pansey's sense of humour, for he made him a baron of the Empire. Previous to this, de Pansey had been one of the earliest recipients of the Légion d'honneur. Soon after he received it, Henrion left Paris to spend some time on his estate at Pansey. On the way he stopped to rest his horse in Épernay. He sat down on a bench, and a crowd gathered around him, curious to know the meaning of the unfamiliar rosette.

'What have you got in your button-hole? Why are you wearing that red ribbon, and what do you use it for?'

'My friends, you ask me for more information than I am able to give,' was Henrion's laconic, and ironic, reply.[4]

And it was Henrion de Pansey who, addressing three of France's most distinguished scientists (Laplace, Chaptal and Berthollet) in 1812, made the wry remark:

I regard the discovery of a new dish, which sustains our appetite and prolongs our enjoyment, as an event of far greater interest than the discovery of a star: we can already see quite enough of those.*[5]

---

*This line is frequently, and carelessly, attributed to Brillat himself: Brillat includes it among the aphorisms at the beginning of *La Physiologie du goût*, but attributes it to Henrion at the end of the book.

As *Archichancelier*, Second Consul, and the man ultimately responsible for the preparation of the new Civil Code, Régis de Cambacérès must have been a figure of keen interest to Brillat. Cambacérès erected *gourmandise* into a system of political philosophy based on the advantages to be derived from lavish entertainment. As Napoleon was too busy to entertain, and indeed was not by nature disposed to the sort of orgies advocated by Cambacérès, he left this to his Second Consul.

Magistrates were aware that the way to attract Cambacérès' favourable attention was by way of his stomach, and those seeking advancement were careful to send him hams from Mainz, truffles from Périgord, pâtés from Strasbourg, duck livers from Toulouse, pullets from Chartres, sausages from Arles, smoked beef from Hamburg, terrines from Nérac, or partridges (*bartavelles*) from near his native city, Montpellier, in the Cevennes.[6]

Cambacérès' meals were sumptuous: the German playwright Kotzebue reported, 'of the seventy or eighty dishes, to taste at least one half of which I had summoned my powers, there was not one which Lucullus or Apicius would have disdained.'[7] Brillat, however, makes no mention of any invitation to the supreme law-lord's table, although it is clear that his writing was influenced by Cambacérès' example.

After his transfer from Versailles Brillat's first lodgings were at No. 19 rue du Mail, the street where he had lived on his return from America and where the Récamiers too had lived until two years before. No. 19 was also occupied by the Club des Étrangers, an establishment where political geography and modern languages had been taught since 1791.[8]

The flat was huge, an entire floor of a Louis XV building (which still exists); but Brillat did not remain there long. Over the next seven years he moved first to the rue Notre Dame des Victoires, and then to the rue du Mont Blanc (today rue du Chaussée d'Antin) where once again he was a neighbour of the Récamiers, before moving to the place where he died, 22 rue des Filles Saint Thomas.[9]

The *Tribunal de cassation* required his presence on only three days a week; he served in each of the court's three chambers in turn. He therefore had plenty of time in which to stroll down to the Café Lemblin at No. 100 Galérie du Beaujolais in the Palais-Royal. Lemblin was to the Bonapartists what the neighbouring Café de Valois was to the monarchists: political differences often led to armed fights in the gardens of the palace. Brillat spent much of his time in the Café Lemblin sipping the famous chocolate produced by the firm of Debauve (a former supplier to the court of Louis XVI) in the rue des Saints Pères. His dog Sultan sat under his chair, and Brillat would roll up the crumb of his bread into a ball for Sultan while he himself nibbled the crusts.[10]

Beauvilliers had re-opened in 1799, and Brillat was able to eat there, as at the Trois Frères Provençeaux, in the company of friends. Twice a week, Brillat ate in a private room at Véfour.* The cafés and eating-houses of the Palais-Royal were able to satisfy all his needs.[11]

The Consulate and the Empire led to a rediscovery of the culinary arts following a Revolution which, according to Grimod, had threatened to destroy even the recipe for a *fricassée* of chicken. Gradually, after 1800, a new generation of chefs came to the fore who were well able to match the talents of those who had developed the the idea of restaurants in the years just prior to the Revolution. Ultimately the process produced the first culinary superstar, in Marie-Antoine Carême, deemed to be the first chef able to perform all branches of the culinary art with equal dexterity.

Not only restaurants multiplied after 1800; Brillat tells us that there was a concomitant explosion of caterers, *pâtissiers*, sweetmakers and grocers – the men and women who people the pages of Grimod's *Almanach des gourmands*. *Sautés à la suprême* were a current vogue, dishes quickly prepared over a spirit-lamp at the dining table.[12] Also developed were *petit-fours*, cakes and biscuits cooked at low temperatures in a small brick oven. Preserving techniques were being perfected and a vogue for greenhouses, partially initiated by Napoleon's wife, Joséphine de Beauharnais, provided a wider variety of fruits and vegetables all year round. In or around the year 1804 the Café Hardy in the boulevard des Italiens invented the *déjeuner à la fourchette*: at any time of the day, the hungry Parisian could stop off for a plate of kidneys or chops, selected on a fork from a display in the window and simply grilled.[13] Another fashion was the 'tea'; according to Grimod, this was a large meal served in the houses of the opulent financiers who had profited so greatly from the years of incessant warfare. For

---

*Véfour is now called the Grand Véfour, and preserves the decoration it possessed in Brillat's time. The seats in the restaurant have copper name-plates referring to the historic clientèle. Not so long ago the author found himself sitting in Grimod de La Reynière's seat, opposite that of Brillat-Savarin. It is unlikely, however, that the two men ever sat at the same table.

Brillat, a meal offered to people 'who have lunched well, presupposes that they are neither hungry nor thirsty: its sole purpose is therefore to pass the time.'[14]

Brillat spent his holidays in Belley; he was not such an old dog yet, and a story about him is recalled by Tendret. It concerned a jape perpetrated against a waning beauty who came to stay in the *gentilhommière* at Vieu. The woman in question was an elderly, flirtatious widow. Brillat-Savarin, overhearing her ask for a servant to be sent to warm her sheets, disguised a friend as a chambermaid and arranged for him to precede the widow upstairs with copper kettle and warming-pan.

As the 'chambermaid' warmed the sheets at one end of the room, the widow, believing herself to be in the presence of 'a person of the sex', as the Church puts it, began to undress, and to search her clothes for lice as she did so. Then, as Tendret tells it,

> suddenly letting fall every vain ornament and veil which weighed so heavily on her, as on Phaedra and so many others, she exclaimed:
> 'Still beautiful, if a bit swarthy! . . .'
> The sheets by now being sufficiently warm, S—— took his leave, carrying with him both the warming-pan and his impressions; he told the story with the line at the end, which made his name, and now (in these parts) when we talk of an old beauty fallen to ruin we exclaim, like the old lady: 'Still beautiful, if a little swarthy!'[15]

II

Many of Brillat's speeches had found their way into print, but he had never attempted a book. In 1801, at the age of 46, he produced a work which, though it might surprise those who only know of *La Physiologie du goût*, is unlikely to have astonished those who knew him at the time: it was entitled *Vues et projets d'économie politique*, by Citizen Brillat-Savarin, ex-Constituent, member of the *Tribunal de cassation* 'and many learned societies'.*

Vues et projets is not in any way an attempt at a system of political economy, but rather a series of helpful suggestions for improvements in certain domains: the civil service; roads; commerce and industry;

---

*The copy in the British Library is inscribed to 'Citizen Taleyrand' [*sic*] in Brillat's own hand. Brillat did not know the Foreign Minister well, but he must have encountered him in the Constituent Assembly.

agriculture; civil and criminal law; the army and finance: all fields in which Brillat, for one reason or another, had taken a particular interest.

Part of Brillat's aim was to tidy up the 'numerous atoms' so displaced by the Revolution that the government found it difficult to wield its authority. This was particularly apparent in the civil service, where the orders of the central government were obfuscated, delayed or scrambled by local officials. Brillat stressed the importance of hope in the work place, and suggested that *aspirants* be attached to prefects and government commissioners, a system which had worked well in Savoy and Piedmont, where unemployed law graduates were attached to the Senates. In the past, civil servants had held the same position for their entire working lives, often handing over the job to their sons, but since the Revolution all that had changed:

> So many requests unanswered because no one has read them! So much business unfinished because no one has classified it! So many accounts unsettled because the documents have been lost! So many offices that have not been reformed or reorganized because of the rapid turnover of departmental heads! . . . it is as a result of the constant flux that venality has reached such a frightening degree that it has almost ceased to be the scandal that it should be.[16]

Brillat was an early advocate of retirement pensions, which until then existed only for soldiers.

He proposed that local businessmen should be encouraged to undertake road repair work; their business interests would provide an incentive. He advocated the rights of pedestrians, recommending that roads be provided with three-foot-wide stone pavements; he might have foreseen motorway halts in his suggestion that benches and shady trees should be provided for weary travellers. He proposed a size limit on coaches and a restriction on the number of horses attached to them, to prevent accidents.

Turning to agriculture, Brillat advocated the establishment of a rural committee in each region to encourage cultivation of the potato. Butchers' meat was more widely consumed since the Revolution, and he was concerned to increase its availability still further; in the Bugey, for example, the peasant diet was still cheese, vegetables, bread and a great deal of wine, four times a day. He advocated the revival of the great studs, and heaped praise on the new Society for the Encouragement of National Industry, of which he was a member. (In *La*

Physiologie du goût he later described one of his inventions, the *irrorateur* which sprinkled scented water on people, maintaining somewhat implausibly that 'the wettest people were the happiest.'[17]

As a bourgeois, and one particularly fond of hunting and shooting, Brillat naturally glossed over some of the adverse effects of the Revolution. The abolition of the laws restricting hunting to fief-holders had led to unimaginable massacres of wildlife. According to Grimod, the pheasant 'was one of the first victims of the democratic system of government adopted in France since 1789; it is however still possible to find the odd one which has escaped from the clutches of revolutionary justice.'[18]

In his chapter on law, Brillat returned to several old themes: a court for every *arrondissement*; the need to keep the judiciary independent of the government (as it had been in France until the Convention had interfered, with disastrous results); the merits of appointing magistrates for life; the drawbacks of juries; the exhibition of condemned prisoners with placards around their necks explaining their crimes (he believed they should not be paraded *en masse*, but brought out one by one, in silence, and their crimes read out to the crowd); the high-minded administration of prisons.

Drawing on his experience of Augereau's army, whose ranks had been swollen by young soldiers with little respect for their superior officers, he favoured a return to a pre-revolutionary structure for the military. One of his odder ideas stemmed from a system existing in the Tsarist armies called an *artel*. The *artel* was a kitty into which every member of a platoon or company put money on a regular basis in order to pay for drink, meat or means of transport. Each soldier's death in battle increased the share of the survivors; according to Brillat's logic, this tended to make the soldier more loyal to his regiment! When a soldier left the colours, his share of the kitty would be given back to him. This system Brillat advocated for the French army.

Finally, Brillat turned to the problem of finding revenues for the state. Many of his ideas were rather ahead of his time. He favoured, for instance, a system of fixed taxation to benefit cash-flow, rather than an annual calculation based on the budget. He called for more money to be raised from indirect taxation, on luxuries like shooting and gambling, not on staples like corn. Overall, *Vues et projets* reveals Brillat's sharp administrative intelligence.

III

But Brillat was not the only Belleysan to produce a first book that year. His achievement was dwarfed by the work of his godson, Anthelme Richerand, who had sketched out his work at the age of only 19. The *Éléments de la physiologie* was a massive success, 'translated into all languages'.[19] By 1858, it had sold more than 30,000 copies, and had brought its author huge fees in his practice, and the title of baron. Richerand, however, did not have the reputation of being a pleasant man. Brillat faulted him only for the speed with which he consumed his food, but a later critic said he was 'jealous, filled with hatred, vindictive, argumentative to the degree that he lost his temper, outrageously critical and unjustly severe . . .'.[20] Richerand's book profoundly affected Brillat: it gave him the structure for his own thoughts and reminiscences as they emerged twenty-four years later in *La Physiologie du goût*.[21]

In 1802 the *Tribunal de cassation* had the important task of ratifying the projected *Code civil*, which was finally published two years later. The *Tribunal* was not directly responsible for writing the *Code civil* (changed to the *Code Napoléon* in 1807), but was consulted. The four men most important in drawing up this much-imitated document were President François-Denis Tronchet, the 75-year-old head of Brillat's court, Félix-Julien-Jean Bigot de Préameneu, Jean-Étienne Marie Portalis, and the marquis Pierre Joseph de Maleville. The different geographical origins of the four chief *rédacteurs* doubtless helped to homogenize the law of the *ancien régime*; Tronchet was a Parisian, Bigot a Breton, and these were regions where customary laws had prevailed; Maleville was a Bordelais and Portalis a Provençal, from regions where written, Roman law had survived. The essential conservatism of the *Code* is not surprising when one considers not only the age of Tronchet, but the fact that he had nobly consented to defend Louis XVI. Portalis had been, like Brillat, a victim of the left-wing *coup d'état* of Fructidor.[22]

The 'observations' made by the *Tribunal de cassation* in 1802 display something of the different views which needed to be reconciled in order to bring French law up to date. Opinions were based both on the laws of the *ancien régime* (which had always been Brillat's advocacy), and on such tenets of revolutionary law as were to be retained, chiefly divorce and mortgage.[23]

Brillat noted that many of the effects of the Revolution were being set aside as the dictatorial power of the First Consul increased. Curiosity even drove the sceptical judge through the doors of the much-abused, much mutilated Cathedral of Notre Dame. On 15 July 1801 a Concordat had re-established the Catholic Church in France, and on 18 April 1802 the disciple of Voltaire attended Mass for the first time in many years:

> Yesterday I spent six hours in Notre Dame, I attended Mass, heard the homily and a *Te Deum*. I don't need to tell you [he wrote to Rostaing] that I went more for reasons of philosophy than for devotion's sake. These are my observations: I saw the famous Regent diamond, shining from the hilt of the First Consul's sword. The throne of the Cardinal *a latere* was lower, smaller and uglier than that of the government. All the clergy went to greet the three Consuls* with the cross at the door of the church. Bonaparte made a present of a mitre, a ring and a crook to each of the bishops and archbishops . . . At the Consular Palace there was a lunch laid out for four only. At the same time the ministers had the task of entertaining the corresponding authorities [i.e., the churchmen]. Among the most remarkable of these was the abbé Bernier,† a prelate who is half French and half Chouan,‡ half priest and half warrior. Anyone who knew what problems he created would never have total faith in his blessing.[24]

One other prelate who was present that day to celebrate the brief Peace of Amiens which halted the war with England was the Archbishop of Paris, the Cardinal de Belloy. The ancient Jean-Baptiste de Belloy was a man who might have reconciled Brillat to the Church. It was following a spectacular salmon at de Belloy's table that the greatest gastronome of the age, Dr Jean-Baptiste Joseph Gastaldy, succumbed to apoplexy. De Belloy 'was fond of good cheer,' Brillat observed. 'Several times I saw his patriarchal eyes light up at some distinguished morsel. On every occasion, Napoleon showed him deference and respect.'[25] De Belloy is also thought to have been the inventor of filter coffee, as we know it today.

---

*Bonaparte, Cambacérès and Charles François Lebrun.

†Etienne Alexandre Jean-Baptiste Marie Bernier, later Bishop of Orléans.

‡A Chouan was a member of the Breton counter-revolutionary group responsible for the civil war in the west of France in 1793.

IV

That year of peace, Brillat-Savarin took his holidays in Belley as was his custom. A glimpse of his rural existence may be gleaned from an undated letter sent to his cousin Madame Roux, who it seems had had the temerity to send Madame Récamier (*not* the famous Juliette, but the wife of Anthelme Récamier, the chief physician of the hospital in Belley) a letter filled with reproaches about Brillat's behaviour, and obviously suggesting that Madame Récamier should give him a severe dressing-down. We do not know the precise nature of the complaint, but every indication would lead one to suppose that it was Brillat's attitude to women which was at fault.

> I have just this minute returned from Madame Récamier's, who let me read your letter. I read it; found it charming; and escaped to write to you – in the twinkling of an eye. These are reflex actions which require no thought, and where the intention is outstripped by the performance.
>
> The two-pronged sermon so warmly recommended to Madame Récamier was not delivered. She didn't have the heart . . . In faith, I think she's frightened of me, and doesn't dare give me lessons in morality when she is on her own.
>
> . . . Believe me, dear Cousin, your letter was very much to the point, and even if I treat the subject lightly in this one, I do need all the compassion that it calls for. One day an antique statue was found in Rome. The antiquarians gathered round it and while they were admiring it, a frightful snake slid out, which had found its way into [the statue] by means of a hole which no one had at first noticed . . .

After this veiled, teasing *cri de coeur* on the subject of his wickedness, Brillat deals with some local gossip. There has been a wedding; he has called upon a relation who is unwell; a worldly prelate has visited Belley:

> For a few days we had M. the abbé de Laurencin in Belley, a poor hermit with an income of 80,000 francs. He had a carriage and four, four lackeys and a fledgling monk with him, the latter played the role of butler or valet. One was either besplattered by the carriage, affronted by the lackeys or elbowed out of the way by the little monk.
>
> In Paris all that would be all very well, but we honest provincials found it in poor taste that one who had taken a vow of poverty had so much money; that the man who had sworn chastity had women in his carriage; and that one who had made a vow to obey had so many

people around him whose orders were to obey him: we cursed the carriage, the lackeys and the baby monk with them.

At the invitation of M. de Sainte Julie, I spent two days in Moulins. I dined well and was delighted with the way I was received by the colonel. I lunched one day with Madame Vuillermet who was actually put between Rubat and me. She is a little woman of seventeen, dark-skinned, fresh and lively; those who look at her in a wholly kindly way find an innocence which makes her appear to possess something which she has clearly lost, connoisseurs penetrate this virginal varnish and detect a capable side which promises a good deal.

Brillat then returns to teasing his cousin Madame Roux. It would seem that her letter spoke of a retreat in a place called Badane where she might retire with just Madame Récamier for company.

Oh! Badane is it? I think you'd be very happy indeed there. The air is pure, the wine is good, the position countrified, it would make a marvellous little retreat. So you're thinking of going on foot! . . . but you forget that it will take you at least half an hour to walk that far. What a deal of vigour and strength you conceal from us! And by such a scabrous path . . . this is the best of all. It is pure heroism! . . . Heavens, haven't I got enough on my plate, do I have to be jealous too? Well, I am . . . You tell me that Madame Récamier would be admitted to your little retreat and that then you would have everything you desired. And what about me? What am I, a dog? No, not entirely, but a man who is good for nothing more than the receipt of sermons. It would seem that when we look for pleasure we go to Badane, and when we're in a bad mood we give the cousin [i.e., himself] chapter and verse. This idea gave me the bile and I shall leave you without saying goodbye.

But he didn't; he kept the letter open, and felt charitable enough to end with some verses. Perhaps the prospect of lunching again with the lady from Moulins had its effect:

As I write I am in the middle of my *toilette*, for I am to lunch at Madame Récamier's with Madame Vuillermet. I can't really make up my mind whether I am serious about her: I've had quite enough heartache, one way or another. All the same I am making the odd adjustment, removing my powder carefully and brushing my clothes attentively. I'll probably say something foolish to her; I'll never understand these things.[26]

V

On 27 December 1803 Brillat and his colleagues were involved once again in a revival of the ceremonial of the law, complete with black cassocks and scarlet gowns, at the opening session of the *Tribunal de cassation*. After a religious service celebrated by the 94-year-old Cardinal de Belloy, the *procureur général* Merlin de Douai* said:

> [The government] is aware that in order to allow justice to blossom, judges must be honoured, and it earnestly desires to inspire in the people sincere veneration. In the solicitude which motivates it [i.e., the government], its constant concern is that the bench should exist in full awareness of its own dignity, right down to the manner in which it robes, and when wearing their severe but noble apparel let the judges never forget that they are the arbiters of the highest interests and the repositories of a formidable power. It is essential that their diction, behaviour and comportment never fall short of that magnificent office with which the law has invested them . . .

Merlin's next line was all the more curious for coming from the lips of the originator of the Law of Suspects and one of the architects of 18 Fructidor:

> In your youth you witnessed the last moments of the pre-revolutionary bar; but almost all of you have problems recalling those glorious days without despairing of ever seeing them return.
>   Take courage generous citizens; a man has been raised by providence. . .[27]

Brillat's social status was improving, with that of high-ranking judges as a whole. The Constitution of the year II had virtually abolished the bench; now, after the see-saw years of the Directory, the bench was not only back where it had been, but was to be treated with the respect which the *noblesse de robe* had been accorded until the eve of the Revolution.

The publication earlier that year of a wholly novel work on food, the *Almanach des gourmands*, had taken Paris by storm. Like the later *Physiologie du goût*, the *Almanach* was unsigned; the author concealed his identity behind the *nom de guerre* 'le vieil amateur' (the

---

*Philippe Antoine Merlin, known as Merlin de Douai (1754–1838). Merlin had the reputation of being the greatest French lawyer of his day.

old [food] lover), but his name, Grimod de la Reynière, was well known to the majority of fashionable Parisians.*

Before the Revolution Grimod had scandalized Paris and his family with a succession of practical jokes which resulted in his father, a wealthy tax farmer, banishing him under a *lettre de cachet* to imprisonment in Lorraine. Grimod did not return to Paris until 1794, at the height of the Terror which had imprisoned his mother and countless relations and executed his uncle, the Chancellor Malesherbes, for the shocking reason that he had had the courage to defend Louis Capet.

The fantastic wealth of the Grimods was no more. All that remained was the family house, the Hôtel de La Reynière. Grimod was compelled to work for his living, writing theatrical reviews which brought him into contact with actresses with whom he fell haplessly, hopelessly in love.

Grimod derived no satisfaction from the Revolution. The insolence of the nobles whom he had detested before 1789 had been replaced by that of the profiteers, the racketeers, the men who made money out of the sufferings of war. Deciding, somewhat tongue in cheek, that there was a need to provide these *nouveaux riches* with a guide to their only passion, Grimod produced the *Almanach des gourmands*. Eight volumes appeared between 1803 and the beginning of 1813, enchanting the public and making a fortune for the author. The first volume alone sold 20,000 copies.[28]

Much has been written by both the Grimodians and the Brillatins about the degree to which Brillat learned from, copied or plagiarized Grimod. In *La Physiologie du goût* Grimod is not mentioned once but, as Pierre Varillon pointed out 35 years ago, it is quite impossible that Brillat did not know of the *Almanach*; it is also highly unlikely that the two should not have encountered one another. Grimod frequented Cambacérès' table, and dedicated the first volume of the *Almanach* to his steward, the gourmand marquis Jean-Pierre d'Aigrefeuille. That Brillat knew d'Aigrefeuille is clear from *La Physiologie du goût*, where the gastronome is depicted inconsolable because of delayed dinner. Brillat also knew the theatrical critic Jean-Louis Geoffroy who, like d'Aigrefeuille, had been a dining companion of Grimod's since the 1780s. Brillat referred to Geoffroy as a 'cynic', perhaps because he attributed faults in literary composition to the consumption of sugar and water.[29] Proof that Brillat not only knew of

---

*Grimod was all the more noticeable for the fact that he had been born without hands.

the *Almanach*, but had actually read it, may be found in one of his letters to Rostaing: 'I've bought you the *Almanach des gourmands*, a book of the rarest merit, both in style and subject matter. [Benjamin, the younger brother of the dead Étienne] Delessert wanted to write a dedication to you but he is so busy that I have never found the opportunity to make him act on it.'[30]

Consciously or unconsciously, on Brillat's part much of Grimod's work had found its way into *La Physiologie du goût* when that was published in 1825.

VI

Brillat's judicial duties kept him busy until the spring of 1804. We next encounter him as one of the judges at the trial of the monarchist plotters Georges Cadoudal, the Polignac brothers, the marquis de Rivière and General Moreau. General Pichegru was spared the formality of a hearing by being strangled in his prison cell in the Temple. Of the twenty conspirators who appeared in the dock, twelve (including the Chouan Cadoudal) were executed, while eight others were pardoned. Brillat reported the conclusion of the case to Rostaing: 'Polignac, La Rivière and Russillon have had their sentences commuted. That should produce an extremely good effect on the French, who like things to be liberal and magnanimous. In general it is believed that little blood will be shed over this business.'[31]

One of those spared was Brillat's former hero, General Moreau. Juliette Récamier knew Moreau through his wife, and as a letter of hers reveals it was Brillat who enabled her to witness the trial. Madame Moreau, the General's wife,

> told me . . . that Moreau had often looked for me among the friends who mingled with the numerous members of the general public who filled the court. I made it a point of duty to attend the trial. The day after our conversation I went along, accompanied by Brillat-Savarin, a judge who is closely related to Monsieur Récamier. The crowd was so vast that not only the court room, but also the avenues leading to the Palais de Justice were packed . . . M. Savarin let me in by a door which opened on to the amphitheatre which faced the accused. I was separated from them by the entire breadth of the room. Much moved by the scene, I rapidly sought out Moreau among those in the amphitheatre. At the instant I lifted my veil, he recognized me, rose and waved. I

waved back with emotion and respect, and then hurried down the steps to the place which had been reserved for me.[32]

Napoleon was not pleased to hear that Madame Récamier had attended the trial. The following day she received a note from Cambacérès informing her that Bonaparte had asked what she was doing there.[33] The First Consul told Cambacérès to 'give the judge [who let her in] a dressing down'.[34] Madame Récamier was enchanted by the risks which Brillat had taken on her behalf. Up until then she had shown no particular interest in her husband's cousin, but as a reward for his actions Brillat received the first of two much-valued presents from the society beauty. 'Madame Récamier has just given me her portrait painted by one of Paris's best painters, Augustin.* He was paid fifty *louis* for it by the beautiful lady. I have put it on my table.'[35]

Brillat was not disciplined, and the wrath of the First Cousul soon blew over. On 14 July 1804 Brillat, together with the rest of the bench, was awarded the Légion d'honneur. Brillat did not treat his sash and buttonhole with the levity of Henrion de Pansey; he was proud to wear his ribbon, and his loyalty towards the First Consul received a decided fillip.

That year Brillat returned to Belley as usual. To celebrate the end of a successful harvest in his vineyard on the Côte-Grêle, Brillat threw a ball at Vieu.

My vintage was pleasant. I've done a lot of shooting and not bad shooting at that. . . . Having promised me in writing that she would come and dance on the Feast of Saint Hubert,† Madame La Bâtie broke her word and stayed in Tallissieu to gossip with Jeanette [unknown]. That afternoon I entertained sixty people to lunch and the same number that evening at dinner. The ball lasted from three in the afternoon to seven in the morning.[36]

His harvest over and the results of his shooting prowess devoured by his sixty guests, Brillat returned to Paris and the court.

The court had changed its name. Earlier that year Brillat had written to Rostaing of the new pomp that was planned by Napoleon, and of his own role in it. At the end of May 1804 Brillat told his friend of Napoleon's decision to make himself Emperor.

---

*Jacques Augustin was best known for his miniatures.

†Saint Hubert is the patron saint of huntsmen.

The First Consul is soon to make a journey to Brussels. I am assured that sometime now the Senate will be given instructions to name him Emperor of the Gauls. General Murat will be appointed Vice-President of the Italian Republic. . . . The fate of the *Tribunal de cassation* has been decided: it is to be called the *Cour de cassation*. The title of Consul is to go. Cambacérès will become *Archichancelier* and President of the Senate . . . there will be eight grand officers of the Empire, and probably eight or twelve marshals of France. The imperial household is to be run on lines roughly equivalent to the court of Louis XV.[37]

A month after Brillat's return to Paris, on 2 December 1804, Napoleon crowned himself Emperor in the presence of Pope Pius VII, and of Counsellor Brillat-Savarin of the *Cour de cassation*.[38]

The new counsellor had much to occupy him that winter. He was an assiduous member of the Society for the Encouragement of Industry and of the Académie Celtique, the forerunner of the Royal Society of French Antiquarians. He still practised his violin, taking stock of changes in technique brought about by Baillot, Professor of Violin at the Conservatoire, when he introduced the longer bow. In an idle moment, Brillat composed a Mass for the church of Saint-Sulpice.[39]

As a result of his act of kindness towards Madame Récamier, Brillat found himself admitted to the inner circle of her acquaintance, a regular dinner guest at the Château de Clichy and at their town house in the rue du Mont Blanc. The house built for the banker Jacques Necker and acquired by the Récamiers in 1798, was the scene of Madame Récamier's sumptuous balls.[40]

The *dîners* of fashionable Paris were getting later and later. They had been pushed into the late afternoon by the sessions of the revolutionary assemblies, and now most people dined at six at the earliest. A midday meal had therefore been instituted as a solid *déjeuner* for those too peckish to wait so long. At six Brillat often found himself ringing the bell at the Hôtel de Necker to be received by cousin Juliette. On one such occasion Madame Récamier told Brillat of the visit she had just made to a gourmand clergyman who, it being a Holy Day of Obligation, was tucking into an abstemious feast of soup with a *coulis* of crayfish, a salmon trout and a tunnyfish omelette. Madame Récamier gave her cousin full details of the priest's omelette, and it later became one of Brillat's culinary specialities.[41]

Brillat toyed with a project of spending some time in Italy, lured by the chance of a different sort of game from that habitually found in the Valromey:

Paris is excessively gloomy; everybody has gone to the country and I myself am off as soon as I can get leave. At the moment thousands of navvies are working either at the Tuileries or on the new roads being built around it.

All you say about Italy does not take away my desire to go there. I am singularly fond of both art and women, and I am told that both those commodities are available in unlimited supply. I hope that I shall not leave this earth without having shown my august features in that land.[42]

If Brillat did visit Italy that summer or autumn, he has left no record of the fact. In his next letter to Rostaing he writes again of the 'improvements' being made to the city by the construction of the rue de Rivoli and other projects, and of the new fashions for men and women. 'I have seen embroidery by the quintal, lace by the kilometre, and diamonds by the heap', not to mention 'pretty tits by the hundred', a result of the prevailing fashion for low-cut dresses. 'I get excited just thinking about it.'

This particularly prodigious feat of voyeurism took place at the Emperor Napoleon's New Year reception. For the time being the Empire retained the revolutionary calendar, and the date of the reception was therefore 23 September. Brillat was pleased to tell his friend that the Emperor had 'twice graciously deigned to address himself to me'.[43]

The same letter relates misfortunes in the Récamier household.

Jacques Récamier has just recovered from an inflammation of the chest, but he got off with a fright. There are few men who would have caused such a sensation by their deaths: every day he had as many as four hundred people leaving their cards at his door, and trade would have regarded his death as a public calamity . . .[44]

The callers' fears were justified: Récamier had overstretched his bank and was on the verge of bankruptcy. On 13 November 1805 he summoned a meeting of his creditors to inform them that he would not be able to meet their payments. His was one of a wave of bankruptcies at the time, which pushed the Emperor to make the Banque de France a state institution.

That autumn, Brillat moved for the last time. His new address was 23 rue des Filles Saint-Thomas* on the corner of the rue de Richelieu.

---

*Now No. 11. The building still stands; the ground-floor shop sells safes and strong-boxes.

The building had been put up in 1738, and had been rented out as furnished rooms until that year; Brillat's apartment, on the first floor, above a chemist's shop,[45] was part of a new conversion.[46]

VII

Brillat must have felt singularly at home above the chemist. He was still as passionately interested in medicine as ever and was delighted to give one or two of his circle advice and prescriptions. He must have felt a particular delight in treating his old Belley friend Antide de Rubat for over-taxing himself in bed. Brillat's cure involved feeding his patient on hot chocolate thickened with egg yolks.[47] Another man who trusted his medical advice was the obese duc de Luynes, whom Brillat had first encountered at the Constituent Assembly. Luynes became a Senator in 1803, and died four years later: he had grown so abominably fat that he had difficulty staying awake for much of the day.[48]

Brillat's interest in medicine led to an equal interest in its practitioners, and he was intensely proud of the achievements of his two godsons. A close friend was Napoleon's physician Jean Nicolas Corvisart, later made an imperial baron for his services. His cures were often of a rough and no-nonsense sort: he prescribed a mixture of egg-yolks and milk for Napoleon's chronic constipation. Bonaparte liked the nostrum so much that he was still addicted to it on Saint Helena. On another occasion, Corvisart found his master suffering from lumbago:

> asking everyone to leave the room, he had the sovereign undressed and asked him to press against the edge of a pedestal table. He then slapped each of his buttocks with as great force as he was able to muster. Surprised and furious, Napoleon turned round sharply, ready to express his disbelief at such insolence. His wrath melted immediately, however, for in turning around so energetically the painful contraction of his back muscles magically disappeared.[49]

Corvisart was not always disrespectful towards Napoleon. Once when the two were shooting at Meudon, near Paris, a local wine was brought to the Emperor. At the first sip, Napoleon grimaced.

'Corvisart,' he said, 'taste this wine for me – and take care, it is bad enough to frighten horses.'

'It's rough.'

'Rough! It's like swallowing a thistle: it must be this year's, wine.'

'Oh no!' replied Corvisart gaily. 'It's next year's, at the very least.'*[50]

Corvisart drank champagne with the 'fine and abundant food for which his cook had a reputation, to the quality of which even Brillat-Savarin in person bore witness.'[51] Corvisart was sent his champagne by a doctor in Bar-le-Duc who wanted to keep in favour with the country's first physician. The wine, however, had a debilitating effect on Corvisart, as Brillat himself observed.

> Doctor Corvisart, who could be extremely nice when he wanted to be, drank only well-chilled champagne. At the beginning of a meal, while the other guests were still busy with their food, he was noisy and full of anecdotes. On the other hand, by the time we had reached dessert and the conversation began to liven up, he became serious, taciturn and sometimes even morose.[52]

The reason for this, according to Brillat, lies in the nature of the wine itself. Champagne 'is exciting in its first effects . . . and stupefying thereafter.'[53] Brillat puts this down to the effect of carbonic gas.

The gourmand doctor was justly proud of his cellar, 'which in its heyday contained shelves which were well provisioned and . . . carefully labelled. Much later, when he could no longer drink even a drop of this bacchic liquor he loved so much, he made it a point of honour not to allow stocks to run down when he was entertaining so that he could give his friends a dignified welcome when they visited him in his retreat. When he died he still possessed four barrels of ordinary wine and four hundred bottles of fine wines of different *crus*.'[54]

Brillat became friendly with Corvisart in 1806, the year of Austerlitz and Jena. Brillat still observed the progress of the imperial armies with pride, glorying in the achievements of his friends and relations. Frédéric Brillat-Savarin was now commanding a battalion in Germany, their nephew Guigard and Prosper Sibuet were in Naples with Joseph Bonaparte, where they met Jacques-Rose Récamier's brother Alphonse, acting as a courier between the Emperor and his brother.

---

*Paris wines never enjoyed much of a reputation. Brillat notes that the most famous of these, Suresnes, was what the Germans call a *Dreimännerwein*: to swallow it you need two men to hold your arms and a third to pour it down your throat.

France is about to be surrounded by princes [wrote Brillat to Rostaing on 30 March]; this is the fruit of our victories: Prince Murat will get Juliers, Cleves and Berg, while Berthier gets Neufchâtel and Valengin. It is believed that Prince Louis will be given Holland, while Prince Joseph has accepted the crown of Naples.

. . . the Emperor told his council that sixty million men were subject to his authority and this calculation is not exaggerated when one thinks that everyone obeys him, from Portugal to Bavaria . . .[55]

On 9 June Brillat sent more news to his friend in Lyon; this time he wanted to tell Rostaing about the visit of the *Cour de cassation* to Louis Bonaparte and his wife, *née* Hortense de Beauharnais, before their departure for Amsterdam.

As a member of the bench, I paid a visit to the King and Queen of Holland. The Queen received us with much grace, and when my name was called King Louis said he already knew of my reputation. I swear that I scarcely know to whom I owe this compliment. I lowered my gaze with a modesty which you would have found enchanting. The royal family is leaving on Wednesday.[56]

Brillat does not tell Rostaing whether the reputation which had reached the ears of Napoleon's brother was that of a solid jurist and former Constituent, or a roguish libertine and gourmand. Perhaps Louis had been told something of his sense of humour. There is a story which belongs to this time concerning a dinner at which the *convives* had received a turkey liberally stuffed with truffles. The old lady sitting next to Brillat asked him where truffles grew: 'A vos pieds, Madame,' was his reply. The old lady was perplexed. To salvage the situation, another guest explained that the judge had meant 'at the feet of charming women'. She was consoled by this compliment, and more so by the person who had issued it. At the end of the meal someone else asked Brillat the same question and, apparently oblivious of the woman who was standing beside him, he replied, 'At the feet of old oak trees'.[57]

Jests of this nature were normally reserved for his holidays in the Valromey. Brillat was back in Belley, as usual, in September, in time to harvest his vineyard. There to greet him at the door of the *gentilhommière* were his gouty sisters, Joson and Padon, who lay in bed all year until the day before their brother was due to arrive, and went back to bed the day following his departure for Paris. Joson and Padon had recently written their wills. Their dear brother

Anthelme was to be the recipient of all their wordly goods. Meanwhile, changes were taking place at Vieu. Later that year Brillat acquired the land of a Madame Pérrachon, adding to his estates in the Valromey.[58]

Brillat must have been still in Vieu when he heard the first news of the French victories over the Prussian armies at Auerstädt and Jena. On 16 October he wrote to Rostaing with boyish pride, expressing his full confidence in the policy of Bonaparte: 'We've beaten the Prussians. We captured 32 pieces of ordnance and 6,000 prisoners; We have killed Prince Louis-Ferdinand and many more. It appears that these are the forward units of their army which we have wiped out in this way.'[59] The Treaty of Tilsit which followed dismantled the achievements of King Frederick the Great.

VIII

Prussia came to have a rather different significance for Brillat-Savarin, for it was a Prussian prince who led to his receiving a second token of affection from Juliette Récamier. Brillat seems to have been instrumental in frustrating a suicide attempt by Madame Récamier while she was in the throes of an emotional entanglement with Prince August of Prussia. He retrieved from her possession both the opium pills by means of which she proposed to kill herself, and a revealing suicide note addressed to her husband.[60]

Madame Récamier's reward to Brillat for his kindness in saving her life and marriage was a terracotta bust of herself. The sculptor, Joseph Chinard, had produced several copies of the original terracotta so that Monsieur and Madame Récamier might give them as presents. Chinard had made drawings for the bust during a visit to the rue du Mont Blanc in 1801, and it was finished by 1805. Later a marble bust was also produced.*[61]

Brillat was very proud of his sculpture. Few in his immediate circle could claim anything remotely comparable to two such personal presents from the most beautiful woman in Paris. When Frédéric Brillat-Savarin and the elderly Dr Dubois came to the rue des Filles Saint-Thomas for a day-long bout of gustatory self-indulgence later that year, Brillat proudly showed off his treasures. He may not, how-

---

*This, and a terracotta, can now be seen in the Musée des Beaux Arts in Lyon.

ever, have anticipated the effect they would have on the old gentleman or his brother:

> They were so enchanted that the thick-lipped doctor kissed the portrait while the captain abused the sculpture in such a licentious way that I was compelled to intervene, for if all the admirers of the original were to do as much, that voluptuously shaped bosom would soon be in the same state as the toe of Saint Peter in Rome, which pilgrims have worn away with their kisses.[62]

Brillat was not expending all his time on frivolous pursuits, as is indicated by a slim pamphlet which appeared in May 1808, under the lengthy title *Théorie judiciaire: fragment d'un ouvrage manuscrit intitulé; Théorie judiciaire par M. Brillat-Savarin, membre de la Cour de cassation et de la légion d'honneur.* The fragment dealt with the selection of judges, and announced that the full work would appear in a few months' time; but it never did, and it is uncertain how much was ever committed to paper. In his pamphlet Brillat opposed the school of thinking which now prevails in France, that the *magistrature* should receive a training different from that of the lawyers who plead before them. Brillat held that it was essential for a judge to have had a wide experience of pleading in the courts before being selected to sit on the bench. Similarly, judges should not be elected to the higher courts until they had served in the pyramid of departmental courts. Brillat was careful to add that judges were not like generals in this respect: while the bench should not be open to candidates under 30 and a *Cour de cassation* judge should be 40 or more, a general might very well show his mettle at a far earlier age. He was well aware that his Emperor was not yet 40.[63]

Brillat further believed that a judge should possess a reasonable private income, which together with his stipends would render him less accessible to bribery. But he should be no Croesus; 'the judge, happy with the pleasures derived from friendship, from the love of science and the arts, should be a stranger to all those transient joys which come from pure luxury, which wear out the soul, dissipate the body and serve no other purpose than to squander fortunes . . .'[64]

Brillat may not have been completely candid about his own pleasures, but the *Théorie judiciaire* was well-timed: while it was with the printer, Napoleon decided to elevate the entire bench of the *Cour de cassation* to the new, imperial nobility. On 26 April 1808 Brillat-Savarin became a *chevalier de l'Empire.*[65]

As recently as 1801, in *Vues et projets*, Brillat had published views somewhat opposed to his pride in this ennoblement. However, even before 1808 he had at times granted himself the tell-tale 'de' of French nobility. In 1803 he had gone so far as to have his 'arms' carved on to his pew in the church at Vieu. Many in the valley must have laughed at his expense, if they remembered his revolutionary speeches on the subject.[66]

Brillat was by no means unique in this hypocrisy: most of his friends would have been delighted to become part of the new nobility of Napoleonic France, even nobles of the *ancien régime*. Visiting him in Vieu, attending Mass with him in his newly carved pew, few of them would have seen anything remotely out of the ordinary. It was all part of the process of forgetting the more embarrassing moments of the revolutionary years.

His trips to the village church were never more than a formality of Brillat's rural life. He was still a sceptic. The real joys of Vieu were the shooting, the feasting and the harmless flirtations which Brillat carried on with the wives of the Belley *notables*. In September there was the pleasure of the quail shoot, up near the village of Hotonnes. In *La Physiologie du goût* Brillat tells us that the best moment was always the harvesting of the grain, when the quail population was condensed into an ever-diminishing parcel of corn. On one of these shoots a sudden strong wind led to the rapid consumption of all the decent wine the huntsmen had loaded on to the 'supply donkey', and when they came to dine off a regal dish of spinach cooked in quail fat, the party had to content themselves with wine from the local tavern, which was 'hardly even as good as the wine of Suresnes'.[67]

Charles Monselet complained that Brillat had an unpleasant habit of appearing at the court with a decomposing woodcock in his pocket, so that he might be able to verify the state of its putrefaction and determine the best moment to put it on the spit.[68] Later writers have contested this. Tendret, for example, says that 'He was too well brought up to inflict on others anything so disagreeable as breathing a foul odour, and he was not ignorant of the fact that an unplucked bird, tied up in a bag and deprived of air, would develop a nasty taste.'[69]

Good taste may have prevented Brillat from bringing decaying game into the court, but he was not scrupulously clean in his person. His early biographer Callet takes Tendret's line about the woodcock, but asserts from the evidence of a Monsieur W. Roux who had it from his grandmother, Madame César Roux, that 'Brillat's hands were so little washed or tended that once, when he was telling the story of having killed a hare ten days before, his interlocutor expressing doubts, Brillat showed her his hands, saying "There you are, see, the blood's still there." ' Callet says, compassionately, that Brillat must have gone through a complete overhaul on his return to Paris, before entering the salon of Madame Récamier.[70]

Tendret is responsible for a glimpse of the light-hearted chevalier de Brillat-Savarin that winter of 1808, at dinner in the noble Faubourg Saint-Germain in Paris. After the meal, the young girls of the household expressed a strong desire to dance,

> but none of them knew music. One of the guests, the abbé de Bombelles, who had been recently elevated to the bishopric of Amiens, sat down at the piano. M. Brillat-Savarin took up a violin and the dancing began, led by this singular orchestra composed of bishop and counsellor from the *Cour de cassation*.[71]

CHAPTER NINE

The Monarchist

I

O N 16 NOVEMBER 1813 Brillat's Empire came to an end. Napoleon engaged the allied armies at the Battle of Leipzig: four days later the haggard Emperor was forced to admit to his first personal defeat in battle.[1] Within six months Prussians, Austrians, Russians and Britons were occupying a defeated France and Brillat had to make some rapid decisions about his future.

For the first time since the Middle Ages, Paris was occupied by foreign troops. While the wild-eyed soldiers of the Allied armies roamed the streets gawping at the unfamiliar luxuries and grandeur of the French capital, their officers availed themselves of the most harmless of the Revolution's many achievements: the restaurants. The most popular were the grandest: Véry, Méot and, above all, Beauvilliers. Brillat must have contemplated this spectacle with distaste, as he later wrote:

> you saw the vehicles of every nation constantly parked in front of his [Beauvilliers'] door. He got to know the generals of all the foreign armies and ended up by speaking all their languages, or at least as much of them as he needed for his business.[2]

Parisian restaurant-goers quit the Palais-Royal in disgust; Brillat and his friends migrated to the Rocher de Cancale in the rue Montorgeuil. Here he is said to have met Talma, and also Grimod de La Reynière, but in the latter's case this is unlikely, for he had already retired to Villiers-sur-Orge.[3] The Rocher de Cancale, however, was certainly Grimod's favourite haunt in Paris, and he summed up the chef Baleine's ability in these terms (it helps to remember that *baleine* means whale):

> M. Baleine is now in a position to swallow the majority of his rivals, like the cetacean of the Holy Writ who engulfed the Prophets, and whose name he bears; these new Jonahs, disgorged and not digested, will be forced to proclaim the glory of the Rocher de Cancale in every corner of the earth. This restaurant is now the Rock of Tenerife in the gourmand universe.[4]

In general, the many changes of regime which had occurred over the past 26 years had made the French very adaptable. Who would have guessed that so many of the leading Terrorists could so easily assume the courtly, devotional character of the Empire? The *Cour de cassation*, entrenched in privilege by the defeated Emperor, decided to grasp the nettle. On 9 April, just six days after Napoleon's abdication and before the king appeared in the city, the *Cour de cassation*

> solemnly quit the Palace of Justice and proceeded in a body to the Tuileries to present their homage to *Monsieur*, the comte d'Artois, the Lieutenant-General of the kingdom. At its head was the First President Muraire, whom the Emperor had just rescued from a lamentable bankruptcy. Immediately next to him, grinning his eternal smile, was the Prosecutor General Merlin [de Douai], who seemed the only man that day to have forgotten that he had voted for the death of Louis XVI. Other regicides were apparent in the cortège: Lamarque, today referring to Louis XVIII as *Louis le désiré*, or Oudot, who had voted for death 'in the interests of humanity', and others.[5]

Henrion de Pansey kept a cool head – after all, he had nothing to conceal from the Bourbons. On Louis XVIII's return he was appointed Minister of Justice, a post he held for only 45 days. On entering the ministry Henrion told his staff, with a 'paternal kindness appropriate to his advanced years':

> *Messieurs*, I am unlikely to remain long enough in your company to do any good; but you may be certain of one thing: that I will do you no harm.[6]

Henrion was as good as his word; virtually the only recorded action of his six-week ministry was the liberation of victims of imperial justice who were languishing in the cells. On leaving office he demonstrated his real political allegiance by becoming president of the council to the duc d'Orléans, later Louis-Philippe, King of the French. In honour of his loyalty to the liberal future monarch, the painter Couder painted Henrion as Principal of the College of Reichenau in Switzerland, where Louis-Philippe taught maths during his years as an émigré.[7]

Brillat was not sanguine. Once again his world had collapsed about him. He returned to Belley and sulked. It would have been uncharacteristic of him, however, to sulk for long. He did two positive things: he wrote a new section for his book on the judiciary, and he sent off a letter to an old friend from the Constituent Assembly, the abbé de Montesquiou.

The paper on judicial theory was published a few months later as *De la Cour suprême; deuxième fragment d'un ouvrage de Théorie judiciaire par Brillat de Savarin, chevalier, conseiller en la Cour de cassation*. Brillat's message is clear from the very beginning: the need to safeguard the law despite changes of regime. 'Everything which is the creation of man carries within it the germ of its own destruction, and legislation, although made to shape the future, is not immune from the ravages of time.'[8] The Supreme Court (read *Cour de cassation*) plays an important role in preventing law from obsolescence, 'seeking to discover the presumed aim of the legislator by reference and cross reference'.[9] Brillat warns against any attempt to revive the *parlements* of the *ancien régime*, with their confusing multiplicity of legal systems: such a revival was being advocated by certain members of the new king's entourage, including the new Minister of the Interior, the abbé de Montesquiou.[10]

Brillat is careful to point out that too slavish a desire on the part of the judges to please the legislature is as dangerous as too hostile an opposition. The courts, he says, should retain their independence (it was a moot point whether the French courts after 1789 had achieved this) from both the legislature and the executive. He condemns the new *Conseil d'état* and any project to invest it with powers to overrule the decisions of the higher courts.

Brillat finishes his short work with a word of guidance for the new king, a plea for him to retain the established bench and not to dismantle the system of justice created by the Revolution and the Empire. The new monarch should bear in mind, he writes,

more than everything else, the lessons of history which teach us that the courts must be sacrosanct, that the judge owes the citizen a total account of his life; that he refuses bravely to countenance any obvious iniquity, that whenever a tyrannical power has sought to oppress the honour, the life and the property of a citizen, its first objective has always been to reduce the power of the judiciary; this was behind the committees [public safety, etc.], lists of *émigrés*, military tribunals [i.e., revolutionary tribunals], police measures, special courts and other creatures of circumstance which have never been employed but for the misery of the people, and which often result in the unhappiness of kings . . .[11]

Brillat probably thought a measured plea of this kind would not be damaging, and might come to the King's attention. How the paper was regarded in official circles is not known. It would seem that it was his letter to the abbé de Montesquiou which did him the most good.

François-Xavier-Marc-Antoine, duc de Montesquiou-Fézensac, abbot of Beaulieu (1756–1832), had been elected to the Constituent Assembly as a member of the first estate. The abbé was not one of those clergymen who had rallied to the third estate; with aristocratic disdain, he held out against joint sessions until the order from Louis XVI enforced them. Even then he fought hard to retain the privileges of his order. After the fall of the Tuileries in August 1792 Montesquiou wisely emigrated to England, returning only after Thermidor, when he instantly became involved in royalist politics. Following Napoleon's abdication he favoured the resurrection of many features of the *ancien régime*, including its legal institutions, the *parlements*. On 26 April 1814 he was named a member of the new king's *Conseil d'état*. On 13 May he became Minister of the Interior.[12]

Brillat wrote to the abbé on 6 October. Having reminded Montesquiou of their acquaintance at the time of the Constituent Assembly, he asked to be recommended to the King; 'the love of the common good, which unites all ex-Constituents', he claimed, made him wish to communicate to Montesquiou his 'fears for the continuation of his position';[13] 'If he had emigrated, it was because of his attachment to the monarchy', he lied boldly.[14] He was careful to use his new aristocratic style, and signed himself 'Brillat de Savarin'. As it turned out, he had had little cause for alarm; except for some of the more outrageous regicides who had found a refuge in the appeal court, the judges were confirmed in their positions in February of the following year.

Even so, this meant a fairly long wait before the now staunchly monarchist judge knew what his fate would be under the Bourbon king. He couldn't spend every day shooting or trying to lure the local matrons into bed so, at 59, he decided to try his hand at fiction. He wrote five stories in all: 'Ma Première Chute', written for Mesdames Boscary de La Grange, 'Le Voyage à Arras', 'Ma Culotte Rouge', 'L'Inconnu' and 'Le Rêve'. Apart from a few fragments, all five have been destroyed.

Persistent forces have been at work to obscure the real, earthy nature of Brillat-Savarin. Published extracts of the letters to Rostaing omit all but a few details from a correspondence which must have been notably frank on the subject of Brillat's dalliance, particularly with whores. Madame de Jubécourt burned Brillat's letters to his friend, the Bugey rake Garan de La Morflans. The *contes* were probably destroyed in the 1920s, a hundred years after the death of their author, at a time when interest in his work was increasing. In the 1890s the *contes* not only still existed, but formed part of a yearly ritual in the Valromey to celebrate the village fair. A lunch was served in the *gentil-hommière* at Vieu, presided over by the bust of Brillat-Savarin:

> We eat at twelve noon. We drink Côte-Grêle, the wine from Brillat-Savarin's vineyard, and we eat the traditional square pâté, called for this reason *l'oreiller de la belle Aurore* (*la belle Aurore's* pillow), named after the mother of Brillat-Savarin, Claudine-Aurore Récamier. After dinner we read some pages from the unpublished stories of this charming, witty author . . .[15]

Even Tendret was of the opinion that the stories were unpublishable. In his delightful book *La Table au pays de Brillat-Savarin* he prints a passage from one of the tales, in which Brillat mocks the sort of prudery which would try to sweep what he saw as harmless ribaldry under the carpet:

> How ridiculous is the convention which would have us refrain from describing in detail those things which are both the most pleasant and the most useful [to society]. There is continual talk of pistols, swords and even cannons. In the story which will follow, *Mesdames*, you will find some highly painted passages, but the words will be chaste, and such as, handled skilfully, could even form part of a homily delivered by the abbé de Lamennais.*[16]

---

*Jean-Marie-Félicité de Lamennais, religious revivalist, author of *Réflexions sur l'état de l'église*.

The destruction of the stories, never confirmed by the family, caused an understandable outrage among Brillatins in the 1920s. In the 1930s, Dr Joseph Récamier wrote:

I am the only surviving person to have heard these stories read in full, by Charles Lenormand in the course of lunch at Châtelard where Georges Brillat lived. This was in 1925. I am convinced that they will be found again one day. I can still see the binding in red leather. Madeleine Brillat must have put them away on the death of her brother, but I don't think they have been burnt.[17]

In the 1920s Curnonsky and Marcel Rouff had made some effort to relocate the stories. At the house of Lucien Tendret's son, Paul, they heard some fragments which were enough to convince them of their literary merit.

They are in the purest tradition of French literature, in our opinion superior to *La Physiologie du goût* – in literary terms – in a style which is fluent, economic, and displays a subtle irony, with a lively vigour, a delicious charm essentially similar to the *contes* of Voltaire or the *Liaisons Dangereuses* . . .

These stories are in the hands of the last descendants of Brillat-Savarin, who swore an oath to their father that they would never publish the masterpieces of their great ancestor on the pretext of their objection to an unbuttoned earthiness which is nevertheless as far from pornography as *grande cuisine* is from a formal banquet. It appears that even now they are preparing to destroy them: literature and French culture have an interest in preventing this sacrilege from being carried out.[18]

Despite the strong words of Curnonsky and Rouff, and the conviction of Dr Récamier, it is the opinion of informed local scholars that the descendants of Brillat's brother François-Xavier did indeed destroy the stories. Apart from the extracts quoted by Tendret and Herriot (see below), one sizeable fragment has survived. Given its unique character it may be well to present it in full. (It appears to owe more to *Tristram Shandy* than to Voltaire.)

The Saint Quentin Inn
A Fragment from 'Voyage à Arras'

Having nothing further to detain me and thinking only of my departure, I was spending the morning dreaming in my bedroom when I was aroused by a gentle tapping at my door. I hastened to open it and there to my extreme delight was Lucie, Lucie indeed: 'What, you? My dearest angel!' I said, drawing her into the room. 'I thought I had lost you forever, I'm besotted with you . . .'

'Monsieur,' she said, blushing, 'I'm very embarrassed. I have obtained a place on the mail coach which is leaving any moment, I have no news of my luggage and I don't wish to lose it and, after all your kindness towards me on the journey, I hope that if it turns up you'll have the goodness to send it on to me; and should it not, do for me only what you would do for yourself.' 'Wicked girl! You know how delighted I am to be of service; however, you will have to understand that if I am to be the errand boy you will have to give me a tip, and that means three full kisses at the very minimum.'

'Good Lord! I have never heard of such a thing!'

'It is the most ancient of practices, and a complete kiss, my dear, is a kiss given and a kiss given back.'

As we spoke, I had taken the adorable creature in my arms, and after one or two objections, she abandoned the prettiest mouth in the world to my kisses.

The poor little thing had scant idea of the intoxicating character of the embraces which she had licensed me to perform; I, on the other hand, was only too aware of their power, and though she had long since paid me my dues in full, I had deliberately failed to keep count. Suddenly, I noticed that tears stood in her eyes and that the pallor of the lily was warring with the pinkness of her complexion . . . (It is never in vain that a professor makes an observation of this sort.)

....

....

Mesdames, it would take you three days to fill in that line and a half, and as the subject matter is of the most scabrous nature, it might heat your imaginations and inflame your senses to such an extent that were the devil to knock at the door during these moments of exaltation, why, who knows? You might even open it!

In faith, I have enough sins of my own without being encumbered with those of persons to whom I can scarcely be said to owe a duty. I shall therefore reveal all, and as for the more scrupulous of my audience, well, let them avert their gaze. For no matter how edifying her previous reading, she will never have heard anything to compare with what follows

....

Lucie remained immobile in my arms, her face was pale, her eyes closed, her cheeks wan, but her bosom heaved, and it is this last symptom which distinguishes a swoon from a fainting fit. This state is not new to me; I was aware of the course of action which the severe rules of masculine honour imposed on me, and I carried it out without so much as a sigh.

I laid out my sweet patient in the position best suited for the cure, and lifting all those veils which might get in the way, feasted my eyes on the treasures which offered themselves to my gaze, thanking God for the rewards which attach to good works. I acted in haste, as I had a vague notion that any further preparation would be vain, and possibly even dangerous.

I was armed to the teeth for this lovely cure, and soon I was installed in a charming nook which seemed expressly made for my use. This was pleasing since I had on other occasions come across examples which had, without question, been created for others.

At the moment when I began to employ my instrument, Lucie's eyes half-opened, but she closed them again immediately, either because she had not entirely recovered consciousness or because she realized that it was too late to put a stop to my activities, or perhaps, indeed, because of a certain ingrained instinct which made her fear to spoil the effects of a remedy which had become so indispensable to her.

I therefore operated, not with the speed of a disciple of Esculapius,* but with the circumspection of a seasoned yet passionate practitioner who proceeds wisely to his goal, and who knows from past experience of this particular field that there is time for everything.

A treatment so expertly given could hardly fail to produce signs of success. Lucie didn't open her eyes; but the rose tints returned to her cheeks, while her lips resumed their normal crimson. She said not a word, but her charming mouth opened in the loveliest way and informed me I was not working for an ungrateful woman. While these things were taking place in the upper hemisphere, events of no less interest were taking place in the Antipodes.

Soon, scarcely perceptible movements informed me that my transports of pleasure were shared; later a shivering sensation from within and some fractured sighs warned me that the time had come; the storm was building up . . . I discharged a volley . . . the fusillade of pleasure rang out loud and clear as a double storm broke over Saint-Quentin.

Dear, sweet, child! May the Heavens bless her with their most exquisite favours for her *gauche* defence, the virginal purity of her charms, her transports of joy, and, above all, for the grace with which she exclaimed when she came to her senses, 'Oh, Lord! And we were going to part for ever.'

I replied with the gentlest of caresses, and it was at this moment that

---

*i.e., of a medical student.

I noticed that in my haste to invade I had neglected her breasts which were worthy of a thousand libations.

Lucie clearly feared the results of this discovery, for, giving the impression of answering a question rather than speaking to me, she said: 'I believe you are expecting a visit from my aunt.'

That idea made me envisage consequences of the most tedious nature, for which I was scarcely prepared. I metamorphosed in the twinkling of an eye.

Together we set about repairing the damage done to Lucie's clothing and general appearance in the fray. She then gave me a look filled with grace and modesty, took my arm, and out we strolled.

'Monsieur,' she said to me on the way, 'if you should ever think of Lucie, do not judge her too harshly; I could not foresee what occurred and the distress you have caused me is a sorrow I shall have to bear, but not a fault for which I should reproach myself.'

My eyes alone could give her a reply for we were reaching our destination – and that language cannot be translated.

The time had come. We found the carriage at the door and the aunt on the threshold: tall, thin, old and swarthy, she certainly had an overwhelming compulsion to complain, but when she saw my grey hair, my height and my decoration her features melted, and she offered me fulsome thanks for a consideration for which I believed myself already amply rewarded . . .

The mail coach was in a hurry to leave and its haste cut short the ceremonial. I placed Lucie inside and gave her a goodbye kiss, I waved to the aunt and thus we said *adieu*.[19]

Fantasy or personal reminiscence? The reader will observe that the hero of this mild pornography is none other than our appeal-court judge: tall, grey-haired, with his Légion d'honneur proudly displayed in his buttonhole. We will probably never know more, unless by some miracle other papers of Brillat's should reappear. The questions remain: if this fragment survived, what were those pieces committed to the flames like? And, to what extent does this fragment provide a key to Brillat's sexuality? To the last question I should say, probably a great deal.

II

In February 1815 Brillat put down his pen and travelled to Paris to join his colleagues in the new, royalist *Cour de cassation*. The need for loyalty to the new sovereign was to be brief: on 1 March Napoleon landed at Antibes and by 19 March, Louis had decided that he could not defend his throne and had fled to Belgium. The King of Elba was once again Emperor of the French.

The judges of the *Cour de cassation* were in little doubt as to the right course of action; on 27 March all 37 members of the bench signed the *adresse Muraire*, referring to Bonaparte as the 'sole true and legitimate sovereign of the Empire'.[20] After news reached them of the outcome of the Battle of Waterloo, the same 37 signed a similar document, known as the *adresse de Sèze*, which pledged support for Louis XVIII. The two documents make amusing reading now; the one, as Balzac put it, 'sullied by ignoble insults against the Bourbons . . .', the other 'filled with curses against the usurper'.[21]

Brillat's apologists have put his behaviour down to what one of them is pleased to call 'the demoralizing effect of revolutions'.[22] In reality, it was just one more example of the political acrobatics so common – perhaps even so necessary – at the time.

However, Brillat was undoubtedly happier under the Napoleonic regime. He had little faith in the Bourbon restoration, dragging his heels in Belley with a fabricated 'indisposition' while he scribbled away at pornography to pass the time away from the fleshpots of the Palais-Royal. Napoleon's return evidently came as a relief. In April Brillat received a letter from his friend Rostaing, who had been in Grenoble when Napoleon arrived there in the course of his triumphal journey through Upper Provence and the Dauphiné. Rostaing, by now a far more convinced adherent of the Bourbon cause than Brillat, had called for a spirited defence of the city. Resistance swiftly collapsed, however, and the people, unable to present the Emperor with the keys to the city, presented him instead with the shattered remains of one of the city gates which they had smashed down with axes in order to let him enter.

Rostaing had written to Brillat to convey his fears for the future, and possibly also to suggest that Brillat might find it difficult to explain away his attitude to the Bourbon restoration. Brillat wrote back to Rostaing expressing his confidence in the Emperor:

> he has easily re-established control and I don't believe the disease is incurable. I have received no response at all to my letters, which have perhaps been stopped or lost. Whatever happens, this is my advice: if you were to find it convenient to attach yourself to the Emperor and to

ask for a position, I would personally take on the responsibility of presenting your suit. Make up your mind.[23]

Rostaing remained loyal to the Bourbons. And despite their long friendship, Brillat's willingness to seek favours from Bonaparte proved the last straw for Rostaing. There is just one more letter from Brillat, sent on 1 May 1816, nearly a year after Louis' resumption of the throne; it is clear from the text that the friendship had come to a bitter end:

Divine Jean-Antoine, having regard to certain recent events, and notably a visit I made to your lodgings the other day at a time when you must have been at home, I fear that a frost has fallen between us. I am annoyed for both of us, for I have already reached, and you will soon be at, an age where a thirty-year-old friendship cannot be replaced.[24]

Rostaing was rewarded by his king with the title of *chevalier de Saint Louis*, and made director of the personnel of the General Staff. In 1846 he died, a baron, at his château at Beyrin in Savoy, at the age of 82.[25]

III

Brillat-Savarin rode the storm. Only those who had voted for the death of the King's brother, Louis XVI, were removed from the *Cour de cassation*.

As Brillat neared 60 his two-month holiday in the Valromey became ever more necessary to him. In Vieu and Belley, not only did the 'delicious egotism' which so appealed to Curnonsky come to the fore, but Brillat's generosity became more noticeable.[26] Richerand contended plausibly that Brillat's homeland 'was his unique passion'[27] – those fertile valleys of the Bugey, those last outcrops of the Jura which finally flatten out as they come up against the meandering Rhône.

On the way down Brillat stopped to see friends near Dijon. Often he stopped for a night at La Burbanche near Pugieu to see his friend Dr Genand. According to Callet, Genand used to tell a story of his old servant Pierre: slipping down to the doctor's cellar one day to enjoy a bottle of his best wine, he was unaware of the doctor himself, concealed behind a cask.

The valet, as we called them in those days, knocked back an ample swig from a bottle of old Manicle and shouted 'A ta santâ, Genand!' ['Your health, Genand!']

'Grâ macie, Pierre' ['Thank you very much, Pierre'], Genand replied in a sepulchral tone. Pierre fainted at the sound of this voice, from beyond the grave as it seemed, and never more did he touch his master's wine.[28]

Before reaching the Bugey, Brillat liked to make a stopover in Bourg to indulge in his passion for the famous fattened poultry of the Bresse, as Dr Roques recounts.

Every year for his holidays Brillat-Savarin said goodbye to the *Cour de cassation* in order to travel to the Bresse to put himself on a diet of *poulardes*. On his return he had put on so much weight that he looked like Ptolemy Physcon, the king of Egypt who was so enormously fat that two horses could hardly manage to pull the chariot which bore him.[29]

Some of that weight must have been put on in the Bugey, but this description by Dr Roques of the obese, gluttonous Brillat hardly conforms with the more modest picture he paints of himself in *La Physiologie du goût*, where Brillat describes his stomach as 'quite pre-eminent'; it is hard to know who to believe, but as Brillat was capable of considerable vanity it is tempting to accept the doctor's view of his girth on his return from the country.

The exterior of the *gentilhommière* in Vieu was considerably altered after Brillat's time. His descendants romanticized the manor, adding towers and medieval artefacts to give it a grander air, but the interior remains substantially as it was. The kitchen is a long, low, sixteenth-century room containing a bread kiln built into the outside wall. The present owner, M. Perrin, whose father bought the house from the Brillats in the 1920s, has done his best to restore it; he has even found some of Brillat's own kitchen equipment, such as his ancient, cast-iron braising pot.

Next to the kitchen another low ground-floor room was the bedroom of Brillat's two gout-ridden sisters, Joson and Padon. Over by the stairs which led to the dining-room and Brillat's own bedroom was the washroom. Brillat's tiny bedroom was tucked into a corner of the dining-room with its elegant cornucopia-decorated chimney-breast. At the far end of the dining-room, set into a tower, was a small maid's room. This has given rise to a local story that Brillat freely availed himself of the maid after the rest of the family and his guests had retired.[30]

The music room was on the second floor. Its chimney-breast is also decorated with delicate carvings, probably dating from the Directory. Indicating the purpose of the room, the bas-relief consists of an open score crossed by violin bows, flutes, recorders and violins.

Out in the garden, in the shadow of an ancient ash tree which shelters morels in the spring, the Brillat family had an ice-house dug so that the food served at Vieu should be reliably fresh, and the old judge need not do without the sorbets he had grown to love at Tortoni and Velloni in the *grands boulevards* of Paris.

When Brillat arrived at the beginning of each September, the household would line up to greet him: Manon, Joson and the old cook from Marignieu, who because of her birthplace was called 'la Marignotte'. As the carriage arrived they would run to meet it as best they could, got up in their finery and dragging their gouty limbs.

Once he had changed his boots Brillat made a tour of the village, stopping to exchange a few words of *patois* with a peasant or having a chat about the prospects for the coming vintage with a *vigneron* who was busy cleaning out his barrels in preparation. '*Moncheu le jzuse qui n'etâ pas fiar*' ('*Monsieur le juge* who was not too stuck up') they called him after his death, admiring his ability to sympathize with their concerns. The tour would continue with enquiries after game to the village huntsmen, a chat with the priest, some local gossip, and a leer at the peasant girls bringing milk to provision the swollen table in the manor house. While he was alone Brillat liked to take long walks in the country, with a volume of Horace in his hand.[31]

But very often there were guests, appreciative of the magnificent table Brillat kept during his leave from the court; his apparently universally recognized generosity in this way is one of his most endearing characteristics. Rostaing remained estranged, ensconced in his house in the Pays de Yenne, but there were other old friends.

Huge feasts were prepared featuring Bresse pullets, game brought in from the Grand Colombier, trout from the river Groin, char from Lake Bourget. Then there were the *plats de la résistance*: thrushes and ducks grilled on vine prunings, *noix* of veal with morels, dishes of crayfish cooked *à la Nantua*, and the *oreiller de la belle Aurore*. Artichokes were a particular favourite of Brillat's; he believed them to have aphrodisiac qualities, a theory contested by Dr Roques:

The famous gourmand ate either one or a brace of artichokes on sitting down to dinner; after this preamble he fell on some kidneys cooked in champagne, some cutlets, then chicken fillets with truffles, and all that moistened with a decanter of Pommard or Côtes du Rhône! During the general heat produced by the need to assimilate this food, he might indulge in one or two reminiscences, some stray impulse; but I will proclaim, loud and clear, the innocence of the poor artichoke ranged against that mass of food.[32]

Brillat also considered Bresse pullets to have an aphrodisiac effect. By his own account, a gourmand's indulgence in the richest food in no way inhibited his sexual performance.

The wine served at Vieu was from his own vineyard on the Côte-Grêle, made from grapes grown high up on the cliff in a light and pebbly soil. The wine took on the colour of onion skin with age, and was light, clear and heady. Locals compared it to the wines of Arbois; in all probability it was a lightly pigmented one made from the *pinot noir* grape.[33]

Brillat took an immense interest in the making of his wine, and had it shipped by the barrel up to Paris, where he tried it out on other members of the *Cour de cassation*. Sending one colleague on the bench a cask of his own wine from the Côte-Grêle he reminds the judge that 'you must remember that you'll have to rack it. In that way you may drink the clearest liquor down to the last drop. People are prone to neglect this precaution and my heart bleeds.' Brillat goes on to tell a story about the owner of the great La Tâche* vineyard in the Côte d'Or which he had heard in his student days or soon after:

> In 1778 M. le prince de Condé with whom he had a quarrel, asked to buy fifty bottles of the 1764 offering him a *louis* a bottle for it. No, the judge replied gravely, I am keeping all I have left to drink with my friends.[34]

After dinner in Vieu the women retired, *à l'anglaise*, and the conversation loosened up. Songs were sung, *patois* poems recited and, occasionally, one of Brillat's *contes* was read. The greatest feast of the season took place on 9 September, the day of the village fair; Brillat's descendants subsequently kept up the custom in honour of their famous ancestor. In Brillat's day, however, it was an opportunity to talk of leases and contracts, to round off a domain with a purchase, or to make an exchange in the interests of rationalizing an estate.

---

*The *grand cru* vineyard in the commune of Vosne.

Occasionally Brillat went out in a curious old coach which belonged to the family. The coach had a leather curtain which obscured the view from one side, but it was open on the other. 'It was in a vehicle of this sort that a badly directed Englishman managed to make a complete circuit of the Lake of Geneva without noticing it.'[35]

When he went shooting Brillat took his rifle, a bolt-action Pauly of the type he had helped introduce into the army, and his new dog, the spaniel bitch Ida. Shooting was for Brillat a way of exciting and satisfying the appetite at the same time. Starting from a point near the ruins of the Charterhouse of Arvières, near Lochieu (the first home of the Brillats), the party would set out early in pursuit of quail, partridge and woodcock. At midday came lunch. On great occasions this was brought out by the women of the party, and a picnic ensued: 'the turkey in its transparent jelly, the homemade pâté, the salad all ready to be tossed'.[36]

When no shooting could be organized, or when the game had gone far beyond the reach of the huntsmen, Brillat sank into his Horace, complaining that the women of the Valromey ('the dragons of virtue', as he described them to Henri Roux)[37] were, sadly, not at all like those blithe spirits 'as white as a ray of the moon on the surface of the sea' described by his favourite poet.

His love of the classics prompted him to make one or two further archaeological digs in the region in the hope of finding more vestiges of the Roman colony in the valley. Traces had been found of temples to Mithras and Cybele, and the house at Vieu was believed to be on the site of the baths. Digging in his orchard one day soon after the Bourbon Restoration, Brillat unearthed a relief of what he believed to be an armed horseman, as well as some columns of the town of Venetonimagus. In a paper written for the *Mémoires de la Société des antiquaires de France* he described his find as a horseman 'brandishing the short sword of the Gauls'. Although the Society of Antiquaries has since lost Brillat's discovery, later research has indicated that the bas-relief represented Epona, a divinity associated with cowsheds and stables.[38]

A la San Roman
La nâ est sur le ran*

---

*'On the Feast of Saint Romanus, the snow is on the bushes.' This must be Saint Romanus of Antioch, 18 November.

Once the snows began to fall and autumn to turn into winter, Brillat would pack his bags and return to his dusty briefs and the *Cour de cassation*.

IV

For all his popularity at home in the Bugey, Brillat failed to make any mark on his Parisian world. Frédéric Fayot, who was slightly acquainted with him at the time, leaves a description of a man largely unnoticed by Restoration society.

> His conversation made little impression; what he said was short, of little interest, and monotonous. He was a tall man, heavy and vulgar with an almost old-fashioned notion of dress. I can see him still: the collar of his shirt put up and framing his neck, his long trousers floating over his shoes; his full, expressionless face revealed nothing, certainly not the piquant wit so explicit in his meditations. I can see him seated in the middle of a group of five or six people in Madame Goulet's bookshop in the former Galeries du Bois,* listening rather than taking part in the conversation, not at all animated in the way that his writings might suggest.[39]

This lack of any desire to speak at length was noticeable also in the *Cour de cassation*. After his death, one of his fellow judges told Philibert Le Duc that, although he had both style and wit, as a judge

> he was a bit short. His reports sometimes left something to be desired. His president, old Lazigny, liked him a good deal, but used to speak his mind. One day Brillat-Savarin had brought his hunting dog with him, which was scratching itself noisily under his seat. Annoyed, he gave it a kick. Lazagny noticed and exclaimed 'Hey, leave your dog alone, it has more to say than you do!'[40]

Brillat did sometimes have problems with his dog Ida, who after sitting under his seat through the court proceedings afterwards took her place under her master at the Café Lemblin, Véfour or the Rocher de Cancale. On one occasion Brillat could not find the end of a report. As he scrabbled around in his bag, looking for the missing papers, Henrion de Pansey whispered across the bench, 'I think Ida has eaten the brief.' When the judges looked down at their feet, they

---

*In the Palais-Royal.

found this to be the melancholy truth. Brillat paid the frustrated client's expenses out of his own pocket.[41]

Nevertheless, Brillat was devoted to his dog. When she grew old and had to be put down, he wrote the following verses on her death:

> Pour te soustraire aux maux de la vieillesse,
> Je suis forcé d'ordonner ton trépas,
> Toi qu'on voyait près de moi sans cesse.
> Je serai seul, tu me suivras pas.
>
> Dans peu d'instants tu vas quitter le monde,
> Tu vas mourir, sans douleur, sans éffroi.
> Quand, à mon tour, dans cette nuit profonde
> Je tomberai, viens au devant de moi.*[42]

In 1817 Brillat's godson Anthelme Richerand used the proceeds of his highly successful medical work to buy a country house at Villecresne, not far from Versailles. Brillat was delighted to have somewhere near Paris to retreat to for the country calm, home-cooking and a little game.[43]

Here Brillat met the *littérateurs* Louis-Simon Auger, the perpetual secretary of the Académie française who threw himself into the Seine in 1829, and the poet François-Nicolas Vincent Campenon, another academician who lived in the village. It was usually at Villecresne that Brillat did his writing; most of *La Physiologie du goût* was written there, and it was Richerand and his wife who were the most insistent that he publish.[44]

It was also at Villecresne that Brillat devised an unusual way of cooking a turbot. The Richerands were perplexed as to how to deal with the giant fish, which would not fit into their oven. Richerand was on the point of cutting it in two when Brillat arrived, his nose in the air, following the aromas of dinner which were seeping out of the family kitchen. It was Saturday evening, and the turbot was intended for the centrepiece of dinner the next day. Richerand was certain there was no other solution to the problem, but Brillat was equally adamant that one existed. 'The turbot will remain whole until its official presentation,' he said.

---

*To save you from the sorrows of old age,/I am forced to have you put down. You who were my constant companion,/I shall be on my own, you will not be at my heel.

In a few moments you will leave this world,/You will die without pain or fear,/When in my turn, into the darkest night/I fall, come to me.

Looking here and there for inspiration, Brillat wandered into the laundry where his eyes fell upon a large cauldron: 'It will cook in steam!' he said. Finding an old wicker hamper big enough to hold the fish, he covered the bottom with shallots and herbs, then laid the turbot on top. A second layer of shallots and herbs was strewn over the fish and an old wash-tub placed on top of the basket to contain the steam. In half an hour the turbot was à *point*.

What Brillat tells us about the steamed turbot comes as no surprise today, when fish is frequently steamed, but in his own time the observations were novel: 'not having been in contact with the boiling water, it had lost none of its essence, and equally, it had absorbed all the aromas from the seasoning.'[45]

On another occasion when Brillat was staying with the Richerands, a fish was the cause of his precipitate departure. Explaining to his worried hosts why he was anxious to fetch his hat and cane, he told them 'I am leaving you for some important business: Henri Roux has just taken delivery of a Strasbourg carp, and we are going to have a discussion about the proper way in which to prepare it.'[46]

Brillat still had friends in the world of high finance, men like Benjamin Delessert, who founded the *Caisse d'Epargne* in 1818. Another financier friend was comte Louis Greffulhe of the leading Parisian banking house of Greffulhe et Montz.* *La Physiologie du goût* relates how Greffulhe asked Brillat to choose between a dinner-party made up of men from the world of letters, or one where all the guests would be scientists. Brillat (not surprisingly) accepted both.[47] Later Greffulhe got so fat from over-eating that he went to Brillat for medical advice. Brillat put him on a diet which made him lose three whole pounds. But Greffulhe was so upset at having to forego so many of his favourite things that he told Brillat he wanted no more diets. He expired soon after.[48]

It is said that the man of letters and musician Jean-Baptiste Antoine Suard died as a result of Brillat's treatment. Suard was the translator of Richardson's novel *Clarissa*; he had taught himself music the better to defend Gluck against the opposing Piccinnists who accused the composer of plagiarism, and had given Brillat some lessons. If Tendret is to be believed, Suard died from apoplexy after consuming gargantuan quantities of the *oreiller de la belle Aurore*. Seeing the old man beginning to suffocate on the pâté, Brillat suggested a glass of

---

*Greffulhe had been an *émigré* like Brillat, but his politics were much further to the right.

hot water. Suard was having none of this: 'Dou vino, dou vino,' he cried out.* Brillat had him brought a full glass of Côte-Grêle; 'Suard drank it off, collapsed and died.'[49] Tendret tells us that the events took place at Vieu: Suard died in Paris.[50]

V

In January 1819 Brillat made Juliette Récamier a present of one of his *contes*. Thanks to the never-ending passion for Madame Récamier among historians we have a fragment of the story; it was sent to the waning beauty with a covering letter from the author:

Madame,
Please receive kindly and read indulgently this old man's work. It is a tribute to a friendship which dates from your infancy and possibly a tribute to a more tender sentiment still . . . How should I know? . . . At my age you no longer dare question your heart too closely.

The author of *L'Inconnu*,
Brillat-Savarin

The fragment which has survived (Madame Récamier's biographer Herriot, the wartime Mayor of Lyon, presumably had access to the full story) is the 'historical preface' of 'The Stranger'.

'As you like novels so much, you ought to write one,' the kind object of my dedicatory epistle said to me one day.

'Dear Cousin,' I replied almost angrily, 'you know perfectly well my duties, my work and my pleasures take up all my time and I do not have the leisure to devote to letters.' She did not press the point, but she looked at me with eyes so full of charm that I was pierced to the marrow.

That same night I woke before dawn; sighing I lit my candle; I made a resumé and feeling inspired I jotted down the first four chapters; the rest tumbled out after them, and three days later I had obeyed my orders. While I laboured with ardour, however, I had to reconcile my extreme desire to please with my devotion to idleness, which is also not without charms: I was therefore reduced to writing an inconsequential novella, one which is no more than the precursor of a more long-drawn-out work. If I may speak a language which I ought to have forgotten by now, to present a novel concealed in a ring.

---

*Suard was from Besançon. His request for wine is in the local *patois*.

That in truth is the origin of the trifle which you are about to read. I place it under the protection of the ladies, and those above all who have small feet, elegant figures, lively imaginations and troubled breathing. Those women will be interested in my stranger, will see him as he was, will supply the missing details of the story and will want to know the author who, covered in glory by his success and anxious to prove his gratitude, will bitterly regret having been born forty years too early.[51]

That is all we know of 'The Stranger'. Was it of the same nature as the 'Voyage à Arras', or something a little less earthy for Madame Récamier and her circle? Once again it would seem that the story was autobiographical.

One thing which emerges from the letter and the dedication is that Brillat's passion for his cousin by marriage had by no means abated. One can almost read a veiled proposal of marriage into the penultimate paragraph, which may or may not be connected with Jacques-Rose Récamier's second bankruptcy, in the spring of 1819.[52]

Brillat was indeed busier than ever with his writing. Later that year his second full-length book appeared, entitled *Essai historique et critique sur le duel, d'après notre législation et nos moeurs, par le Chevalier J. A. Brillat de Savarin, ex–Constituent, conseiller à la Cour de cassation, membre de la Légion d'honneur, de la Société d'encouragement pour l'industrie nationale, de la Société royale des antiquaires de France, de la Société d'émulation de Bourg, etc., etc.*

Following the restoration of the Bourbons there was an outbreak of duelling between Bonapartists and Royalists. As a member of the *Cour de cassation* Brillat was involved in the case of Pierre Auguste Ferret, an ardent Royalist who challenged Bonapartist Mathieu-Brutus Caselles to a duel in Montpellier in 1818. Ferret was an experienced fencer but four years older than Caselles, who fatally wounded him. The political nature of the duel made it a thorny issue for the Courts, and after passing backwards and forwards through the criminal and appeal courts of Montpellier and Toulouse, it came before the *Cour de cassation* in Paris. The issues raised by the case prompted Brillat-Savarin to write the *Essai sur le duel*.[53]

The difficulty of the case arose from the fact that although Ferret had been killed, it was he and not Caselles who had issued the challenge. Brillat for one did not believe this to constitute *homicide volontaire*, as murder is defined by article 295 of the *Code pénal*. The political climate in France was sensitive and it was thought prudent to err on the side of clemency when it came to former republicans and

Bonapartists, to prevent them rising in open revolt. Caselles was acquitted; he later became prominent during the Revolution of 1848, and was a deputy under Napoleon III.[54]

Brillat's *Essai* included a full analysis of duelling, and its history from Frankish times. The duel had originated in civil law and remained the province of the upper classes, forbidden to the *bourgeoisie*. Here, Brillat shows that he was as proud of his bourgeois heritage as of his newly acquired noble garb:

> Although during sixty years [under Louis XIV] the third estate shed rivers of blood to maintain the throne; although it was in their bosom that was born the mass of geniuses who, in the arts and the sciences, contributed to carrying the French nation to the peak of European civilization, it was not supposed at that time that a point of honour could have any effect on a commoner; no matter how seriously they had been offended, the resort to arms was rigorously barred to them.[55]

Brillat was inclined to approve of duelling in certain cases, 'for it is well known that the rudest people are not always the bravest'. He also believed that the duel 'prevented' murders: 'better the sword than the stiletto'.[56] He put his faith in public opinion, which increasingly shunned duelling, removing the gloss of honour which had made it respectable. Brillat's opinion was of its time, marking the transition between an aristocratic ethic and a bourgeois one: eleven years after his death the *Cour de cassation* finally decided that any case of duelling called for formal punishment.[57]

The year 1819 was a busy one for Brillat: he was all at once lover, historian, farmer and jurist. His holidays that year must have been particularly welcome. He did not, however, return to Belley and the Valromey; a letter to Lucien Tendret's father, a Belley advocate, makes it clear that he had just spent a month shooting in Champagne. He wrote as he was passing through Paris to stay in 'the splendid château of one of my friends, where I shall hunt, drink, eat and play music as much as I please.' He also predicted a good vintage for that year, 'If the commonly held dictum "A good September, a wine to remember" has any truth to it.'[58]

Later that month Brillat wrote to a cousin in Lyon, Philippe Delphin, giving the latest news about Madame Récamier. Following Récamier's bankruptcy in May, the marriage had broken up and Madame Récamier had moved from under her husband's roof and now convened her court in the Abbaye-aux-bois.

Your uncle, my cousin Jacques, has just finished moving house, a shift which was accompanied by difficulty, annoyance and embarrassment. The household is now in a wholly strange situation with husband living in the rue du Vieux Colombier . . . and Madame Récamier in the Abbaye-aux-bois. Her apartment is not very comfortable, but she's happy with it; it is there where we will start dining again once the kitchen has been organized; for the time being there has been no house-warming as no cook has so far been engaged . . .[59]

VI

Brillat was still devoted to the interests of Belley and the Valromey. Any *bugiste* who knocked at his door was rewarded with a few coins. On his name day, 26 June, all those *dépaysé bugistes* who had the misfortune to live and work in the capital were invited to a sumptuous meal at the rue des Filles Saint-Thomas.

anxious to give his guests a pleasant surprise by serving them a product from their homeland [wrote Lucien Tendret] he had a barrel of his Côte-Grêle brought up . . . by his old mare Babet, led by his farmer, Angelot, wearing his low, black wide-brimmed hat and dressed in a coat made of long stalks tied together with a green weed called *blache* in the Bugey.[60]

At the end of a meal where one presumes local specialities were the order of the day, all those around the table were enjoined to sing a celebratory song about the Ain, of Brillat's own composition.[61]

If the Bugey beckoned, Paris too had its pleasant side, wholly different from the provincial society of the Valromey. The women there he now dismissed as 'dragons of virtue', but in Paris the Palais-Royal could offer excellent nourishment in that line by way of an appetizer before a visit to the many cafés and restaurants arrayed around the formal garden and the ramshackle Galérie du bois. Under the arcades of the Palais-Royal, Brillat could stroll into Véry, Véfour, the Trois Frères Provençeaux, Beauvilliers, Méot or the Boeuf à la mode. Not so far away there was Robert, and beyond the place des Victoires was the Rocher de Cancale. On the *grands boulevards*, too, a crop of famous eating-houses had begun to appear with Henneveu's Cadran Bleu. Henneveu was the son-in-law of Le Gacque, one of the first restaura-teurs, who still had his premises in the Tuileries.

Many of these restaurants already had their specialities. Le Veau qui tette, for example, was a past-master at mutton trotters. The Boeuf à la mode was famous for the meridional *gras double* (mutton stomach lining); the Trois Frères Provençeaux prided itself on Provençal food, with dried cod (*morue*) a speciality; Véry was better known for its liberal use of truffles; Le Rocher de Cancale for its fish and fresh oysters; and the Cadran Bleu for 'the mysterious boudoirs on the fourth floor'.[62]

When France was invaded by the Allies, Paris was subjected to foreign influences which benefited its cuisine: the beefsteak came back into fashion and Brillat was happy to indulge again in the punches and Welsh rabbits he had grown to enjoy in New York. From Germany there was *sauerkraut*, from Hamburg dried beef and from the Black Forest 'fillets' – a game speciality Brillat had encountered during his time on Augereau's staff. The Spanish introduced the *olla podrida*, an all-encompassing stew (literally 'rotten soup') containing different sorts of meat, vegetables, lentils, chickpeas and cabbage; Malaga raisins and peppered hams also arrived from Spain. The Italians were responsible for macaroni, Parmesan cheese, Bologna sausages, *polenta*, ices and liqueurs. The Russians had brought their dried meats, smoked eels and caviar; the Dutch herrings, dried cod, cheeses, curaçao and anisette; from India came curries, rice, and sago. Brillat also mentions 'the wines of Schiraz' [*sic*].* In his long list he also praises wines from the Cape (Constantia), American potatoes, yams, pineapples, chocolate, vanilla and sugar. All these imports, says Brillat, made Paris a better place in which to live.[63]

Not so the Allies themselves. Although he was happy to entertain a Croat captain in 1815 who taught him the principles of the steak *tartare* (the Tartars allegedly pulverized raw meat under their saddles as they rode), Brillat was less happy with the English. The English Croesus was a standard feature of the Restoration, a large, blotchy-faced individual, regorging gold and tending to eat, and above all drink, to excess. This type of Englishman tends to creep into the novels of Balzac, and into the miscellany of the *La Physiologie du goût*. The Parisian traders knew well the value of English gold, and the delicatessens of the period, like Madame Chevet's in the Palais-Royal,

---

*The Syrah grape, responsible for the Hermitage and Côte du Rhône wines beloved of Brillat, is supposed to have originated at Shiraz in Persia, or at Syracuse. In the Rhône valley some authorities dispute this, claiming that the grape is indigenous to Côte-Rôtie to the south of the city of Vienne.

stocked certain goods which were well beyond the pocket of most Frenchmen, even a judge, but presented no problem to the visiting English.[64]

Madame Chevet's little corner premises in the Palais-Royal were as popular with Brillat as with other gourmands, such as Grimod. Madame Chevet once said that the thought of Brillat's death upset her; he must have been a faithful customer. Another favourite of Brillat's was the *pâtissier* Achard – if he could get there before everything had been bought up by the rapacious English. When he failed he had to console himself with the local baker, Limet.[65]

In March 1825 Brillat's friend the chevalier de Borose died when lightning struck the tree under which he had taken shelter from a storm. His death was much regretted by Brillat.[66] Borose was a discriminating host and a fine Grimodian. He also had a daughter who caught the eye of the 69-year-old Brillat, although she can't have been more than 16 at the time. On New Year's Day she received a pair of slippers from her father's friend, and after Borose's death Brillat continued to show a lively interest in her studies, her harp-playing and her growing band of admirers. With the seventh decade of his life drawing to a close, Brillat's mind turned to love.

> Charmant amour, divinité trop chère,
> Ah! Dans mon coeur demeure un jour!
> Songe enchanteur, ravissante chimère,
> Voudrais-tu me quitter sans retour?
>
> T'ai-je jamais préferé la fortune?
> Pour tes autels, ai-je épargné les fleurs?
> Ah! Laisse-moi t'en offrir encore une!
> Refuses-tu cette grâce à mes pleurs?
>
> Philinte allait en dire davantage,
> Mais il se tut car l'amour s'envola.
> Il s'enrichit, fut puissant, devient sage.
> De n'aimer, plus rien ne le consola.*[67]

---

*Charming Eros, dearest divinity,/Spend one more day in my heart!/Enchanter of my dreams, lovely chimera/Would you leave me for ever?

Have I ever preferred riches to you?/ Have I not strewn flowers at your altar? Please let me offer just one more?/Will you refuse a tearful man that favour?

Philintus would have said more,/But he fell silent as Eros had flown away. He grew rich, was powerful, became wise./But nothing could console him for being without love.

Brillat, however, was not only thinking about the end of love; he was working hard at another project. More and more weekends were spent at Villecresne, and by the end of the spring the final corrections had been made to the manuscript which was to bring him immortality: *La Physiologie du goût.*

CHAPTER TEN

'The Fathers of the Table'

L A PHYSIOLOGIE DU goût would not have been written but for the special circumstances of Brillat's life and time. The Estates General had summoned him from his provincial backwater and thrust him into the centre of the world's political stage; the Terror hounded him out of France and sent him on a voyage of discovery to the far side of the Atlantic; the Empire introduced him to unforeseen pomp and splendour: all this in the course of a quarter of a century. Brillat was indisputably a product of the Revolution, and the same might be said of gastronomy. Before the Revolution there were cookery books and treatises on carving and serving food, but only after 1789 were there commentaries, gourmand breviaries and gastronomic theories.

A solid classical education was common to those Frenchmen whom Sainte-Beuve described as 'the fathers of the table'. Like Brillat, they knew from their reading of the classics that Archestratus had produced a 'gourmand geography' based on his travels round the Mediterranean in the age of Pericles, but that this text had been lost. The first classical source was Apicius, not the book allegedly written by a contemporary of Tiberius, but a treatise written at the end of the fourth or the beginning of the fifth century AD. Apicius' *De re coquinaria libri decem* is a cookery book, but many of the recipes contained in its ten volumes seemed as disgusting to eighteenth-century palates as they do to ours: stuffed wombs and udders, dormice and boiled ostrich, capons' testicles with asafoetida, and all stuffed with rue, endless rue.[1]

Attempts to recreate Apician meals were usually treated as a joke in the eighteenth century. Far more interesting to the gastronomically minded was Pliny's *Natural History*. In their own 'gourmand geographies' both Etienne Montucla and Grimod de La Reynière were imitating Pliny. Pliny's work explained the origins of some of the delights of Western gastronomy, such as the first oyster beds.[2] From Pliny they learned the Roman method of force-feeding geese to make *foie gras*;[3] of Umbrian cheeses the size and weight of truckles of *parmigiano reggiano*;[4] and the secrets of Roman viticulture: here were their gastronomic roots.

However, a better idea of Roman and even of Greek food may sometimes be gleaned from the poets the eighteenth-century French read at school. Brillat read Horace constantly, to the end of his days; nor did he have to look far to find other references to a simpler form of Roman cookery, as far from the baroque concoctions of Apicius as France was from Tierra del Fuego.

Frenchmen of Brillat's time took little interest in medieval recipe books. Brillat includes a few paragraphs on the Middle Ages in *La Physiologie du goût*, but his analysis lacks conviction. In the *Manuel des amphitryons*, Grimod lauds the influence on French food of the Italian Renaissance, in the person of the 14-year-old Catherine de Medici, bride of the future Henri II. Catherine brought with her to France many delicious things, including liqueurs, parsley, and haricot beans. She even brought the fork.

In terms of the invention of dishes, the period of Louis XV was far more productive than that of Louis XVI or the Revolution (which was even destructive, as we have seen). It was the mixture of sex and gourmandise at the court of Louis XV that created its gastronomic culture. Noblewomen seeking the King's favour would present him with dishes invented in their honour, making a direct connection between sex and food. Even during the Empire most of the *grande cuisine* served by chefs like Robert, Laguipière or even Carême was derived from the court cooking of the great Bourbon monarch. Apart from encouraging restaurants (and that was inadvertent), the Revolution added only gastronomic literature to the world of food and the kitchen.

The man who coined the word gastronomy, and for that alone is called the 'first father of the table', was the provincial lawyer Joseph de Berchoux. His importance lies more in his use of the word than in the verses he collected together under the title *La Gastronomie: poème en quatre chants*; a somewhat flatulent epic as these lines on the Roman gourmand Lucullus make clear:

> Rassasié d'honneurs, usé par la victoire,
> Il se mit à ses festins, son étude et sa gloire.
> La terre lui fournit, de l'aurore au couchant,
> De ses productions le tribut succulent.
> A l'art de sa gloire elles furent soumises . . .
> Et l'Europe lui doit les premieres cérises.*[5]

Berchoux' moment of glory was swiftly eclipsed by the publication, on New Year's Day 1803, of the first volume of the *Almanach des gourmands*. 'Le vieil amateur' (Grimod) had been inspired to write by his publisher Maradan. He put the book together in a matter of weeks, which may explain its slightly scrappy content. Its preface left those who bought the work in no doubt as to its purpose.

> The upheaval that has taken place in the distribution of wealth as a natural result of the Revolution has transferred old riches into new hands. As the mentality of these overnight millionaires revolves around purely animal pleasures, it is believed that a service might be rendered them by offering them a reliable guide to that most solid part of their affections. The hearts of the greatest number of rich Parisians have been suddenly transformed into gullets, their sentiments are no more than sensations, their desires, appetites; it is therefore with the idea of most usefully serving them that we give them, in these few pages, the best possible means of drawing the greatest profit for their penchants and their pockets.[6]

Mocking his low-born readers proved a profitable formula for the noble Grimod, and the *Almanach* was an overnight success, finding a wide readership not only in France but also, in a pirated edition, in Germany. Even in England it did not go unnoticed: Thomas Love Peacock read it with evident pleasure, and most of the novelist's later works include a gourmand clergyman whose ideas owed something to Grimod.[7]

The most original feature of the first edition of the *Almanach* was its nutritive calendar, which gave details of what was best at every moment

---

*Satiated with honours, and worn out by victory,/He retired to his feasting, his studies and his glory./Morning noon and night the earth provided him/With the tributes of its succulent creation./They were put to work for the art of his glory . . ./And Europe owes to him its first cherries.

of the year. Later editions of the work are often marred by careless presentation, a sign of fatigue on the part of an author forced to serve up regular novelties on the basis of one inspired idea.

The *Almanach*, which appeared eight times over the years 1803–13, was initially supposed to appear annually, providing fresh funds of gastronomic observation, kitchen tips, bacchic chants and recipes. In 1806 Grimod moved into the world of magazines as well. The *Journal des gourmands et des belles* was the first ever cookery magazine. Although Grimod enjoyed a monthly meal at the Rocher de Cancale at the paper's expense, his collaboration was short-lived, and by the end of the year his column had been reallocated to one 'Gastermann', the pseudonym of a hack writer named Reveillière.[8]

By 1808 Grimod was at work on two major projects, the *Manuel des amphitryons* and the *Dictionnaire de la cuisine*. Only the *Manuel* was published. It was divided into three parts: an excellent short history of the table, a treatise on the carving of different animals (including the *rarissime* European bustard), and a series of suggested menus using the formal dishes of the *ancien régime*. As with the *Almanach*, the *Manuel*'s chief joy lies in the author's irreverent *aperçus*. It is a great pity that Grimod never produced his dictionary, since his style lent itself to that form of writing. Even the notes for the book have been lost; but we do know that Grimod was the inspiration behind the *Grand dictionnaire de la cuisine* published by Alexandre Dumas *père* in 1872; the creator of the Count of Monte Cristo actually visited the aged gourmand at the Château de Brinvilliers sometime before his death in 1837.[9]

The last volume of the *Almanach* appeared on New Year's Day 1813, when the crumbling Empire was in no mood for its frivolities. Grimod's work had attracted official disapproval more than once in its ten-year history, but a heavily censored press was now even more priggish and critical. Suffering perhaps from hurt pride, or simply deciding his idea had run its course, Grimod retired to Villiers-sur-Orge where he had bought a small estate. In the last 24 years of his life few people outside his circle of friends gave a thought to this gastronomic pioneer.

This loyal circle contained two other 'fathers of the table', the marquis de Cussy, formerly a member of Grimod's *Jury dégustateur*, and Dr Joseph Roques. Louis de Cussy was a career army officer and courtier who had rallied to the Empire. Napoleon made him a palace 'prefect' and an imperial baron. De Cussy got on well with Bonaparte, even going so far as to interest the Emperor in one or two of his 365 different ways of preparing a chicken. Later, he admitted that trying to get the Corsican to pay more attention to the table was a wasted effort:

> Napoleon ate without thinking, above all without selection: he ate to fill his belly and cared little about taste. He was able to understand gastronomy, but a sensual existence would have been incompatible with a life so active.*[10]

In 1814 de Cussy was detailed to accompany the Empress Marie-Louise to Vienna. Loyal to Napoleon, he disliked Marie-Louise's attitude to her husband and when they reached her designated Duchy of Parma, he asked to leave her service. He arrived back in Paris on 20 March 1815, the very day that Napoleon returned to the Tuileries, and once again assumed his prefectorial position. Naturally his loyalty to Bonaparte was irreconcilable with serving the restored Bourbon, and de Cussy spent his last 22 years as a private citizen, enjoying good food and wine. Roques tells us that he died, like the Emperor Hadrian, from 'a surfeit of doctors'.[11] As he lay on his deathbed his interest in good cheer was undiminished. The day before he expired, he received a visit from a nephew come from the war in Algeria:

> 'You are most welcome,' said the dying man, raising his gaze in gentle pleasure. 'What is the news of the army? How are the young [Orléans] princes faring? We're going to have a good scrap, no?' Then he paused, and in a weak voice added, 'Have you seen much game over there?'[12]

Nothing of de Cussy's gastronomic writing appeared during his lifetime, but Frédéric Fayot published extracts from de Cussy's *Art culinaire* in his *Classiques de la table*. They reveal a gentle old sensualist who enjoyed food, wine, restaurants and women in a way Brillat would have appreciated. De Cussy did not, for example, believe (a view he shared with Grimod) that one could be a gourmand before the age of 40 – the age which, according to Brillat, one might aspire to the highest ranks of the judiciary. 'Love for the table is a passion which one does not feel until the age of 40, and one is certainly no expert until then . . . an elegant table is the last ray of sunlight to tease the valetudinarian.'[13]

---

*The great chef Carême also remarked on Napoleon's sobriety: 'He preferred Bordeaux wines and drank little. He was sober to such a degree that a glass of madeira would turn his face pink.'

That de Cussy had a robust appetite is revealed by his 'model dinner'.

1. Soup. 2. A few substantial dishes with sauces, a few small ones with *purées*. 3. Meat essences with layers of vegetables, some meat reductions, and ices [!]. 4. Hot pâtés. 5. Roasts, grilled meats and salads. 6. Vegetables and sweetmeats and large cold dishes; these last are here for formality's sake only, you store up trouble for yourself by eating them. For these dishes select fine wines which are dry, simple, straightforward and intoxicating: nothing sweet, not even a dribble of sugary wine![14]

Later on de Cussy gives us a better indication of what these wines should be:

When the connoisseur is modest and very abstemious, he contents himself with a bottle of Haut Brion, Léoville, Latour or Laffitte [*sic*] from the 1827 or the 1834 vintages, where the exquisite finesse [of the wines] surpass even that of the comet year [1811].[15]

Joseph Roques' contribution to the history of gastronomy has been neglected by later writers. Roques, a doctor, met Grimod and later de Cussy in the last years of their lives when he was fleeing the angry husband of a patient he had seduced. It was probably Roques who told Grimod about Brillat-Savarin, whom he had known slightly for some time. Roques was also responsible for introducing de Cussy to the chef Carême.

Roques brought a medical eye (genuine, not amateur like Brillat's) to questions of food. His *Histoire des champignons comestibles et vénémeux* broke new ground for gastronomic literature, introducing the French to the huge variety of mushrooms for the first time. His four-volume *Nouveau traité des plantes usuelles* is one of the most delightful, and most useful, food books of all time: in it he explains, fruit by fruit, vegetable by vegetable, the uses of plants in both surgery and kitchen. Recipes and anecdotes are scattered throughout the book and add to its charm.

The works of both de Cussy and Roques appeared after Brillat's *La Physiologie du goût*, which to some extent prepared the ground for an effusion of works concerned with food and eating. But a book which preceded Brillat's and owed nothing to the French approach to gourmandise was Carl-Friedrich von Rumohr's *Der Geist der Kochkunst*, published in 1822. Born in Schleswig-Holstein, von Rumohr was brought up at the elegant court of the Elector of Saxony at Dresden, but later the need to superintend the family estates sent him back to Lübeck. Rumohr was an art historian of note, so *Der Geist der Kochkunst* was published under the name of his cook, Joseph König to avoid ridicule by those who believed food books unworthy of a serious intellectual. He advocates a simplicity in gastronomic matters, much as the Prussian Winckelmann had pointed the way back to the Greeks in artistic style. Not surprisingly, perhaps, the German 'father of the table' lacks the frivolity of a Grimod or a Brillat.

Instead, von Rumohr solemnly advocates a return to the methods of Homeric Greece and Augustan Rome, aided by the technical improvements of the modern age. The Ancients, he claims, 'touched cookery without shame or fear' in their simple, healthy approach to the preparation of food. There is little to please the gourmand or the glutton there.

In another respect, too, von Rumohr's work is distinctive in approach compared with Brillat and the French masters. Rumohr is aware of the expression of national identity through food. Brillat, although forced abroad by the Terror, looks at the foods of other countries only in the light of what they may do to expand the heritage of France. Rumohr makes the essential connection between food and ethnography.

In 1825 Richerand told Brillat, 'The very word gastronomy makes everyone's ears prick up; it's the current fashion.' The doctor was encouraging Brillat to finish his book, a book which had been planned for the past two years or more but about which the judge – fearing for his reputation – had reservations. The 'current fashion' was the result of a remarkably successful piece of literary plagiarism performed by two young writers, Horace-Napoléon Raisson and Léonce Thiessé. Honoré de Balzac was a close collaborator of theirs, and it seems likely that he too had a hand in the work.*

The book in question was the *Nouvel Almanach des gourmands*, first published in 1825 and re-edited in 1826 and 1827. While Brillat

---

*The first edition of Balzac's *La Physiologie du mariage* was published in 1826. Balzac later denied that there had been any plagiarism in the title of the book. The expanded edition of *La Physiologie du mariage* which appeared in 1829, however, shows obvious signs of Brillat's influence. Balzac never concealed his admiration for Brillat, but his references to the judge in *La Comédie humaine* are often contradictory. In *La Peau de chagrin*, for example, Brillat is referred to as both an ascetic and a hedonist of the Cambacérès school. For *La Physiologie du mariage* see *La Physiologie du mariage pré-originale 1826*, edited with an introduction by Maurice Bardèche (Paris, 1940).

was encouraged by its success, the hermit of Villiers-sur-Orge was justifiably furious. Engaged with de Cussy's help on the preparation of a ninth edition of the *Almanach*, Grimod described the book as 'brigandage.'[16] In 1827 he published a prospectus for the new edition, and the authors of the *Nouvel Almanach* ran for cover. In later editions of the *Nouvel Almanach des gourmands*, however, Raisson and Thiessé took the opportunity of plundering a new book, presenting its anecdotes as their own. This book was by the man they respectfully hailed as the 'Voltaire of gastronomy' – Jean-Anthelme Brillat-Savarin.[17]

CHAPTER ELEVEN

Swansong

I

'*LA PHYSIOLOGIE DU goût* . . . par un professeur' appeared at the beginning of December 1825, at the expense of its anonymous author as the publishers doubted its commercial viability. They were wrong. The public showed immediate interest, both in the book and in an author who could pen such a lively 'treatise', at once theoretical and practical, on the art of choosing, preparing and digesting all that which serves as food for mankind.[1]

That Brillat had been working on the book for some time is clear from a letter written in 1823 to his friend Garan de La Morflans:

> I am still working on the book. I have the structure in my head and I make little trips to the country – to Madame de Villeplaine's house, the Château de La Grange – to escape from the interruption of people asking for favours. I hope it will be printed some time in 1824. *Physiologie du goût*, or meditations on transcendental gastronomy . . . It is a slight work which will have to make its way in the world.[2]

But Brillat was wracked by doubts. He worried about how the *Cour de cassation* would view the frivolous nature of some of the contents. He was worried that the work in its final version was not as good as it might have been. As he explained to Professor Portal, another of his medical friends, who had been physician to Louis XVIII:

> Alas . . . Someone stole my manuscript and I had to start again from scratch, looking through my memoirs, adding the reminiscences of

people with whom I have been in correspondence over the years. Despite all my efforts, several chapters have been lost.[3]

La Physiologie du goût, dubbed by Balzac 'an *olla-podrida* which defies analysis', was largely an essay in fashionable science. What makes it delightful is the irrepressible tendency of the author to include passages of amusing personal history to break up the text. After 20 aphorisms (some of which strongly echo Grimod de la Reynière),* a curious dialogue between the author and Dr Richerand which serves as an apology for publication, a tribute to the medical fecundity of Belley, and a preface, the book proceeds to 30 'meditations', followed by 27 'variétés' in the guise of anecdotes.

Brillat makes it clear from the outset that he has no interest in writing a cookery manual. He is an amateur doctor, he tells us, and much of the science will be medical. While the preface is mockingly pedagogical, Brillat cannot forbear entirely from braggadocio. He tells the reader of his myriad talents, of his many languages, and the many countries he has visited. He also makes a spirited defence of neologisms in language: 'When I have need of an expression and I fail to find it in the French compartment, I look in the neighbouring one.'† He is happy to borrow words or phrases from English, German or Spanish in a way that must have appalled the Académie française of the day, and might indeed shock their successors.

As well as borrowing from other languages, Brillat prides himself on the words he invents: *irrorateur* for his scented sprinkler, from *ros, roris*, dew; *esculent* from *esca*, food; *garrulité* from *garrire*, to chatter. Balzac particularly appreciated this bold trait of Brillat's, which provided him with words like *truffivorous* for a truffle eater; *obsegenous*, for something tending to put on weight (Bresse pullets, for example); or the verb to *indigest*.[4]

In later editions of Brillat's book a great deal of the physiological information was cut out as it was considered too arid for the general reader. Ever since the publication of *La Physiologie du goût* there has been debate in medical circles on the value of Brillat's information, so it is worth looking at his sources.[5]

'Physiology' was a fashion of the period. In medical terms

---

*Compare Grimod's 'There are a thousand people who can cook well to one who knows how to dress a roast' with Brillat's 'On devient cuisinier, mais on naît rôtisseur.'

†Brillat's self-congratulation on his foreign languages sometimes verges on the absurd. For example praising the pike of the Rhône: 'Gut! gut! gut! (Germ.)'.

'physiology' meant philosophical, as opposed to descriptive, science, Brillat had learned from his principal source, Richerand's *Eléments*. It was Richerand's stated purpose to join philosophy to medicine:

> Without philosophy, medicine becomes a branch of comedy and satire; the eternal and worthy butt of the spiciest jokes and the bitterest sarcasm.[6]

Brillat's aphoristic style was borrowed not only from Grimod: Richerand too was partial to aphorisms. Life, for example, he defined as 'a collection of phenomena proceeding from one another over a limited period within an organism'.[7] Richerand also inspired in his godfather an interest in sleep and dreams:

> In a perfect state of sleep sensual perception . . . is totally suspended. In this state a more or less complete veil is cast over our sensual organs. We know that we become hard of hearing, that smell and taste are numbed, and that sight is obscured.[8]

Richerand, too, was concerned with questions of nutrition and taste. We find similar appraisals and definitions in the two authors' work, down to a condemnation of the vegetarian echoed in Brillat's second 'meditation'. Like Brillat, Richerand saw nourishment as a need to 'repair the losses . . . which take place during the day'.[9] He analysed man's meat intake, demonstrating the similarity of man's feed to his organic make-up, and deducing a vital need to consume flesh. Richerand was also intrigued by the differences of taste which make one man like something which another will shun, 'asafoetida, for example'.[10]

Brillat, however, did not learn only from Richerand. As a sort of medical 'groupie' he 'collected' medics such as Corvisart and the anatomist Jules Cloquet. Through his other godson Anthelme Récamier he knew Pierre Jean Georges Cabanis, Mirabeau's physician and the author of the *Rapports du physique et du morale de l'homme*, a book which provided Brillat with a hundred insights later to appear in his own *Physiologie*. From the great eighteenth-century naturalist le comte de Buffon came Brillat's notion of a 'genesic' sense, a sixth sense said to bring men and women together and lead, ineluctably, to reproduction.

Buffon was not the only eighteenth-century thinker who contributed to Brillat's view of the world; we have witnessed his devotion to Voltaire. The *philosophes* in general had instilled in him a belief in the principle of 'perfectability', a belief akin to positivism. Brillat extended this principle to cover the senses, and held that one sense could compensate for another, more feeble one. In an attempt to prove his point, Brillat conducted experiments with taste, guessing that without the nose the palate is next to useless.

If some of the science Brillat had absorbed through his conversations with doctors and his deep reading of Gall, Lavater and Buffon was adequate, he was poorly served for biochemistry, which at that stage was in its infancy. The fifth meditation is 'riddled with errors'.[11] Brillat did not understand albumen, fats, or hydrocarbons, didn't know that there was no chemical relationship between sugar and flour. Medical commentators think better of his analysis of dieting, but it has to be said that his interest in obesity seems to have been but an extension of his interest in women: Brillat preferred them on the podgy side.

Medical men who have analysed *La Physiologie* since Brillat's death tend to the view that its broad lines are correct and have stood the test of time. His medical contemporants, however, were not always so approving. Roques, for example, thought Brillat 'a little credulous on matters of hygiene' and often irresponsible in his dietary suggestions. Brillat advises women who eat an ample lunch to swallow a cup of cocoa, suggesting they will then have totally digested it by dinner time (three hours later). Roques comments:

> Without a doubt he is talking about some sort of amazon endowed with a super-energetic stomach; either that or they were pulling the professor's leg . . . This is what we may term a perfidious piece of advice. M. Savarin had an implacable appetite, a cast-iron stomach, and a belly of enormous capacity . . .[12]

Elsewhere Roques questions Brillat's somewhat disingenuous advice to dieters to abstain from floury foods:

> Our physiologist . . . expounded on the manner of curing that form of obesity which doctors called physconia. He expressly forbade all forms of flour and rarely ate them himself, yet he loved feeding himself with pullets fattened on floury substances; was this not a case of pulling the wool over the reader's eyes?[13]

II

If Brillat's science has been generally approved by later writers, opinions on his style have varied. Local authors, perhaps overly proud of the most famous son of Belley, tend to excess in their praise, often echoing Balzac's view: 'All these trifles are expressed in a style so concise, so light, so picturesque, but above all so limpid and sunny, that you imagine *rancio** wine in a coloured crystal glass.'[14] Rumohr also approved: 'an ingenious work', he wrote in 1832, 'which appeared recently and which contains some important passages'.[15] But Rumohr emphasizes the chief fault of *La Physiologie du goût*, its bittiness. If, as some authors suggest, it is modelled on a dinner, everything is as it was in Louis XIV's time – hundreds of heavy dishes are all placed on the table at the same time.

In an aggressively pro-Grimodian article in the *Revue des deux mondes*, the writer Pierre Varillon dissents from the general praise:

Today *La Physiologie du goût* is practically unreadable. It should be noted that the quotations that are made from it are restricted to twenty aphorisms placed at the front of the book, and even these are generally wrongly quoted, like the most famous of the lot: 'A dessert without cheese is like a beautiful woman with only one eye!' in which 'dessert' is always changed to 'meal'. With the exception of some nicely turned passages or the best-told anecdotes, the body of the text is so heavy and so long that the merest commonplaces have become long-winded gibberish. Let us open the book at random: 'We mean by foodstuffs, the substances which, when introduced into the stomach, may be broken down by the digestive juices and thereby repair the losses made by the human body by usage'; 'By washing over the human race, the torrent of time has never ceased to bring with it new perfections of which the cause, always active albeit rarely visible, is to be found in the demands of our senses which, over and over again, require that they should be pleasantly occupied.' Worse still is that the judicious remarks – for there are some – are drowned in page after page of the author's self-satisfaction in his personal talents, all of which ends in making the book intolerable.[16]

Brillat emerged as something of a cult figure in the years immediately following the First World War, thanks to the similarly Ptolomy-Physcon-like figure of 'Curnonsky' (the gastronomic writer Maurice Sailland), whom Varillon describes as one of

a little band of parasites whose double chins had suffered during four years of war and who wanted to get back their pot bellies as swiftly as possible. The redistribution of wealth offered them easy game, but

---

*A wine of the Madeira type.

first they had to create a means and it was to this end they laboured, with the support of a few crafty tradesmen who knew what might be in it for them. The mass of people, who are used to talking about all subjects with the same incompetence, fell into the trap. With high-sounding mystique [the members of the group] exchanged addresses, and recipes such as *pré-salé* lamb *à la Villeroy* for a *Demidoff* pullet, salmon cutlets poached in Jurançon against pike in *beurre blanc* in the manner of Nantes . . . To crown the edifice, all that remained was to create a high priest of this new religion, and to endow it with an evangelist . . . Anthelme Brillat-Savarin.[17]

There has naturally been some debate on the relative merits of Brillat and Grimod. Balzac's view has become the standard one. 'Brillat-Savarin's humour', he claims, 'has a higher degree of Atticism.' Despite a certain fondness for aphorisms, there is a vast gulf between the two styles: Grimod likes to shock or outrage his readers with outlandish comparisons and metaphors. He calls a pike 'the Attila of the fish ponds', a wild boar 'a wild republican' or a carp 'a dish for a prince, or at the very least a *louche* republican purveyor on his third bankruptcy'.[18] Grimod is at a disadvantage in that his wit is scattered over a dozen volumes, whereas Brillat's sallies are all contained in the one volume that has brought him fame.

The late nineteenth-century gastronomic writer and poet Charles Monselet puts forward the view that

Between Grimod de La Reynière and Brillat-Savarin there is the difference between the heavy and the delicate eater. Grimod de La Reynière was a Rabelaisian, permanently famished (although with certain preferences), a man who couldn't stop himself from throwing a longing glance at the wedding feast of Gamache. His enthusiasm knew no bounds, even pushing him to exclaim at one point, 'You'd eat your own father in that sauce!' And he would have done what he said. Brillat-Savarin draws the line there: he wouldn't have eaten anybody, no matter how good the sauce.[19]

But Monselet is simply confusing the man and the style. The truth is probably the other way round.

III

Although de Cussy was a close friend of Grimod's he did not, in *L'Art culinaire*, enter the Brillat *vs* Grimod debate. But he does present a portrait of Brillat-Savarin which is far from the air-brushed version given by Monselet and his followers in this century. De Cussy makes one or two criticisms in as gentlemanly way as possible, adding that to 'point out a few small spots on the sun is not to lessen the force of its rays'.[20] When they met at the end of that year, Brillat proposed a snack of two dozen oysters, already taken from their shells and arranged in advance on the plate. The Norman de Cussy erupted at the very thought: 'Professor, what are you thinking of! Oysters open and detached! I shall excuse you because you were born in the Ain department!'

Brillatins dismiss as jealousy Carême's condemnation of him as a man with no knowledge of food 'who simply filled his stomach';[21] as to Baudelaire's criticism that he knew nothing of wine, *La Physiologie du goût* may say little about it, but as his letters amply prove, Brillat was both interested in wine, and well-informed.[22]

Brillat's compatriot, the proto-Socialist Charles Fourier, envisaged a major role for the pleasures of the table in his communes or phalasteries. Eating, he wrote, was both the first and the last pleasure given to man. But the heavy diet proposed by Brillat did not impress him. 'Savarin was a simplist,' he wrote, ignorant of 'gastrosophy . . . the art of combining the refinements of consumption and preparation with rivalries and hygienic methods'. Fourier was determined that everyone in his commune, 'Harmony', would learn how to cook; even the poorest inhabitant would select his meals from a menu containing twelve different sorts of soup, twelve different sorts of bread and wine, a dozen meat and vegetable dishes, all fashioned as lightly as possible. Fourier's vision, like that of Rumohr, anticipates the modern notion of healthy eating.[23]

Few people today bother to read *La Physiologie du goût* from cover to cover; it is a book for dipping into at random (indeed, an *olla podrida*). Read in this way, the tiresome stretches of science lose their importance and the passages of reminiscence come to the fore. There is much that is charming in Brillat's swansong: the wild turkey shoot in the Blue Mountains, which remained one of his favourite memories of exile; the theory of frying and its picture of the professor at work (an image borrowed by Cyril Connolly in *Enemies of Promise*?); the quail hunt on the plain at Hotonnes; the captain and the doctor feasting under the bust of Madame Récamier; the reminiscences of Belley before the fall; the day spent with the Cistercians of Saint-Sulpice; and the seduction of the wife of the *conventionnel* Prost.

Finally, we are left with the image of the benevolent former President of the *Cour de cassation*, Henrion de Pansey, smiling down on the work and its author.

I do not believe the sciences will be sufficiently honoured or properly represented until I see a cook sitting under the dome of the Académie française.[24]

CHAPTER TWELVE

The End

I

TWO YEARS PASSED before Grimod de La Reynière read *La Physiologie du goût*; he was amazed. 'My illustrious friend,' he wrote to Cussy, 'I have bought and read with extreme pleasure *La Physiologie du goût* written by poor M. Brillat-Savarin, who hardly outlived his triumph. It is a book on higher gastronomy compared to which my *Almanach des gourmands* is nothing more than a miserable rhapsody. How is it that a talent so deep, so pithy, was so late in revealing itself? *Did the author die of indigestion?*'[1]

It was not exactly indigestion, which would indeed have been a suitably ironic end; the irony lay in Brillat's death a mere two months after the publication of his one major work.

In September 1825 the judge travelled down to Vieu and the Valromey as usual. A letter to Henri Roux dated 22 September gives a picture of Brillat's rural existence near the end of his life:

> I am living as is my wont here, eating well and receiving anyone who calls. As I am observing a Friday fast I am in touch with someone at Lake Bourget, and I am at present taken up with the problem of how to deal with a char weighing five pounds . . .
>
> There is practically no game. Every day it is killed by poachers, and even more by dogs who hunt all by themselves and teem over the countryside.
>
> The harvest will be good, all the conditions are right as a result of some rain which fell on Paris[!]; I am picking the Côte-Grêle on the 26th; I shall be making my wine by a new method of my invention and I

think it will be just right next March. I shall have two tuns sent up, and we shall drink them, GOD WILLING!

The estate is looking good; I have four horses, two fat oxen and a plethora of bullocks, cows and heifers. As for the house, it is fragrant, since there are at least ten young girls aged from sixteen to twenty staying here.[2]

Brillat quit Belley for the last time as the snows began to fall. On his return to Paris his mind was still on sex and agriculture. He wrote to a colleague at the *Cour de cassation*:

I have a lovely big mare and I should like to give her a handsome husband, but I had no idea of the difficulties involved.

I have an idea that you might know personally the man who owns the stud near Versailles. Would you be kind enough to give me a word of introduction to him so that I can dispense with the majority of the formalities; a recommendation always saves a lot of time.[3]

Less than a month after Brillat's return to Paris, the first copies of *La Physiologie du goût* appeared. The shock was felt most by his fellow judges at the *Cour*:

The publication of the new code caused a great commotion among the members of the bench [wrote a contemporary]. They decided that their dignity had been compromised. Fortunately the counsellors could not reverse the verdict of their *confrère*. Were they not too skilled a body of men to fail to recognize *in petto* the sublimity of the work? Besides which, how could they begin to judge this mixture of gravity and humour which disconcerted both those who wanted to dismiss it too lightly and those who wanted to take it too seriously?[4]

Brillat's friend (and godson) Richerand, whose science made up such a large part of the 'serious' side of *La Physiologie du goût*, observed how the news of Brillat's new book was received in his own social milieu, among the grave doctors, the retired literary liberals of the Café Lemblin, and the little coterie of Madame Récamier:

In fashionable society people were completely astonished to find in his book such a breadth and variety of knowledge of the rarest kind, even for a man of letters. For them Brillat was just a nice man. How was it possible that this man who, as soon as he had carried out the austere duties of his profession, abandoned himself fully to the charms of society composed of delightful women (resembling the old man of Teos gambolling amid the graces); how was it, they asked, that he could have learned so much from study and meditation?[5]

Brillat must have enjoyed the attention which publication brought him. In the last month of 1825, people who had previously ignored him as a large old legal gentleman who took a back-seat role in the court of Juliette Récamier suddenly decided that they wanted to shake his hand and learn something from him.

One who made his acquaintance at this time was the marquis de Cussy. De Cussy dined with Brillat on New Year's Eve 1825. The old nobleman had done his homework and had dipped deep into *La Physiologie du goût*. On being presented to the judge, de Cussy immediately took up cudgels against the fifteenth aphorism: 'On devient cuisinier, mais on naît rôtisseur.'

> The fifteenth aphorism of *La Physiologie du goût* was the object of a long discussion between the professor and me and it ended in a way which doubly flattered my self-esteem. In this skirmish before the advance positions, I obtained two big advantages: the benevolent respect of the author and the gift of a copy of the book enriched by a few words of dedication.
>
> The controversial article XV is still as it was in the first edition, death having surprised the professor so soon afterwards that he was left no time to substitute, for this bizarre if pithy idea, the truth, which is so well known that, in his own study, from his own advice and under his own eyes even, I wrote it down in the copy with which the professor had honoured me. This is the primitive text: 'On devient cuisinier, mais on naît rôtisseur', a parody of the illustrious Latin author: 'nascuntur poetae, fiunt oratores.'
>
> Now let us look at the variant which was adopted after a long debate . . . 'On devient cuisinier, on devient rôtisseur, mais on naît saucier.' After all, what is a *rôtisseur*? He is a man who manipulates, who lives by routine observation, who has no contact with precise science except one or two superficial notions of physics needed to calculate the heat required for each joint, or to avoid confusing the effect of coal and charcoal or even wood itself . . . [after all] one does not treat a spit holding a joint of beef weighing twenty pounds like one carrying twenty ortolans, or better still, robins, fig-eaters or larks.
>
> What is the *saucier*? An enlightened chemist, a creative genius, the cornerstone of the monument to transcendental cuisine, to use the professor's ingenious expression. No sauce, no redemption, no cookery.[6]

De Cussy talked Brillat round; the genius of the kitchen, they decided, was the *chef-saucier*. An emendation was planned for the second edition: 'I am obeying the author's wishes,' wrote de Cussy. 'I am the executor of his oral testament; perhaps I should have made these revelations earlier?'[7]

Despite being bearded in this way in his study, Brillat ended the year on a happy note, revealed in a letter to Dr Anthelme Récamier written at the beginning of the New Year. The letter shows that his attitude to religion had been undergoing a slight change in the last year of his life. The anticlerical Brillat of 1793 had not, however, entirely relinquished his Voltairean cynicism, though he had ceased to bay for the clergy's blood.

A marriage was being arranged between Dr Récamier and Brillat's cousin, Elisabeth Brillat, and the doctor had written to his godfather hoping to bring him back to the Church. Brillat-Savarin wrote back with news of how Récamier's brother, and envoy, had delivered the doctor's proposal of marriage:

the petitioner delivered the proposal, to which Eliza replied, 'Monsieur, I have always prayed to Heaven that I should marry an honest man and God has heard my prayer,' at which your brother asked for permission to kiss [her], which was graciously given.

My niece will certainly be a good wife: she is pious, circumspect, very orderly and possesses a vast range of that domestic knowledge which provides half the charm of matrimony.

You see, dear doctor, that I have placed piety uppermost, and I would have had I written to anyone other than yourself. This is my theory: while there is no such thing as a good wife without religion, on the other hand, this sentiment must be contained; prayer must not descend to the level of pleading for favours, and I think that a woman is better off at home with her husband and children than in the pocket of her father confessor.

You will see by my conclusion, dear doctor, that your last letter, which was brimming with good sense, has not totally brought me round to your way of thinking, but *Gutta cavat lapidem* ['the drop hollows the stone'].[8]

The final month of Brillat's life mingled a lukewarm observance of the laws of the Church with deference to another of his least favourite causes – the monarchy. Since the restoration of the Bourbon monarchy, the presence of high-ranking officials and members of the King's court at the expiatory Mass for Louis XVI on 21 January had been *de rigueur*. By some ruse, Brillat-Savarin had so far managed to escape this performance each year; if this was because to attend would have troubled his conscience, it may be a sign that he had approved the

Convention's decision to execute Louis. His attendance *now* proved fatal.

This year, 1826, the President of the *Cour de cassation*, Romain de Sèze, was adamant that Brillat should attend the Mass. De Sèze had defended Louis XVI, and demonstrated his attachment to the dead king by adopting the Temple prison surrounded by *fleurs-de-lys* on his coat of arms. It is a mystery, given de Sèze's presence on the bench, how Brillat managed to avoid the ceremony for so long.

De Sèze wrote to Brillat on 18 January. According to Balzac his letter was friendly, mocking, but resolute: 'Dear Colleague, your presence on this occasion will be no less pleasant for us *by virtue of its being for the first time.*'[9]

A rather stricter, crosser and less graceful version is also known, dated 20 January. Perhaps both letters were sent. For this, de Sèze removed his kid gloves.

> I have noted your absence from the ceremony of the 21st January on several occasions. His Majesty has been informed of the fact and the Minister [of Justice] is not pleased. I shall therefore be satisfied to see you tomorrow at the *Chapelle expiatoire.*[10]

The *Chapelle expiatoire* had been completed especially for the ceremony of that year. The chapel stands on the site of the cemetery where Louis' head and body were buried under a layer of quicklime in January 1793. Although the bones of the King and Queen were subsequently sent to Saint-Denis in 1815, it was decided to acquire the site of the graveyard and to build a monument on it. The inauguration of such an important tribute to Charles X's dead brother was taken very seriously indeed, and probably accounts for something of de Sèze's tone.[11]

Brillat was already suffering from influenza. It must have been very cold that day, as the service led not only to Brillat's end, but also killed off two other counsellors from the court, Robert de Saint Vincent and the *avocat-général* Marchagny. Pneumonia developed almost immediately; Brillat collapsed in the street near the church of Notre Dame des Victoires as he made his way back to the rue des Filles Saint-Thomas.[12]

II

Perhaps, as he lay dying, Brillat's mind turned to the moral fortitude in the face of death which he had witnessed in his great-aunt Christine.

Like her, he had no particular fear. At the end of the previous year Brillat had written to Garin de La Morflans on this subject: 'Sorrow becomes less acute at the last moment; and this leads me to hope that when nature comes to blow out my lamp, it won't need to have two goes at it.'[13]

For the time being Brillat was conscious, and well enough to hazard a diagnosis of his illness. He described himself as being 'quite the victim . . . [of the infection], with an inflammation of the eyes and a dose of 'flu in my chest which tosses me about like an earthquake'.[14] A week later it must have been clear to the amateur doctor that his condition was not just 'flu'. His friends began to gather at his bedside, sensing that the end was near.

As so many of his closest circle were doctors, Brillat was not short of medical attention during his final hours. To do justice to Drs Récamier, Richerand, Manjot and others, it does not appear to have been a question of 'too many cooks spoiling the sauce'. In his speech at Brillat's graveside, Roux recalled his last words.

Addressing the dead Brillat, he remembered him as he lay 'surrounded by your friends, who quarrelled over the right to look after you; to spend nights by your bedside; and to relieve your sufferings. We will always recall the firm resolution with which you saw your last hour approach, and that sublime response, worthy of a philosopher, which you made to the doctor who was showing you the blood that he had just drawn from your veins to impress on you the gravity of your illness: "Oh well, dear doctor, if needs be we will know how to die." '[15]

The moment of death arrived on the night of 1 February 1826. Richerand, who was at his side, also wrote later of the remarkable, philosophic calm with which the old judge faced the end: 'He left life like a well-fed guest leaving a banquet – *tanquam conviva satur* – without regret, without weakness . . .'[16]

In the Palais-Royal the news profoundly affected Fontaine, the owner of the Café Lemblin. Madame Chevet may have wept a tear for the old judge who had been so faithful to her cluttered little shop. The restaurateurs, too, were conscious of the loss of more than just a few *louis*. A gloom fell over the *Cour de cassation* and the salon of Madame Récamier; the professor so recently come into his intellectual estate had disappeared for ever.

Meanwhile, Brillat's brothers Frédéric and Xavier disposed of his property. Xavier was already established in Pugieu with his family.

Later his progeny would inherit Vieu, and destroy the manuscripts of the judge's *contes*.

The colonel, Frédéric, is rumoured to have dismissed *La Physiologie du goût* with the comment, 'What the hell shall we do with that? Let's get rid of it.'[17] The rights were sold to the publisher Sautelet for 1,500 francs. (Brillat's Stradivarius fetched twice that sum from Henri Roux.)[18] Sautelet's first edition had sold out by 1828; a new edition appeared in 1829, others in 1834, 1835, 1838 and 1839.[19] The book has never subsequently been out of print.

Brillat's tomb is at Père Lachaise, 28th Division, 1st Line, facing 39 No. 4;[20] but his monument is his book *La Physiologie du goût*. 'One might be tempted to write on the spine of *La Physiologie du goût*,' said Balzac, ' "here lies the soul of the late Brillat-Savarin".'[21]

There remains one other monument to the author, judge and revolutionary politician, on the leafy *promenoir* of his home town, Belley. Surrounded by a group of frolicking *putti*, the bust of the city's most famous son stares out into the Bugey, smiling wistfully at the region he once fought hard to protect and which remained his passion until his dying day.

Notes

Chapter 1

1. Pierre-François Gaçon, *Histoire de Bresse et du Bugey à laquelle on a réuni celle du Pays de Gex du Franc-Lyonnais et de la Dombe* (Bourg-en-Bresse, 1825; reprinted 1989).
2. Quoted in André Abbiateci and Paul Perdrix, *Les Débuts de la révolution dans les pays de l'Ain (1787–1790)* (Bourg-en-Bresse, 1989).
3. Brillat-Savarin, *Mémoire sur l'archéologie de la partie orientale de l'Ain* (Paris, 1820).
4. Abbiateci and Perdrix, *Les Débuts.*
5. Brillat-Savarin, *Mémoire.*
6. Brillat-Savarin, *Mémoire.*
7. *Ibid.*
8. Information from M. David Genin of Belley. M. Genin informed me that forty years ago there were still small boys coming to school for the first time who spoke no French.
9. Brillat-Savarin, *Mémoire.*
10. *Ibid.*
11. *Ibid.*
12. Curnonsky and Marcel Rouff, *La France gastronomique. Guide des merveilles culinaires et des bonnes auberges françaises. La Bresse–Le Bugey–Le Pays de Gex* (Paris, 1921).
13. Quoted in Lucien Tendret, *La Table au pays de Brillat-Savarin* (1892; reprinted, Le Coteau, 1986).
14. Curnonsky and Rouff, *La France gastronomique.*
15. Tendret, *La Table.*
16. *Ibid.*
17. *Ibid.*
18. Brillat-Savarin, *La Physiologie du goût* (Paris, 1825; reprinted 1982, ed. Jean-François Revel). All further references are to the 1982 edition.

19. Tendret, *La Table*.
20. For the victory of the Large White and Landrace pigs over the ancient breeds of Britain, see Julian Wiseman, *A History of the British Pig* (London, 1986).
21. Tendret, *La Table*.
22. *Ibid.*
23. *Ibid.*
24. For the cheeses of the modern department of the Ain, see Patrick Rance, *The French Cheese Book* (London, 1989).
25. Tendret, *La Table*.
26. *Ibid.*
27. Brillat-Savarin, *Physiologie*.
28. Maurice des Ombriaux, *La Physiologie du goût et Brillat-Savarin* (Paris, 1937).
29. Brillat-Savarin, *Mémoire*.
30. Curnonsky and Rouff, *La France gastronomique*.
31. *Ibid.*
32. Brillat-Savarin, *Mémoire*.

Chapter 2

1. Archives Départementales de l'Ain, Series L. Thierry Boissel (*Brillat-Savarin*, Paris, 1989) makes out that Brillat was born on 2 April. This is clearly untrue.
2. See P. Dominjon, *La Compagnie des Avocats du Bugey* (Le Bugey, 1988).
3. A. Callet, *Brillat-Savarin, ses origines, sa famille, son enfance* (Le Bugey, 1920).
4. Françoise Wagener, *Madame Récamier 1777–1849* (Paris, 1986).
5. Abbiateci and Perdrix, *Les Débuts*.
6. Callet, *Brillat-Savarin*.
7. Jules Baux, *Nobiliaire du département de l'Ain (XVIIe et XVIIIe siècles), Vol II. Bugey et Pays de Gex* (Bourg, 1864).
8. Callet, *Brillat-Savarin*.
9. Donald Attwater, *Dictionary of Saints* (Harmondsworth, 1965); and John Kelly, *Dictionary of Popes* (Oxford, 1986).
10. Tendret, *La Table*.
11. Des Ombiaux, *La Physiologie*.
12. Callet, *Brillat-Savarin*.
13. *Ibid.*
14. *Ibid.*
15. Docteur Charles Picquet, 'Un homme illustre du département de l'Ain: Docteur J-F Coste' *Annales de la société d'Emulation et d'Agriculture de l'Ain*, 1901.
16. Picquet, 'Un homme illustre'.
17. *Ibid.*
18. Thierry Boissel, *Brillat-Savarin* (Paris, 1989). As usual, Boissel gives absolutely no evidence to support his assertion.
19. Callet, *Brillat-Savarin*.
20. Information from M. Perrin, the present owner of the *gentilhommière* in Vieu.
21. Callet, *Brillat-Savarin*.
22. Gilles Bressot (ed.), *Les Conventionnels de l'Ain* (Bourg, 1989).
23. Abbiateci and Perdrix, *Les Débuts*.

24. Brillat-Savarin, *Vues et profets d'économie politique* (Paris, 1801).
25. Abbiateci and Perdrix, *Les Débuts*.
26. Boissel, *Brillat-Savarin*; and Brillat-Savarin, *Physiologie*.
27. Tendret, *La Table*.
28. *Ibid*.
29. Brillat-Savarin, *Physiologie*.
30. *Ibid*.
31. Micheline Ribière in *La France à Table*, No. 74. Quoted in Henri Gault and Christian Millau, *Guide gourmande de la France* (Paris, 1970).
32. Brillat-Savarin, *Physiologie*.
33. *Ibid*.
34. *Ibid*.
35. *Ibid*.
36. LeRoy's work was published in 1758. Dora Wiebenson, *Sources of Greek Revival Architecture* (London, 1969).
37. Brillat-Savarin, *Mémoire*.
38. Boissel, *Brillat-Savarin*. No source is given.
39. Brillat-Savarin, *Mémoire*.
40. Brillat-Savarin, *Physiologie*.
41. *Ibid*.
42. R.J. White, *The Anti-Philosophers* (London).
43. Quoted many times, notably in Callet, *Brillat-Savarin*, Tendret, *La Table*, and by Marcel Rouff in the *Mercure de France*, 1 February 1923.
44. Callet, *Brillat-Savarin*.
45. The date usually given is 1775. However, I agree with Boissel, *Brillat-Savarin*, that given the date of his first pleading in Belley, it was more likely to have been in 1774 that he went to Dijon.
46. Boissel, *Brillat-Savarin*.
47. Denis Varaschin, *L'Ain de Voltaire à Joubert* (Bourg, 1988).
48. Brillat-Savarin, *Physiologie*.
49. For Guyton de Morveau see J. Tulard, J.-F. Fayard and A. Fierro, *Histoire et dictionnaire de la Révolution française 1789–1799*.
50. Quoted in Tendret, *La Table*.
51. Wagener, *Madame Récamier*.

Chapter 3

1. Charles Monselet, Introduction to *La Physiologie du goût* (Paris, 1879).
2. Henri Roux, *Notice nécrologique sur Brillat-Savarin*, (Paris, 1826).
3. Fernand Payen, 'Brillat-Savarin, conseiller à la Cour de Cassation, gastronome et gastrologue', lecture, Paris, 1925.
4. Payen (note 3 above) is presumably the source for Boissel, who repeats the assertion about the boar.
5. Dominjon, *Ibid*.
6. Archives de l'Ain; see also Abbiateci and Perdrix, *Les Débuts*.
7. For the situation in the *Parlement* of Bordeaux, see William Doyle, *The Parlement of Bordeaux and the End of the Ancien Régime, 1771–1790* (London, 1974).

8. Dominjon, *La Compagnie*.
9. *Ibid*.
10. Abbiateci and Perdrix, *Les Débuts*.
11. Brillat-Savarin, *Physiologie*. For Grimod on the Cistercians, see Giles MacDonogh, *A Palate in Revolution: Grimod de La Reynière and the Almanach des Gourmands* (London, 1987). See, in particular, 'Abbot for a Day' and 'Canon Fodder' among Grimod's *contes*.
12. Brillat-Savarin, *Physiologie*.
13. Tendret, *La Table*.
14. *Ibid*.
15. Brillat-Savarin, *Physiologie*.
16. *Ibid*.
17. *Ibid*.
18. Quoted in André Abbiateci, *Crise économique et révolution* (Le Bugey, 1988).
19. *Ibid*.
20. Archives de l'Ain, series 3E 03543. Papers of the notary Garin of Champagne en Valromey.
21. Abbiateci, *Crise économique*.
22. *Abbiateci and Perdrix, Les Débuts*.
23. Simon Schama, *Citizens: A Chronicle of the French Revolution* (London, 1989). Schama's quotation is from Stendhal, *The Life of Henri Brulard*.
24. Norman Hampson, *Prelude to Terror* (London, 1988).
25. Quoted in E. Dubois, *Les Préliminaires de la Révolution dans l'Ain. Les cahiers de doléances des bailliages de Bourg, Belley et Gex et de la sénéchaussée de Trévoux* (Bourg, 1913).
26. Abbiateci and Perdrix, *Les Débuts*.
27. *Ibid*.
28. *Ibid*.
29. *Ibid*.
30. Dubois, *Les Préliminaires*.
31. *Ibid*.
32. *Ibid*.
33. Général E. Vautrey, *Un Militaire égaré en politique. Jacques de Clermont-Mont-Saint-Jean, baron de Flaxieu en Bugey, député de la noblesse du Bugey en 1789* (Le Bugey, 1988).
34. Hélène Perceveaux, *L'Abbé Aimé Favre. Deputé à l'Assemblée Nationale Constituante (5 mai 1789–30 septembre 1791)* (Le Bugey, 1988).
35. Dubois, *Les Préliminaires*.
36. B. Dominjon, *Joseph Bernard Delilia. Deputé du Tiers Etat (1789–1791) avant et après son mandat* (Le Bugey, 1988).
37. Dubois, *Les Préliminaires*.
38. *Ibid*.
39. *Ibid*.
40. *Ibid*.
41. *Ibid*.
42. *Ibid*.
43. *Ibid*.
44. Perceveaux, *L'Abbé Aimé Favre*.
45. Vautrey, *Un Militaire*, quoting Bellod, *Livre de Raison*.

Chapter 4

1. F. Lorin, 'Brillat-Savarin Versaillais et Seine et Oisien', *Revue de l'Histoire de Versailles et Seine et Oise. 24e Année*, January–March 1922.
2. Schama, *Citizens*.
3. Brillat-Savarin, *Vues et projets*.
4. Quoted in Lorin, 'Brillat-Savarin'.
5. Edna Hindie Lemay, *La vie quotidienne des députés aux Etats Généraux* (Paris, 1987).
6. For the day-to-day events of the Assembly see Jacques Godechot, *La Révolution française; chronologie commentée 1787–1799* (Paris, 1988). Boissel explains Brillat's absence from the chamber by suggesting that he had 'flu and was cured of his illness by Dr Guillotin, the inventor of the 'Louison' or 'Saint Guillotine'. It is hard to know whether this is the truth or simply one of Boissel's fantasies.
7. Quoted in Philibert le Duc, *Histoire de la Révolution dans l'Ain*, 6 vols. (Bourg, 1879), Vol. 1.
8. Schama, *Citizens*. See also Jacques Hillairet, *Dictionnaire historique des rues de Paris*, 3 vols. (Paris, 1963).
9. See Hampson, *Prelude to Terror* (Oxford, 1988).
10. 'Lettre de Monsieur Brillat-Savarin, Député du Bugey, à ses commettans [*sic*], concernant le récit de ce qui c'est passé à Paris et à Versailles, depuis le départ de M. Necker, jusqu'à son retour.' Versailles, 30 July 1789.
11. Schama, *Citizens*.
12. *Ibid.*
13. 'Lettre de Monsieur Brillat-Savarin'.
14. *Ibid.*
15. Quoted in Godechot, *La Révolution*.
16. 'Lettre de Monsieur Brillat-Savarin'.
17. Quoted in Abbiateci and Perdrix, *Les Débuts*.
18. Eugène Dubois, *Histoire de la Révolution dans l'Ain. Volume I: La Constituante (1789–1791)* (Bourg, 1931).
19. Abbiateci and Perdrix, *Les Débuts*.
20. See Georges Lefebvre, *La Grande Peur de 1789. Suivi des Foules Révolutionnaires*, with an introduction by Jacques Revel. (Paris, 1988).
21. Dubois, *Histoire*, Vol. 1.
22. Abbiateci and Perdrix, *Les Débuts*.
23. Dubois, *Histoire*, Vol. 1.
24. Report to the justices quoted in Abbiateci and Perdrix, *Les Débuts*.
25. *Ibid.*
26. Boissel, *Brillat-Savarin*. Boissel says Brillat left Paris after the vote on 4 August, returning before 26 August.
27. Dominjon, *La Compagnie*.
28. The poem has been printed many times, notably by Philibert Le Duc and Abbiateci and Perdrix. The latter use a modernized text. I have used that in Varaschin, *L'Ain*.
29. Boissel, *Brillat-Savarin*.
30. Brillat-Savarin, *Essai historique et critique sur le duel* (Paris, 1819).
31. *Ibid.*
32. *Ibid.*
33. *Ibid.*

34. Quoted in *Réimpression de l'ancien Moniteur*, Vol. 1 (Paris, 1840).
35. *Ibid*. Also 'Motion de M. Brillat-Savarin, député du Bugey, sur la nouvelle division des Provinces'.
36. Quoted in Michel Peronnet and Henri Plagne, *La Révolution dans l'Ain* (Le Côteau, 1989).
37. Dubois, *Histoire*, Vol. 1.
38. *Ibid*.
39. *Ibid*.
40. *Ibid*.
41. Alphonse Martelain, *Départements et districts. Notes inédites sur la formation du district du Bas Bugey* (Le Bugey, 1988).
42. *Mémoires de Bailly*, eds. Berville and Barrière, 3 vols. (Paris, 1821).
43. Emile Le Houck, *Vie de Charles Fourier* (Paris, 1978). See also Jonathan Beecher, *Charles Fourier, the Visionary and His World* (Berkeley and Los Angeles, 1986).
44. Monique Lansard, 'Un Bicentenaire gourmand. Celui de la naissance des restaurants de France', *Echos des Relais et Châteaux*, No. 23, Spring–Summer 1989.
45. MacDonogh, *A Palate in Revolution*.
46. Brillat-Savarin, *Physiologie*.
47. *Ibid*.
48. *Ibid*.
49. Grimod de La Reynière, *L'Almanach des gourmands*, 1803. Quoted in MacDonogh, *A Palate in Revolution*.
50. Brillat-Savarin, *Physiologie*.
51. See two books by René Héron de Villefosse: *Histoire et géographie gourmandes de Paris* (Paris, 1956); and *L'Antiversailles, ou le Palais-royal de Philippe Egalité* (Paris, 1974).
52. De Villefosse, *Histoire et géographie*.
53. Boissel, *Brillat-Savarin*. Brillat is not mentioned in Michael Kennedy, *The Jacobin Clubs in the French Revolution* (Princeton, 1982).
54. Archives Municipales de Belley, Affaires Militaires, 1L 215–19.
55. Archives Municipales de Belley, Letters to Brillat-Savarin.
56. *Ibid*.
57. *Ibid*., 29 March.
58. *Ibid*., 12 April.
59. *Ibid*., 6 May.
60. *Ibid*.
61. *Réimpression de l'ancien Moniteur*, No. 114.
62. Boissel, *Brillat-Savarin*.
63. *Réimpression de l'ancien Moniteur*, No. 216.
64. 'Discours de M. Brillat-Savarin, membre de l'Assemblée nationale, deputé du Bugey, sur la manière d'organiser les Tribunaux d'appel. Prononcé le 23 juillet 1790,' Paris.
65. *Réimpression de l'ancien Moniteur*, No. 223.
66. Quoted in Alexis de Tocqueville, *L'Ancien Régime et la Révolution* (Paris, 1856).
67. Abbiateci and Perdrix, *Les Débuts*.
68. Archives Municipales de Belley, Letters to Brillat-Savarin.

69. Brillat-Savarin, *Essai*.
70. Michaud, *Biographie universelle* (1843). The article is Balzac's.
71. Dubois, *Histoire*, Vol. 1.
72. Quoted by Justin Lesage in *Visages de l'Ain*. Special issue devoted to Brillat-Savarin, January–March 1955.
73. Archives Municipales de Belley, Letters to Brillat-Savarin.
74. Archives Nationales, F3 (II) Ain 4.
75. Brillat-Savarin, *Essai*.
76. *Ibid.*
77. Quoted in Schama, *Citizens*.
78. Quoted in Picquet, 'Un homme illustre'.
79. Quoted in Dubois, *Histoire*, Vol. 1.
80. *Réimpression de l'ancien Moniteur*, No. 151.
81. Dubois, *Histoire*, Vol. 1.
82. Pierre Labracherie, 'L'Aventure révolutionnaire', *Visages de l'Ain*, January–March 1955.
83. Dubois, *Histoire*, Vol. 1.
84. See Hampson, *Prelude to Terror*.
85. Quoted in Boissel, *Brillat-Savarin*.
86. Archives Municipales de Belley, Letters to Brillat-Savarin, 19 and 24 July 1791.
87. Hampson, *Prelude to Terror*.

Chapter 5

1. Substitute Général M. Aynes, 'La Vie prudente et sage de Brillat-Savarin. Discours prononcé devant le cour d'Appel de Caen. Audience solonelle de rentrée du 16 septembre 1955.' Also comte Stanislas de Clermont Tonnerre, 'Opinion sur le conseil [*sic*] de Cassation. 24 mai 1790.'
2. Richerand, Introduction. *La Physiologie du goût* (Paris, 1847); and des Ombiaux, *La Physiologie*. Also Archives Nationales: emigration, Ain. Series F.7 4827, No. 44. The file contains a letter from the municipality of Belley attesting to the fact that Brillat was permanently resident in Belley from 20 January 1792 to 12 Frimaire of the year II (for the revolutionary calendar I have used *Concordance des calendriers grégorien et républicain* (Librarie Historique Clavreuil, Paris, 1983).
3. A. Chagny, Le Général Sibuet (Le Bugey, 1934); and Brillat-Savarin, *Physiologie*.
4. Brillat-Savarin, *Physiologie*.
5. *Ibid.*
6. *Ibid.*
7. *Réimpression de l'ancien Moniteur*, No. 241.
8. Dubois, *Histoire*, Vol. II.
9. Brillat-Savarin, *Physiologie*.
10. Archives Communales de Belley, Révolution 29.
11. Archives Départmentales de l'Ain, L III.
12. Le Duc, *Histoire*, Vol. II.
13. Archives Départmentales de l'Ain, Belley, Acquéreurs de Biens Nationaux, Table 759.

14. Archives Communales de Belley, 29 Révolution.
15. Archives Départementales de l'Ain, Rubat letters.
16. Quoted in Norman Hampson, *Danton* (Oxford, 1978).
17. Archives Nationales, AAI0 385.
18. The Constitutions are printed in Tulard, Fayard and Fierro, *Histoire*.
19. Archives Départementales de l'Ain, Rubat letters. Also Dubois, *Histoire*, Vol. III.
20. Varaschin, *L'Ain*.
21. Dubois, *Histoire*, Vol. III.
22. *Ibid.*
23. Archives Municipales de Belley, Register of meetings.
24. Bressot, *Les Conventionnels*; and Dubois, *Histoire*, Vol. III.
25. See Philippe Boutry, *Sociétés politiques des pays de l'Ain* (Le Bugey, 1988).
26. Dubois, *Histoire*, Vol. III.
27. Dubois, *Histoire*, Vol. III.
28. Dubois, *Histoire*, Vol. III.
29. Quoted in *Les Girondins*, ed. Michel L'Héritier (Monaco, 1949-50).
30. Quoted in *ibid*.
31. Tulard, Fayard and Fierro, *Histoire*.
32. Archives Nationales, AF II 83, Comité de Salut Public, Gouly. Dubois, *Histoire*, Vol. III.
33. Quoted in Dubois, *Histoire*, Vol. III.
34. Le Duc, *Histoire*, Vol. III.
35. Pierre Labracherie, 'L'Aventure Révolutionnaire'.
36. Archives Nationales, AA10 385.
37. Dubois, *Histoire*, Vol. III.
38. Archives Communales, Affaires Militaires de Belley, 1L 215-19.
39. Dubois, *Histoire*, Vol. III.
40. *Ibid.*
41. *Ibid.*
42. Archives Communales de Belley, Révolution 12.
43. Dubois, *Histoire*, Vol. III.
44. *Ibid.*
45. Archives Communales, Affaires Militaires de Belley, 1L 215-19.
46. *Ibid.*
47. Dubois, *Histoire*, Vol. III.
48. *Ibid.*
49. Le Duc, *Histoire*, Vol. III.
50. *Ibid.*
51. *Ibid.*, Vol. IV.
52. *Ibid.*, Vol. IV.
53. Varaschin, *L'Ain*.
54. Louis-Marie Debost, *Une Agonie de soixante quinze jours. Journal inédit. Août 1793 - Avril 1794. Avant propos et notes de G. Lenôtre* (Paris, 1932).
55. Archives Communales de Belley, Révolution 12; and Anon., 'Franche-Comté et Monts Jura', *Revue régionale mensuelle*, Besançon, March 1922.
56. Dubois, *Histoire*, Vol. IV.
57. *Ibid*; and Archives Communales de Belley, Révolution 12.
58. Debost, *Une Agonie*.

59. Dubois, *Histoire*, Vol. IV.
60. Brillat-Savarin, *Physiologie*.
61. For Brillat's meeting with the magistrates in the Billet trial, see Anon., 'Franche-Comté et Monts Jura'; abbé Fromond, 'Le Voyage de Brillat-Savarin dans le Jura, octobre 1793', *Revue Viticole de Franche Comté et de Bourgogne*, 1900; and Roger Sorg, 'Stephanie-Louise de Bourbon-Conti', *Revue de l'Histoire de Versailles*, 1960.
62. *Mémoires historiques de Stephanie-Louise de Bourbon-Conti écrits par elle-même*, 2 vols. (Paris, 1798).
63. See Wilhelm Kosch, *Deutsches Theater Lexicon*, Vol. 2 (1960).
64. Brillat-Savarin, *Physiologie*.
65. *Ibid.*
66. Labracherie, 'L'Aventure Révolutionnaire', insists that Prost was at university with Brillat. For Brillat's connection with Amondru, see Anon., 'Franche-Comté et Monts Jura' and Fromond, 'Le Voyage'.
67. Brillat-Savarin, *Physiologie*.
68. Fromond, 'Le Voyage'.
69. Brillat-Savarin, *Physiologie*.
70. *Ibid.*
71. *Ibid.*
72. Labracherie, 'L'Aventure Révolutionnaire'.
73. Archives Communales de Belley, Révolution 12.
74. Dubois, *Histoire*, Vol. IV.
75. *Ibid.*
76. Archives Nationales, AAIO 385.

Chapter 6

1. Archives Communales de Belley, Révolution 12.
2. *Ibid.*
3. See D. Bollet's essay in *Les Conventionnels*, ed. Bressot.
4. Dubois, *Histoire*, Vol. IV.
5. *Ibid.*; and Labracherie, 'L'Aventure Révolutionnaire'.
6. Archives Nationales, Comité de Salut Public, AF 1183, Gouly. Also quoted in Dubois, *Histoire*, Vol. IV. Versions of the texts alter after Thermidor when Marat becomes 'le prétendu ami du peuple . . .'
7. *Ibid.*
8. Dubois, *Histoire*, Vol. IV; and Archives Communales de Belley, Révolution 12.
9. Archives Nationales, Comité du Salut Public, AF II 83, Gouly.
10. On Albitte see R. Perceveaux, *Albitte la Terreur* (Le Bugey, 1988); and Jacques-Philippe Giboury, *Dictionnaire des régicides 1793* (Paris, 1989).
11. Archives Nationales, AAI0 385.
12. Brillat-Savarin, *Physiologie*.
13. *Ibid.*
14. *Ibid.*
15. *Ibid.*
16. Chanoine Chagny, 'Lettres d'Anthelme Brillat-Savarin à Jean-Antoine de Rostaing', *Annales de la Société d'emulation et d'agriculture d'Ain*, 1955.

17. Archives Nationales, AAI0 385.
18. See I.N. Phelps Stokes, *New York Past and Present: Its History and Land-marks, 1524–1939* (New York, 1939).
19. Chagny, 'Lettres'.
20. A Whitridge, *Brillat-Savarin en Amérique*, trans. abbé M. Juilleron (Le Bugey, 1937).
21. *Ibid.* see also P. Pezou, *Brillat-Savarin et la Musique* (Le Bugey, 1949): 'Je doute que la perspective de figurer parmi les exécutants de l'orchestre d'un théâtre en planches ait poussé beaucoup de européens à émigrer.'
22. Sim Coppins, 'La Page Blanche ou Brillat-Savarin observateur de la jeune République americaine', *Visages de l'Ain*, January–March 1955. Coppins imagines Brillat's stay in America as there is so little evidence of what he did there.
23. Michel Poniatowski, *Talleyrand aux Etats Unis, 1794–1796* (Paris, 1967); and Chagny, 'Lettres'.
24. Roux, *Notice*.
25. Brillat-Savarin, *Physiologie*.
26. *Ibid.*
27. R. Szramkiewicz, *Les Régents et Censeurs de la Banque de France nommé sous le Consulat et l'Empire* (Geneva and Paris, 1974).
28. For Delessert see Paul Antoine Cap, *Eloge à Benjamin Delessert* (Paris, 1849); Alphonse de Candolle, *Notice sur Benjamin Delessert* (Geneva, 1847); and *Notice sur la vie de Delessert* (Paris, 1847).
29. Moreau de Saint Méry, *Voyage aux Etats Unis d'Amérique, 1793–1798*, ed. Stewart Mimms (New Haven, 1913).
30. Brillat-Savarin, *Physiologie*.
31. *Ibid.*
32. *Ibid.*
33. *Ibid.*
34. *Ibid.*
35. *Ibid.* See also Archives Nationales, Emigration Ain, F.7. 4827, No. 44, and Archives Départementales de l'Ain, Emigrés, LIII.
36. Archives Nationales, Emigration Ain, F.7. 4827, No. 44, and Archives Départementales de l'Ain, Emigrés, LIII.
37. *Ibid.*
38. *Ibid.*
39. Archives Départementales de l'Ain, LIII.
40. Archives Nationales, Emigration Ain, F.7. 4827, No 44.
41. Chagny, 'Lettres'.
42. Four of Brillat's letters to Rostaing from America were reprinted in Charles Jules Dufay, 'Lettres inédites de Brillat-Savarin (1795–1796)', *Revue de la Société Littéraire, Historique et Archéologique du Département de l'Ain*, 1873. First letter, 12 October 1795.
43. Chagny, 'Lettres'; Dufay, 'Lettres', 25 October; and Brillat-Savarin, *Physiologie*.
44. Dufay, 'Lettres'.
45. Brillat-Savarin, *Physiologie*.
46. *ibid.*
47. Dufay, 'Lettres'.
48. *Ibid.*

49. Brillat-Savarin, *Physiologie.*
50. *Ibid.*
51. *Ibid.*
52. *Ibid.*
53. Dufay, 'Lettres'.
54. See Raoul Florentin, 'Brillat-Savarin et les Femmes', *Visages de l'Ain*, January–March 1955.
55. Dufay, 'Lettres'. Dufay censors the letter, especially in the parts where Brillat's concupiscence is mentioned. These missing elements may be found in Chagny's transcriptions, see 'Lettres'.
56. Whitridge, *Brillat-Savarin.*
57. *Ibid.*
58. Brillat-Savarin, *Physiologie.*
59. Archives Nationales, Emigration Ain, F.7. 4827, No. 44.
60. *Ibid.*
61. Dufay, 'Lettres'.
62. Archives Nationales, Emigration Ain, F.7. 4827, No. 44. It is reprinted in Whitridge, *Brillat-Savarin.*
63. Archives Nationales, Emigration Ain, F.7. 4827, No. 44.
64. *Ibid.*
65. Bernard Trapes, *Brillat-Savarin, un méconnu surprenant* (Moulins, 1983).
66. Chagny, 'Lettres'.
67. Brillat-Savarin, *Physiologie.*
68. *Ibid.*
69. Poniatowski, *Talleyrand.*
70. Coppins, 'La Page Blanche'.
71. Poniatowski, *Talleyrand.*
72. See the memoirs of Larochefoucauld-Liancourt, Talleyrand, Moreau de Saint Méry, and so on. Nor is there any allusion to Brillat in the biographies of Volney or Dupont for this period. Nonetheless, Boissel, *Brillat-Savarin*, not only contends that they met: he actually reports their conversations.

Chapter 7

1. Gauthier gives the time of Brillat's arrival as the 'début du mois courant', i.e., Fructidor IV, which means that Brillat could have arrived as early as 18 August 1796. See Archives Nationales, Emigration Ain, F.7. 4827, No. 44.
2. For his address, *ibid.* See also Hillairet, *Dictionnaire*, for the Récamier household.
3. Archives Nationales, Emigration Ain, F.7. 4827, No. 44.
4. Chagny, 'Lettres'.
5. Archives Nationales, Emigration Ain, F.7. 4827, No. 44.
6. Chagny, 'Lettres'; and des Ombriaux, *La Physiologie.*
7. *Ibid.*
8. Chagny, 'Lettres'.
9. Roux, *Notice.*
10. For Richerand and Stendhal see *Visages de l'Ain*, 1962.
11. Archives Départementales de l'Ain, Emigrés LI44.

12. Archives Nationales, Emigration Ain, F.7. 4827, No. 44.
13. *Ibid.*
14. 'Rapport J.L.N. Vaillant. Deputé du Pas de Calais. 23 Messidor. year IV.'
15. *Ibid.*
16. Archives Nationales, AF III 431 pl. 2465, No. 55.
17. *Ibid.* See also *Journal des débats et des décrets*, No. 465 and Jean-Louis Halperin, *Le Tribunal de cassation et les pouvoirs sous la Révolution (1790–1799)* (Paris, 1987).
18. Archives Départementales de l'Ain, Emigrés, Ll45.
19. Archives Nationales, Emigration Ain, F.7. 4827, No. 44.
20. Francois Villaret, 'Avocat à la cour de Paris. Brillat-Savarin avocat et homme politique', *La Vie Judiciaire*, No. 479, 18 June 1955.
21. Louis-Sebastien Mercier, *Le Nouveau Paris* (Paris, 1806).
22. *Ibid.*
23. *Ibid.*
24. *Ibid.*
25. *Ibid.*
26. *Ibid.*
27. *Ibid.*
28. MacDonogh, *A Palate in Revolution.*
29. Barras, *Mémoires.*
30. *Ibid.*
31. Letter of 1814 to the abbé de Montesquiou. Brillat was discreet about his dismissal from the court. He mentions it again in his request to return to the court on 19 January 1800 (29 Nivose VIII). The application is included in Charles C. [Charles Cousin], *Voyage dans un grenier à bouquins, faïences, autographes et bibelots* (Paris, 1878).
32. Chagny, 'Lettres'.
33. A. Callet, *Brillat-Savarin et La Physiologie du goût* (Le Bugey, 1914).
34. Brillat-Savarin, *Physiologie.*
35. *Ibid.*
36. Chagny, 'Lettres'.
37. Brillat-Savarin, *Physiologie.*
38. *Ibid.*
39. Chagny, 'Lettres'. Parts are also printed in des Ombiaux, *La Physiologie.*
40. Chagny, 'Lettres'.
41. *Ibid.*
42. Chagny, 'Lettres'.
43. *Ibid.*
44. Varaschin, *L'Ain.*
45. Chagny, 'Lettres'.
46. Aynes, 'La Vie prudente'; and Payen, 'Brillat-Savarin'.
47. Lorin, 'Brillat-Savarin'.
48. *Ibid.*
49. *Ibid.*
50. Brillat-Savarin, *Physiologie.*
51. *Ibid.*
52. Lorin, 'Brillat-Savarin'.
53. Boissel, *Brillat-Savarin.*

54. Lorin, 'Brillat-Savarin'.
55. *Ibid*.
56. 'Observations adressés au Corps Législatif par les Tribunaux civil et criminel du Département de Seine et Oise.' No date.
57. Chagny, 'Lettres'.
58. Archives Départementales de l'Ain, Emigrés, L140.
59. Archives Départementales de l'Ain, Emigrés, L142.
60. Quoted in Aynes, 'La Vie prudente'.
61. Quoted in Lorin, 'Brillat-Savarin'.
62. Chagny, 'Lettres'.
63. *Ibid*.
64. Aynes, 'La Vie prudente'.
65. 'Discours de M. J. Cornudet', 14. Ventose An VI (Paris).
66. *Ibid*.
67. 'Discours de M. G.T. Abolin (Haute Garonne)', 26. Floréal An VI (Paris).
68. Undated document accompanying *ibid*.
69. Archives Nationales, AF IV. 10, Minutes des Actes, 18 Germinal An VIII.

Chapter 8

1. 'Procès-verbal d'installation du Tribunal de cassation du Ier Floréal an VIII de la République' (Paris).
2. Roux, *Notice*.
3. *Oeuvres judiciaires du Président Henrion de Pansey, annotées par une Société de jurisconsultes et de magistrats. Avec une notice biographique par M. Rozet, avocat* (Paris, 1843).
4. *Ibid*.
5. Brillat-Savarin, *Physiologie*.
6. See Pierre Vialles, *L'Archichancellier Cambacérès* (Paris, 1908).
7. August von Kotzebue, *Journey from Berlin to Paris* (English translation, London, 1803).
8. Hillairet, *Dictionnaire*.
9. Lorin, 'Brillat-Savarin'.
10. Callet, *Brillat-Savarin*.
11. *Ibid*.
12. MacDonogh, *A Palate in Revolution*.
13. *Ibid*.
14. Brillat-Savarin, *Physiologie*.
15. Tendret, *La Table*.
16. Brillat-Savarin, *Vues et projets*.
17. Brillat-Savarin, *Physiologie*.
18. MacDonogh, *A Palate in Revolution*.
19. Brillat-Savarin, *Physiologie*.
20. Isidore Bourdon in *Dictionnaire de la conversation et de la lecture* (Paris, 1852–1858), Vol. XV.
21. Jean Armand Laroche, *Brillat-Savarin et la médecine. Thèse pour le doctorat de médecine* (Paris, 1931).
22. Romuald Szramkiewicz and Jacques Bouineau, *Histoire des Institutions. Droit*

et société en France de la fin de l'Ancien Régime à la Première Guerre mondiale (Paris, 1989).

23. 'Observations du Tribunal de cassation sur le Project de Code Civil. Paris An X.'
24. Chagny, 'Lettres'.
25. For Gastaldy, see MacDonogh, *A Palate in Revolution*. The quotation is from Brillat-Savarin, *Physiologie*.
26. The letter is printed as an appendix to *Le Bugey*, 1948.
27. 'Procès-Verbal de l'audience publique et solennelle du Tribunal de cassation présidé par le Grand Juge et Ministre de la justice. Tenue le 6 Nivose An XI.'
28. MacDonogh, *A Palate in Revolution*.
29. Brillat-Savarin, *Physiologie*.
30. Quoted in Ned Rival, *Grimod de La Reynière, le gourmand gentilhomme* (Paris, 1983).
31. Chagny, 'Lettres'.
32. Madame Lenormant, *Madame Récamier, les amis de sa jeunesse et sa correspondance intime* (Paris, 1872), and the same author's *Souvenirs et correspondance tirés des papiers de Madame Récamier* (Paris, 1860; second edition).
33. *Ibid.*
34. Callet, *Brillat-Savarin*.
35. Chagny, 'Lettres'.
36. *Ibid.*
37. *Ibid.*
38. *Ibid.*
39. Pezou, *Brillat-Savarin*.
40. Hillairet, *Dictionnaire*.
41. Brillat-Savarin, *Physiologie*.
42. Chagny, 'Lettres'.
43. *Ibid.*
44. *Ibid.*
45. Callet, *Brillat-Savarin*.
46. Hillairet, *Dictionnaire*.
47. Brillat-Savarin, *Physiologie*.
48. *Ibid.*; and Lorin, 'Brillat-Savarin'.
49. Paul Ganière, *Corvisart, médecin de Napoléon* (Paris, 1951).
50. Jean Bourguignon, *Corvisart, premier médecin de Napoléon* (Lyon, 1937).
51. Ganière, *Corvisart*.
52. Brillat-Savarin, *Physiologie*.
53. *Ibid.*
54. Ganière, *Corvisart*. See also Charles Hemmerlé, *Un Hommage à Jean-Nicolas Corvisart* (Reims, 1931).
55. Chagny, 'Lettres'.
56. *Ibid.*
57. Callet, *Brillat-Savarin*.
58. Archives Départementales de l'Ain, Notaire Garin, 3EO3539.
59. Chagny, 'Lettres'.
60. Wagener, *Madame Récamier*. The letter is in the Bibliotèque Nationale in Paris (NAF 14087). Madame Récamier's handwriting is so mean and cramped, however, that it quite defeated the author.

61. Madeleine Rocher-Jauneau, *L'Oeuvre de Joseph Chinard (1755–1813) au Musée de Beaux Arts de Lyon* (Lyon, 1978).
62. Brillat-Savarin, *Physiologie.*
63. Brillat-Savarin, *Théorie judiciaire* (Paris, May 1808).
64. *Ibid.*
65. Patrice Boussel, 'Du barreau de Belley à la Cour de cassation,' *Visages de l'Ain*, January–March 1955.
66. A Callet, *Les vacances en Bugey de Brillat-Savarin* (Le Bugey, 1919).
67. Brillat-Savarin, *Physiologie.*
68. Monselet, Introduction to *La Physiologie.*
69. Tendret, *La Table.*
70. Callet, *Vacances.*
71. Tendret, *La Table.*

Chapter 9

1. Vincent Cronin, *Napoleon* (Harmondsworth, 1973).
2. Brillat-Savarin, *Physiologie.*
3. MacDonogh, *A Palate in Revolution.*
4. *Almanach des gourmands*, quoted in MacDonogh, *A Palate in Revolution.*
5. Avocat-général Brunhes, *Un magistrat célèbre, Brillat-Savarin. Discours de rentrée, Cour d'appel de Rouen* (Rouen, 1951).
6. Henrion de Pansey, *Oeuvres.*
7. *Ibid.*
8. Brillat-Savarin, *De la Cour suprême* (Paris, 1814).
9. *Ibid.*
10. *Dictionnaire des Parlementaires Français* (Paris, 1889–91).
11. Brillat-Savarin, *De la Cour suprême.*
12. *Dictionnaire des Parlementaires.*
13. *Visages de l'Ain*, January–March 1955. Extracts from the letter to the abbé de Montesquiou are published here.
14. Aynes, 'La Vie prudente'.
15. Tendret, *La Table.*
16. Quoted in *ibid.*
17. Florentin, 'Brillat-Savarin'.
18. Curnonsky and Rouff, *La France gastronomique.*
19. The passage has been printed at least twice: once by Marcel Rouff at the same time as the future of the papers was most in question (i.e., the Brillat-Savarins had probably not yet destroyed them), in the *Mercure de France*, February 1926. The passage was reprinted in Liège in 1950. It is entitled: *Voyage à Arras. Le Relais de Saint Quentin de Brillat-Savarin.*
20. Brunhes, *Un magistrat.*
21. Balzac, op. cit. in Michaud, *Biographie universelle.*
22. Payen, 'Brillat-Savarin'.
23. Chagny, 'Lettres'.
24. *Ibid.*
25. *Ibid.*
26. Curnonsky, 'Eloge de Brillat-Savarin à l'Académie des gastronomes', Paris, 30 January 1934.

27. Richerand, Introduction to *Physiologie*.
28. Callet, *Vacances*.
29. Joseph Roques, *Nouveau traité des plantes usuelles, spécialement appliqué à la médecine domestique et au régime alimentaire de l'homme sain et malade* (Paris, 1837).
30. I am extremely grateful to M. Perrin of Lyon who showed me round his country house, coming all the way from Lyon to do so. M. Perrin is a mine of information on Brillat-Savarin.
31. Callet, *Vacances*.
32. Roques, *Nouveau traité*. There is also a discussion of aphrodisiacs in A.A. Löwenthal's essay on Brillat-Savarin: 'Feinschmecker oder Vielfrass', *Gesammelte Werke* (Tübingen, 1962), Vol. IV.
33. Callet, *Vacances*.
34. C. Joly, *Brillat-Savarin Oenophile* (Paris, 1959).
35. Callet, *Vacances*.
36. Brillat-Savarin, *Physiologie*.
37. Quoted in Callet, *Vacances*.
38. Callet, *Brillat-Savarin*; and Emile Thévenot, 'La Déese de Brillat-Savarin', *Visages de l'Ain*, 1962.
39. M.F. Fayot, *Les Classiques de la table* (Paris, 1843).
40. Philibert Le Duc, 'Brillat-Savarin poète', *Revue de la Société littéraire, historique et archéologique du département de l'Ain*, 1884.
41. Tendret, *La Table*; and François Villaret, 'Avocat'.
42. Quoted in Tendret, *La Table*.
43. Lorin, 'Brillat-Savarin'.
44. Lorin, 'Brillat-Savarin'; and Brillat-Savarin, *Physiologie*.
45. *Ibid.*
46. Denis Guillot, Président de la chambre à la Cour d'appel de Grenoble, 'M. le Haut-Conseiller Brillat-Savarin. Discours.' 16 September 1958.
47. See Szramkiewicz, 'Les Régents'.; and Brillat-Savarin, *Physiologie*.
48. *Ibid.*
49. Tendret, *La Table*.
50. For Suard see A. Suard, *Essai de mémoires sur M. Suard* (Paris, 1820), or Julian Rushton's article in the *New Grove Dictionary of Music and Musicians*, ed. Stanley Sadie (London, 1980).
51. Quoted in Edouard Herriot, *Madame Récamier et ses amis, d'après de nombreux documents inédits*, 2 vols. (Paris, 1905; second edition).
52. Szramkiewicz, 'Les Régents'.
53. Louis Augustin Barrière, *L'essai sur le duel de Brillat-Savarin* (Le Bugey, 1985). See also Docteur C.G. Collet, 'Essai historique et critique sur le duel de Brillat-Savarin, *Revue de la Société littéraire, historique et archéologique du département de l'Ain, 1954*.
54. *Callet, Brillat-Savarin.*
55. Brillat-Savarin, *Essai*.
56. *Ibid.*
57. Barrière, *L'Essai*.
58. Quoted in Lorin, 'Brillat-Savarin'.
59. Herriot, *Madame Récamier*.
60. Tendret, *La Table*.

61. *Ibid.*
62. Brillat-Savarin, *Physiologie.*
63. *Ibid.*
64. *Ibid.*
65. *Ibid.*
66. Brillat-Savarin, *Physiologie.*
67. Florentin, 'Brillat-Savarin'.

Chapter 10

1. Barbara Flower and Elizabeth Rosenbaum, *The Roman Cookery Book. A Critical Translation of The Art of Cookery by Apicius, for use in the study and the kitchen* (London, 1958).
2. *The Natural History of Pliny*, trans. John Bostock and H.T. Riley, 6 vols. (London, 1855), IX, 81.
3. *Ibid*, X, 27.
4. *Ibid*, X, 97.
5. Joseph Berchoux, *La Gastronomie* (Paris, 1801).
6. MacDonogh, *A Palate in Revolution.*
7. See my article on Grimod and Peacock, 'Two Gastronomes, One After the Other', *World Gastronomy*, Vol. 14, 1989.
8. MacDonogh, *A Palate in Revolution.*
9. See the preface to Dumas' *Grande Dictionnaire de la cuisine* (Paris, 1872).
10. Marquis de Cussy, *Art culinaire* in *Les Classiques de la table*, ed. Frédéric Fayot (Paris, 1843).
11. Roques, *Nouveau traité.*
12. Fayot (ed.), *Les Classiques de la table.*
13. De Cussy, *Art culinaire.*
14. *Ibid.*
15. *Ibid.*
16. Rival, *Grimod.*
17. Horace-Napoléon Raisson, *Code gourmand. Manuel complet de gastronomie* (Paris, 1827).

Chapter 11

1. Dr Carry, *Bibliographie de Brillat-Savarin* (Le Bugey, 1922).
2. Callet, *Brillat-Savarin.*
3. Dr Poumies de La Siboutie, *Souvenirs d'un médecin de Paris*, quoted in C.G. Collet, 'Brillat-Savarin, fût-il un causeur spirituel? Mérite-t-il sa réputation d'écrivain?', *Annales de la société d'émulation de l'Ain*, 1955.
4. See the essay of Professor Louis Trénard in *Actes de colloque l'héritage des lumières: Volney et les idéologues. Université d'Angers, 14, 15, 16, 17 May 1987* (Angers, 1988). See also Balzac in Michaud, *Biographie universelle.*
5. On Brillat and medicine see Jean Armand Laroche, 'Brillat-Savarin et la médecine', thèse pour le doctorat de médecine, Paris, 1931; Dr M. Armand, 'La médecine dans Brillat-Savarin', *Annales de la société d'émulation de l'Ain*, 1909; and Claude Georges Collet, 'Brillat-Savarin, biographie des

médecins bugistes', *Société française de l'histoire de la médecine*, 1955.

6. Anthelme Richerand, *Nouveaux éléments de la physiologie* (Paris, 1825; ninth edition).
7. *Ibid.*
8. *Ibid.*
9. *Ibid.*
10. *Ibid.*
11. Laroche, 'Brillat-Savarin'.
12. Roques, *Nouveau traité.*
13. *Ibid.*
14. Balzac in Michaud, *Biographie universelle.*
15. Rumohr in 'Joseph König. *Der Geist der Kochkunst, überarbeitet und heraus-gegeben von C.F. von Rumohr. Zweite vermehrte und verbesserte Aufgabe*' (Stuttgart and Tübingen, 1832).
16. Pierre Varillon, 'Grimod de La Reynière et *La Physiologie du goût*', *Revue des deux mondes*, May–June 1955.
17. *Ibid.*
18. MacDonogh, *A Palate in Revolution.*
19. Monselet, Introduction to *La Physiologie.*
20. De Cussy, *Art culinaire.*
21. Quoted in Gault and Millau, *Guide Gourmande de la France.*
22. Baudelaire, *Les Paradis artificiels* in *Oeuvres complètes* (Paris, 1961).
23. Beecher, *Charles Fournier.*
24. Brillat-Savarin, *Physiologie.*

Chapter 12

1. Rival, *Grimod.*
2. Callet, *Vacances.*
3. *Ibid.*
4. Jules Paton in *Dictionnaire de la conversation et de la lecture* (Paris, 1852–8), Vol. III.
5. Richerand, Introduction to *Physiologie.*
6. Cussy, *Art culinaire.* The passage is quoted by Tendret in *La Table.*
7. Cussy, *Art culinaire.*
8. Florentin, 'Brillat-Savarin'.
9. Balzac in Michaud, *Biographie universelle.*
10. Villaret, 'Avocat'.
11. Hillairet, *Dictionnaire.*
12. Lorin, 'Brillat-Savarin'.
13. Callet, *Brillat-Savarin.*
14. Trapes, *Brillat-Savarin.*
15. Roux, *Notice.*
16. Richerand, Introduction to *Physiologie.*
17. Tendret, *La Table.*
18. *Ibid.*
19. Trapes, *Brillat-Savarin.*
20. See *Guide bleu* (Paris, 1924).
21. Balzac in Michaud, *Biographie universelle.*

Index